Fundamentals of Inventory Management and Control

Third Edition

Fundamentals of Inventory Management and Control

Third Edition

Max Muller

Gary Langenwalter

© 2004, 1998 American Management Association International. All rights reserved. This material may not be reproduced, stored in a retrieval system, or transmitted in whole or in part, in any form or by any means, electronic, mechanical, photocopying, recording, or otherwise, without the prior written permission of the publisher.

ISBN-13: 978-0-7612-1350-5
ISBN-10: 0-7612-1350-3

Printed in the United States of America.

Contents

About This Course	ix
How to Take This Course	xi
Pre-Test	xiii

1. Inventory as Both a Tangible and an Intangible Object — 1
Learning Objectives
Introduction
The Tangible Nature of Inventory
   The Purpose of Inventory
   Types of Inventory
   Inventory Costs
Tracking the Paper Life
Electronic Data Interchange
Recap
Review Questions

2. Inventory as Money — 17
Learning Objectives
Introduction
Accounting for Inventories
How Inventory Is Valued
Inventory on the Balance Sheet
Inventory on the Income Statement
Ratio Analyses and What They Mean
Obsolete Stock
   Why You Have Been Told Not to Dispose of It
   Problems with Convincing Decision-Makers That "It's Gotta Go"

© American Management Association. All rights reserved.

Arguments in Favor of Disposing of Dead Stock
Methods of Disposal

Ordering Cost and Purchasing

Recap

Review Questions

Answers

3. Physical Location and Control of Inventory 39

Learning Objectives

Introduction

Common Locator Systems
Memory Systems
Fixed Location Systems
Zoning Systems
Random Location Systems
Combination Systems

Item Placement Theories
Inventory Stratification
Family Grouping
Special Considerations

Location Addresses and SKU Identifiers
Significance
Keys to Effectively Tying Together SKUs and Location Addresses

Recap

Review Questions

4. The Basics of Bar Coding 73

Learning Objectives

Introduction

Elements of a Bar Code Symbol
Structure of a Generic Bar Code Symbol

Symbologies
Discrete and Continuous Symbologies
Symbology Summary
Popular Symbologies Found in the Inventory World

Scanning Basics

Printing Basics

Bar Code Applications

Examples of Using Bar Codes
Receiving/Shipping
Tracking Multiple Activities at the Same Time in a Manufacturing Setting
Using Barcodes as Part of a Maintenance Program
Bar Coding, Physical Inventory, and Cycle Counting

Recap

Review Questions

© American Management Association. All rights reserved.

5. Planning and Replenishment Concepts   95

Learning Objectives
Introduction
Inventory Types
Three Approaches to Replenishing Inventory
   Lean/JIT
   ERP/MRP II
   Reorder Point/EOQ
Recap
Review Questions

6. Why Inventory Systems Fail and How to Fix Them   131

Learning Objectives
Introduction
Inventory System Failures—Example Case
Metrics
   Inventory Record Accuracy
   Fill Rates
Tools with Which to Uncover System Dysfunctions
   Run Charts
   Flow Charts
   Variance Reports
Cycle Counting
   Cycle Count Methodologies
   Control Group Cycle Counting Method
   Location Audit Cycle Counting Method
   Random Selection Cycle Counting Method
   Diminishing Population Cycle Counting Method
   Product Categories Cycle Counting Method
   A-B-C Analysis Cycle Counting Method
   When to Count
   Who Should Count
Recap
Review Questions

Appendix A—Inventory	167
Appendix A—Formulas	175
Appendix B	183
Bibliography	185
Glossary	189
Post-Test	197
Index	203

About This Course

As one course among many offered in the American Management Association's curriculum, *Fundamentals of Inventory Management and Control, Third Edition,* has been written to introduce the new stockroom/warehouse manager, the nonfinancial inventory control individual, or the small business owner to the fundamental nature of inventory from a financial, physical, forecasting, and operational standpoint. The ultimate goal of this course is to present immediately usable information in the areas of forecasting, physical control and layout, and problem recognition and resolution. These materials should enable you to:

- Understand that modern practice discourages holding large quantities of inventory and encourages only having amounts on-hand required for current needs.
- Grasp the significance of controlling actual, on-hand inventory as both a physical object (shelf count) and as an intangible object (record count and monetary worth).
- Understand the fundamental differences between finished goods inventories in the retail/distribution sectors and raw materials and work-in-process inventories found in the manufacturing environment.
- Apply basic formulas to calculate inventory quantities.
- Recognize and analyze dysfunctions within your own operation.
- Employ basic problem-solving techniques toward issue resolution.
- Control the physical location of inventory in a more efficient manner.

Max Muller has served as chief executive or operations officer for companies distributing products as diverse as food to automated teller machines to safety equipment. In the world of education, Mr. Muller has developed or revised more than nineteen seminars in the areas of warehousing, inventory control, facilities management, project management, employment law, and occupational safety and health. These courses have been presented to more than 100,000 people throughout the United States, England, Canada, and Scotland. Mr. Muller has published articles in several business magazines. He is an attorney and an authorized General Industry Outreach Trainer of the Occupational Safety and Health Administration, U.S. Department of Labor.

Gary Langenwalter, CFPIM, CIRM, has more than 25 years' experience assisting manufacturers to integrate people, processes, and technologies to create competitive advantage. He is founder and president of Manufacturing Consulting Partners and combines a systems approach with sensitivity toward the human element.

He has assisted clients across the entire manufacturing spectrum, from agricultural chemicals, bio-pharmaceuticals, board games, casters, and centrifuges, to tie-down straps, tooling for plastic injection molding, ultrasonic test equipment, window treatments, and wood furniture. He has led classes nationally on Lean, ERP, and leadership/management and has been a member of the steering committees of both Lean and Process industry groups of APICS.

Mr. Langenwalter has written *Enterprise Resources Planning and Beyond: Integrating Your Entire Organization,* and was the lead author of the *Repetitive Scheduling Training Aid.* He co-authored the *Handbook of Material and Capacity Requirements Planning.* He earned an MBA from Michigan State University in Production Management and a BA from the University of Oregon in Industrial Management.

How to Take This Course

This course consists of text material for you to read and three types of activities (the pre-/post-test, in-text exercises, and end-of-chapter review questions) for you to complete. These activities are designed to reinforce the concepts brought out in the text portion of the course and to enable you to evaluate your progress.

Pre- and Post-tests

A pre-test and post-test are included in this course. Take the pre-test before you study any of the course material to determine the amount of prior knowledge you have on the subject matter. Submit one of the scannable answer forms enclosed with this course for grading. On return of the graded pre-test, complete the course material. Take the post-test after you have completed all the course material. By comparing results of the pre-test and the post-test, you can measure how effective the course has been for you.

To have your pre-test and post-test graded, please mail your answer forms to:

American Management Association
Educational Services
P.O. Box 133
Florida, NY 10921

All tests are reviewed thoroughly by our instructors and will be returned to you promptly.

The Text

The most important component of this course is the text, for it is here that the concepts and methods are first presented. Reading each chapter twice will increase the likelihood of your understanding the text fully.

We recommend that you work on this course in a systematic way. Only by reading the text and working through the exercises at a regular and steady pace will you get the most out of this course and retain what you have learned.

In your first reading, concentrate on getting an overview of the chapter's contents. Read the learning objectives at the beginning of the chapter first. They act as guidelines to the major topics of the chapter and enumerate the skills you should master as you study the text. As you read the chapter, pay attention to the headings and subheadings. Find the general theme of each section and see how that theme relates to others. Don't let yourself get bogged down with details during the first reading; simply concentrate on remembering and understanding the major themes.

In your second reading, look for the details that underlie the themes. Read the entire chapter carefully and methodically, underlining key points, working out the details of examples, and making marginal notations as you go. Complete the exercises.

Activities

Interspersed within the text of each chapter you will find a series of activities. These activities may take a variety of forms, including essay, short answer, charts, and questionnaires.

The Review Questions

After reading a chapter and before going to the next, work through review questions. Answering the questions and comparing your own answers to those given will assist you in grasping the major ideas of that chapter. If you perform these self-check exercises conscientiously, you will develop a mental framework in which to place material presented in later chapters.

Grading Policy

The American Management Association will continue to grade examinations and tests for one year after the course's out-of-print date.

If you have questions regarding the tests, the grading, or the course itself, call Educational Services at 1-800-225-3215, or send an e-mail to ed_svcs@amanet.org.

Pre-Test

Fundamentals of Inventory Management and Control
Third Edition

Course Code 95020

INSTRUCTIONS: *Record your answers on one of the scannable forms enclosed. Please follow the directions on the form <u>carefully</u>. Be sure to keep a copy of the completed answer form for your records. <u>No photocopies will be graded.</u> When completed, mail your answer form to:*

American Management Association
Educational Services
P.O. Box 133
Florida, NY 10921

1. Counting a small cross-section of your inventory frequently is called:
   (a) annual physical inventory.
   (b) fair valuation determinism.
   (c) cycle counting.
   (d) inventory stratification.

2. A chart that analyzes the sequence and relationships of product moving through an inventory system is a:
   (a) run chart.
   (b) pareto chart.
   (c) flow chart.
   (d) variance report.

3. In EOQ, the cost of carrying inventory and the cost of acquiring inventory:
   (a) should be within 10 percent of one another.
   (b) are unrelated for purposes of purchasing and stocking.
   (c) should be equal, whenever possible.
   (d) cannot be calculated with any degree of certainty.

4. Human-dependent inventory location systems are:
   (a) fixed.
   (b) random.
   (c) memory.
   (d) combination.

5. Locating items within a facility according to product characteristics is arrangement by:
   (a) Pareto analysis.
   (b) family grouping.
   (c) items affected by market conditions outside the control of your organization's operations.
   (d) demand for items outside of their normal review cycle.

6. Sending routine business transactions between computers over telephone lines is called:
   (a) EDI.
   (b) file sharing.
   (c) ordering.
   (d) ERP.

7. Bar coding is:
   (a) a digital method of achieving automatic identification.
   (b) an optical method of achieving automatic identification.
   (c) an analog system.
   (d) dependent on digital duplexors.

8. From an accounting viewpoint, inventory is a (an):
   (a) liability.
   (b) appurtenance.
   (c) necessity.
   (d) asset.

9. The number of pennies per inventory dollar per year a company is spending to house its inventory is its:
   (a) ordering cost.
   (b) carrying cost.
   (c) rentable space cost.
   (d) usable space cost.

10. A bill of materials is most like a:
    (a) bill of lading.
    (b) production schedule.
    (c) packing slip.
    (d) recipe.

11. In a real-time inventory software system, items are allocated to a specific order at:
    (a) the time of system update.
    (b) the time of data input.
    (c) the time of customer service telling the customer that the items will ship.
    (d) the time of order shipment.

12. The necessity of planning around the largest quantity of an item that will be in the facility at one time is a characteristic of which product locator system?
    (a) Fixed
    (b) Random
    (c) Memory
    (d) Combination

13. The ratio computed as (Current Assets – Inventories) / Current Liabilities is called the:
    (a) current ratio.
    (b) inventory turnover ratio.
    (c) assets/liabilities ratio.
    (d) quick ratio.

14. Which inventory management system views inventory as waste?
    (a) ERP
    (b) ABC
    (c) ROP
    (d) Lean

15. Honeycombing is:
    (a) the warehousing situation where storage space is available but is not being fully utilized.
    (b) an order selection technique.
    (c) a pick-pack technique for order assembly.
    (d) a stock storage technique where floor stacked items are placed next to flow-through racking.

16. In which stock locator system does nothing have a home, but you know where everything is?
    (a) Fixed
    (b) Random
    (c) Memory
    (d) Combination

17. Materials entered into the production process but not yet completed are:
    (a) inventory stratification.
    (b) work in stasis.
    (c) work in process.
    (d) flow through.

18. A key reason an annual physical inventory is not useful in resolving inventory system problems is:
    (a) the audit trail is too long.
    (b) counters are unfamiliar with the system.
    (c) inventory valuation is tied to a single event.
    (d) every stockkeeping unit is counted.

19. Lean concepts dictate that:
    (a) organizations should not carry inventory in excess of what is needed for immediate needs.
    (b) organizations should carry no less than one week's worth of product requirements at any time.
    (c) organizations should organize their purchasing strategies around one week's worth of product movement.
    (d) organizations should only purchase a six-month supply of raw materials at any one time.

20. "F.O.B. origin" indicates that title to product will pass at:
    (a) the time the items arrive at the customer's site.
    (b) the time an order is originated and accepted.
    (c) the time items leave the shipper's dock.
    (d) the time an order is filled at the supplier's stockroom.

21. Which of the following is not a bar-code symbology?
    (a) UPC
    (b) Code 39
    (c) Code 128
    (d) Code 2000

22. The method of inventory that is most closely tied to actual physical flow of inventory is:
    (a) LIFO
    (b) FIFO
    (c) average cost
    (d) standard cost

23. Your company manufactures wooden chairs and tables. Which of the following is an example of dependent demand?
    (e) A one-time customer order for six chairs and one table
    (f) A standing customer order for 20 tables and 120 chairs every month
    (g) An internal requirement for 60 feet of dowel to make the rungs for 12 chairs
    (h) A customer order for one finished rung to replace a broken rung in their chair

24. Which has the greatest scope?
    (a) MRP II
    (b) ERP
    (c) MRP
    (d) ERP II

25. In reporting *up* a chain-of-command the amount of detail supplied differs from level to level in what way?
    (a) The amount of detail increases.
    (b) The amount of detail decreases.
    (c) The amount of detail remains fairly constant.
    (d) The amount of detail is not related to the direction of the information flow.

Inventory as Both a Tangible and an Intangible Object

Learning Objectives

By the end of this chapter, you should be able to:

- Analyze the tangible nature of your inventory.
- Describe how an item manifests itself as an intangible record count throughout an inventory system.
- Explain why inventory accuracy depends on understanding both *where* an item is physically and *how* that location is reflected in the organization's records.

INTRODUCTION

This chapter provides you with a basic understanding of the nature of inventory as both a tangible, physical item actually kept within the facility ("real life" or "shelf count") and an intangible item existing within the company's records ("paper life" or "record count"). Since you frequently make purchasing, sales, customer service, production planning, and other decisions based on whether or not *your records show* an item as being in-house, an item's paper life can be just as important as its real life.

Self-Assessment 1–1

Understanding Your Inventory

Instructions: Answer each of the following questions by checking "Yes," "No," or "Don't Know."

1. Several times per week I am asked to locate product that appears in my company's records but cannot actually be found.	Yes [ ] No [ ] Don't know [ ]
2. My company receives various items in one pack size but stores them in a different size, e.g., received as a single master case but stored as four cartons (which had been in the case).	Yes [ ] No [ ] Don't know [ ]
3. Everyone within my organization has immediate access to the following information on their computer screens or a paper copy: items on-hand, items on-order, items allocated, items in-transit, items actually available for sale or use.	Yes [ ] No [ ] Don't know [ ]

If you answered "Don't Know" to Questions 2 or 3, you are urged to discuss Question 2 with your organization's purchasing agent and Question 3 with the information technologies manager. For a discussion of the significance of understanding who within your organization actually has access to various items of information regarding inventory (for example, quantities on-hand, quantities allocated, etc.), see Chapter 6, *Why Inventory Systems Fail and How to Fix Them*.

THE TANGIBLE NATURE OF INVENTORY

All organizations keep inventory. *Inventory* includes a company's raw materials, work in process, supplies used in operations, and finished goods. Inventory can be something as simple as a bottle of glass cleaner used as part of a building's custodial program or something complex such as a mix of raw materials and subassemblies used in the manufacturing process.

For organizations that sell inventory directly (manufacturers, distributors, and retailers), the inventory itself is usually the primary value they add to the customer. These organizations also provide product information, customer support, pricing, and discounts and rebates as part of their total customer interface. However, if the inventory is not available when the customer wants it, the customer will be disappointed and may start looking for another supplier.

For other organizations (for example, banks, schools, hospitals, and the military), inventory is not the primary reason for being in business. However, these organizations must have the inventory they need when they need it, or they will not be able to function effectively or efficiently. Imagine banks without new account forms, schools with no textbooks, hospitals with no bandages, or the military with no uniforms.

Traditional-thinking organizations assume that they must carry inventory in stock in order to meet demand. Furthermore, accounting systems treat inventory as an asset, which adds value to the company. However, companies that embrace lean, just-in-time (JIT), and/or supply chain concepts understand that they don't necessarily have to carry inventory in stock. They are only required to have access to it when they *need* it. These companies understand that in many instances information can replace physical inventory and that information is much less expensive than actual inventory. Retailers don't carry substantial inventories of items just in case they decide to have a special promotion; instead, they plan the promotion in advance and have the manufacturer deliver the inventories just in time for the sale. Manufacturers understand the seasonality of their goods; they make snow blowers in time for the fall/early winter selling season and sandals and swim suits in time for late spring/summer. In fact, some mail-order or Internet-based retailers actually carry no stock themselves. They take orders from the customer, then have their suppliers drop-ship directly to the customer.

With that understanding, this course presents both the classic inventory management and control techniques and an overview of newer approaches.

The Purpose of Inventory

So why do you need inventory? As we will explore in Chapter 5, just-in-time (JIT) and lean consider most inventory to be *waste*. The only inventory that is required is that which is actually being processed in a manufacturing environment or being delivered to a customer in a distribution environment. Leading companies in all industries recognize that inventory usually indicates a potential area of improvement; it is a symptom rather than an asset.

Traditional approaches to inventory management include six reasons for carrying inventory. While each of the reasons seems valid, especially in the short term, each reason also represents a failure to operate in the most efficient or effective manner. Let's examine the six categories, with the idea that each one is showing your company how you can improve.

1. *Process buffer:* Inventory should be used to buffer processes only at strategic points. As viewed by a supply chain, a warehouse or distribution center is really just a process buffer—goods arrive in batches (pallets, truckloads, cartons, and so on) and are "processed" (distributed to the customer) in smaller lots. In a manufacturing company, processes frequently operate at different rates, thereby requiring inventory buffers. Over the long term, processes should be brought into synch with each other.

2. *Fluctuations in demand:* This inventory allows a supplier to satisfy customer demand that is higher than expected. However, inventory is an expensive substitute for information. When you can see actual usage of your product by the end customer as well as inventory levels in the supply chain, you can satisfy your customers while carrying minimal inventories. This approach requires you to reduce your lead times and those of your suppliers. You can use this same approach to help your suppliers reduce their inventories, and therefore their costs. As you will see in Chapter 5, another way to reduce the need for this type of inventory is to reduce the

resupply time. If the supply lead time can be reduced to one day or less, much less inventory is required.

3. *Unreliability of supply:* In the short run, inventory can (and should) be used as a buffer against unreliable suppliers (both internal, in your own company, and external, your outside suppliers). In the long run, you can work with suppliers to insure their reliability, or you can—and should—replace them. The total cost of supplier unreliability is usually far greater than any savings in purchase price. The best suppliers deliver "perfect" materials directly to the desired location inside your company on schedule. This is equally true for internal suppliers in a manufacturing company. If varying quality is a root cause of unpredictability, it should be addressed by an appropriate quality initiative (for example, Six Sigma or Total Quality Management).

4. *Price protection:* Buying large quantities at one time has been a traditional hedge against price increases. You can (and should) negotiate pricing and long-term contracts with key suppliers, but you should request multiple deliveries. As your suppliers implement lean practices, they will strongly prefer to ship smaller quantities at frequent intervals, rather than asking you to take delivery of the entire purchased amount at once. Pricing agreements should also include the possibility of cost reductions, automatically passing on the the supplier's cost reductions.

5. *Quantity discounts:* Some suppliers offer discounts for buying large quantities. Quantity discounts work just like price protection. Quantity discounts are being replaced today by key supplier agreements, in which you agree to purchase your entire year's usage of various product families from one supplier in exchange for highly favorable pricing, superb service, impeccable quality, and rapid response and delivery. This reflects a culture of partnering with key suppliers rather than treating them as adversaries.

6. *Lower ordering costs:* Traditionally companies looked at at ordering costs as a necessary cost that should be traded off against carrying costs. However, today's preferred way to lower ordering costs is to eliminate all non-value-added steps in the ordering cycle. Value stream mapping is a technique of flow-charting all steps in a process (such as placing an order), calculating the total cost and total elapsed time, then identifying all those steps that don't really add value in the customer's eyes and deciding how to eliminate them (Rother and Shook, 1998).

Types of Inventory

Inventory falls into four basic categories: raw materials, finished goods, work in process, and transit inventories.

- *Raw materials:* These items are purchased from a supplier and are unchanged.
- *Finished product:* This product is ready for current customer sales. It can also be used to buffer manufacturing from predictable or unpredictable market demand. In other words, a manufacturing company can make up a supply of toys during the year for predictably higher sales during the holiday season.

- *Work in process (WIP)*: Items are considered to be WIP during the time raw material is being converted into partial product, subassemblies, and finished product. WIP should be kept to a minimum. Most WIP occurs from such things as queuing bottlenecks, work delays, long movement times between operations, missing components, and unavailability of tooling and machines.
- *Transit inventory:* This is inventory en route from one place to another. It could be argued that product moving within a facility is transit inventory; however, the common meaning of the term related to items moving within the distribution channel toward you (but outside of your facility) or en route from your facility to the customer.

Important issues related to transit inventory are when and how it appears in your records. In other words, when and where does it show up in your record count? Test your current knowledge of transit stock by completing Self-Assessment 1–2: Understanding Transit Stock.

Self-Assessment 1–2

Understanding Transit Stock

Instructions: Answer each of the following questions by checking "Yes," "No," or "Don't Know."

1. My company buys product F.O.B. origin.	Yes [ ] No [ ] Don't know [ ]
2. My company buys product F.O.B. destination.	Yes [ ] No [ ] Don't know [ ]
3. My company's accounting/inventory software displays data fields showing items on hand, items in transit *but not yet counted* as being a part of existing stock, items allocated, items actually available for sale/use.	Yes [ ] No [ ] Don't know [ ]
4. My company's accounting/inventory software displays data fields showing items on hand, items in transit *but counted* as being a part of existing stock, items allocated, items actually available for sale/use.	Yes [ ] No [ ] Don't know [ ]
5. My company uses electronic data interchange.	Yes [ ] No [ ] Don't know [ ]

If you answered "Don't Know" to Questions 1 or 2 in this Self-Assessment, discuss these issues with your purchasing agent or financial officer. If you answered "Don't Know" to Questions 3, 4, or 5 in this Self-Assessment, discuss these issues with your information technologies manager.

DISCUSSION

Transit stock highlights the need to understand not only how inventory physically moves through your system, but also how and when it shows up in your records. If, for example, 500 widgets

Self-Assessment 1–2 continues on next page.

6 FUNDAMENTALS OF INVENTORY MANAGEMENT AND CONTROL

Self-Assessment 1–2 continued from previous page.

appeared as part of existing stock while they were still en route to you, your record count would include them while your shelf count would be 500 short.

How could stock be recorded as a part of inventory before it actually arrives? To answer that question, you must ask, "When did title to the widgets transfer to you?" Did title transfer when the product left the shipper's dock or did it transfer only after the items arrived at your site and were signed for? If title transferred when the product left the shipper's dock and it was then counted as part of your total inventory, your total record count would not match your shelf count. If (a) a stock-keeper did not understand that the item's paper life had floated ahead of its real life, (b) did not have breakdown of items on hand, on order, in transit, and immediately available, and (c) found a mismatch between the shelf and record counts, then she or he might make inappropriate adjustments.

The *Uniform Commercial Code* (*UCC*) governs the transfer of title to product. The UCC has been adopted by most states. Article 2 of the UCC covers the sale of goods.

What Article 2-319 States	What It Means
(1) Unless otherwise agreed, the term *F.O.B.* (which means "free on board") at a named place, even though used only in connection with the stated price, is a delivery term under which:	
(a) when the term is F.O.B. the place of shipment, the seller must at that place ship the goods in the manner provided in this article and bear the expense and risk of putting them into the possession of the carrier; or	This is F.O.B. origin and means that title shifts to the buyer when the goods are delivered to the carrier. Risk of loss while the product is in transit then shifts to the buyer. When the buyer receives notice of the shipment having been made, the goods are then often shown as being a part of the buyer's total inventory. The transit inventory now has a paper life within the buyer's system even though it is still not in the buyer's facility. Buyers will purchase F.O.B. origin in order to control shipping methods, timing, and costs.
(b) when the term is F.O.B. the place of destination, the seller must at his own expense and risk transport the goods to that place and there tender delivery of them in the manner provided in this article.	This is F.O.B. destination and means that title and risk of loss while the goods are in transit stay with the seller until the product reaches the buyer's dock and is accepted. Unless the buyer's system reflects items in transit, the goods have neither a real nor a paper life within the system.

Other categories of inventory should be considered from a functional standpoint.

- *Consumables:* Light bulbs, hand towels, computer and photocopying paper, brochures, tape, envelopes, cleaning materials, lubricants, fertilizer, paint, dunnage (packing materials), and the like are used in many operations. These items are often treated like raw materials.

- *Service, repair, replacement, and spare items (S&R items):* These are after-market items used to "keep things going." As long as a machine or device of some type is being used (in the market) and will need service, repair, etc., in the future, these items are never obsolete. S&R items should not be treated like finished goods for purposes of forecasting the quantity level of your normal stock.
  - Quantity levels of S&R items are based on such considerations as preventive maintenance schedules, predicted failure rates, and dates of various items of equipment. For example, if an organization replaced its fluorescent tubes on an as-needed, on-failure basis, it would need a moderate supply of these lights on hand at all times. However, if the same company relamped all of its ballasts once per year, it would buy a large quantity of tubes all at one time and only keep a small supply on hand on an ongoing basis.
  - Since S&R items are never "obsolete" or "dead" until the equipment or device they are used for is no longer in service, these items should not be included in calculating dead stock levels. See Chapter 2, *Inventory as Money, Arguments in Favor of Disposing of Dead Stock.*
- *Buffer/safety inventory:* This type of inventory can serve various purposes, such as:
  - Compensating for demand and supply uncertainties.
  - Holding it to "decouple" and separate different parts of your operation so that they can function independently of one another as shown in Exhibit 1–1. The amount of inventory in each buffer should be balanced against the business need. It is not necessary to have inventory in all potential buffer areas.
- *Anticipation stock:* This is inventory produced in anticipation of an upcoming season—for example, fancy chocolates made up in advance of Mother's Day or Valentine's Day. Failure to sell in the anticipated period could be disastrous because you may be left with considerable amounts of stock past its perceived shelf life.

Inventory Costs

Inventory brings with it a number of costs. These costs can include:

- Dollars to acquire it
- Space to store it
- Labor to receive, check quality, put away, retrieve, select, pack, ship, and account for it
- Deterioration, damage, and obsolescence
- Theft

Inventory costs generally fall into two categories: ordering costs and holding costs. *Ordering, or acquisition, costs* come about regardless of the actual value of the goods. These costs include the salaries of those purchasing the

Exhibit 1–1
Points Along the Channel of Distribution Where Buffer Stock May Be Used to Decouple Operations

From	Purpose	To
Suppliers	Allows Procurement time to prepare purchase orders, place orders, and control timing and modes of delivery. Protects against uncertainties in lead times.	**Procurement (Purchasing)**
Production	Provides Marketing/Distribution with product to sell while Production is producing items for future sale. Immediate customer satisfaction.	**Marketing/Distribution**
Distribution	Offers the intermediary items to deliver to the consumer/end user.	**Intermediary (UPS, truck line, rail line, etc.)**
Intermediary (UPS, truck line, rail line, etc.)	Satisfies the consumer/end user with product while it is waiting for deliveries from the intermediary.	**Consumer/end user**

product, costs of expediting the inventory, and so on. For a complete discussion of ordering costs see Chapter 5, *Planning and Replenishment Concepts*.

Holding, or *carrying*, *costs* include the cost of capital tied up in inventory (the opportunity cost of money[2]), storage costs (rent, for example), and costs of handling the product (equipment, warehouse and stockkeeping staff, stock losses/wastage, taxes, etc.). For a complete discussion of carrying costs see Chapter 2, *Inventory as Money*.

TRACKING THE PAPER LIFE

In order for you to gain an understanding of the relationship between an item's real life and its paper life within your own system, you should follow a single item on its path through that system. In other words, track an item's physical movement through your facility while noting what is happening to its paper life during that same time period. You will discover instances in which one of these lives moves ahead of the other and instances of system errors—when an item is moved but no paperwork authorizes that action, for example.

---

[2] If you have $2 million tied up in inventory, you cannot earn money (that is, interest) on that money. If you could earn 10 percent interest on that $2 million, you could earn $200,000. Not being able to earn that $200,000 is an opportunity cost.

Exhibit 1–2 provides an example of what could happen if an item's paper life and real life begin to leapfrog one another without the stockkeeper understanding the process.

---

 xhibit 1–2

When Real Life and Paper Life Leapfrog

Carr Enterprises operates six days per week, Monday through Saturday. Its inventory system is updated at 4:45 p.m. every day. In spite of the daily updating, the record count and the shelf count in small stock room #1 are often out of balance.

Carr's warehouse manager, Nate, has decided to count everything in small stock room #1 every Friday. He does so for two months. At the end of that time he is angry—the numbers still don't match.

Carr hires ace inventory detective Shawn to help track down the source of the problem. Nate is flabbergasted. He believes he is counting very carefully; if there is a problem it is with the "computer." Nate declares to anyone who will listen that "the computer is always wrong."

On Monday at 5:15 p.m., Shawn suggests that they examine an item that seems to be out of balance from the previous week's count.

Nate declares, "I'll show you one." Thrusting a brand new inventory stock status report in front of Shawn's nose, Nate states, "Look at these widgets. It says there are 12 of them in stock. When we counted them last week there were 12 of them. I looked at this report this morning and it said there were 13 of them. Now it says there are 12 of them, but I just looked in the stock room and there are actually 15 of them. See, I told you—the computer's always wrong."

Shawn asks if he can see Nate's count sheet with the widgets on it from the previous week. The count sheet looks like this:

Stock Status Report					
Location	Part Number	Description	U/M	Quantity	
AB1002	9063	Gidgets	ea	127	
AB1003	2164	Gadgets	ctn	36	
AB1004	1878	Widgets	ea	~~10~~	12
AB1005	9201	Doodads	dz	98	
AB1006	5769	Whoohahs	pkg	~~105~~	101

Shawn asks what the notations mean.

Nate replies that when the wrong quantity was on the count sheet he would cross it out, write in the correct quantity, and turn the sheet in to Data Entry.

Shawn asked when Nate turned his sheets in. Nate replied, "Friday—why?"

Shawn said, "I understand that you turn the sheets in on Friday. I'm asking, what time do you turn them in?" Nate says he does it at about 5 p.m. Thinking Shawn is criticizing him, Nate defensively states, "Hey, they're busy in Data Entry from 4:30 or so. They're doing cutoff and updates, stuff like that. So I wait until they're done."

Exhibit 1–2 continues on next page.

10 FUNDAMENTALS OF INVENTORY MANAGEMENT AND CONTROL

Exhibit 1–2 continued from previous page.

Shawn asks when Nate's count sheets are keyed into the system. Nate says he doesn't know.

Shawn asks the data entry clerk Hillary when Nate's sheets are keyed in. Hillary replies that she doesn't put Nate's work on the front burner, if Shawn knows what she means. Shawn persists. He asks again, "Who keys Nate's count sheets in and when are they done?" Hillary replies that she works on Saturday but leaves the sheets for Carolyn, the other data entry clerk, to input on Monday.

Shawn asks Hillary if she entered any widgets into the system on Saturday. She says she entered 3 of them into the system on Saturday.

Shawn asks Carolyn how she handles inputting Nate's information. She replies that she pulls up the item on her computer screen, checks to see if the total in the computer matches Nate's handwritten amount. If it doesn't, she changes the amount in the system to match Nate's number.

Shawn charts out the flow of real life and paper life for the widgets, and comes up with the following:

Day	Record Count	Shelf Count	Notes
Friday—close of business	10	12	At the start of business on Friday the system believes there are 10 widgets. There are actually 12. Nate does not note a plus or minus amount on his count sheet. He crosses out the 10 and writes in 12. He does not turn in his count sheets until after the system has been updated for that day. At the close of business on Friday the system still believes there are 10 widgets. There are actually 12.
Saturday—close of business	13	15	No one enters Nate's information on Saturday. Nate does not know this—he hasn't checked. Three widgets are added into the system on Saturday. At the close of business on Saturday the system believes there are 13 widgets in stock. There are actually 15.
Monday—morning	13	15	Monday morning's stock status report reflects Saturday's numbers. During the day on Monday, Carolyn wipes out the record of 13 and enters the quantity of 12 from Nate's sheets.
Monday—close of business	12	15	When the system is updated at 4:45 p.m. on Monday, the stock record and new stock status report reflects that there are 12 widgets. There are actually 15. When Nate began counting on Friday the system was off by 2, and when all was said and done it was off by 3!

As can be seen from the example in Exhibit 1–2, an item's real life and paper life can leapfrog around one another. It is important to understand that these lives can exist independently of one another; to comprehend your own system, you must trace how both product and information move through the system.

The moral of this story: If you are going to note stock quantity changes but there will be intervening inventory events before anyone inputs the

© American Management Association. All rights reserved.

information, you must use a "plus/minus" notation system, for example, +3; –4; ±0. When you use a plus/minus notation system, the data entry clerk will add or subtract from the then-current amount, which will already include any intervening events.

Activity 1–1
Tracking the Paper Life

Instructions: At each stage of the flow chart below, note:

1. Where is the item physically?
2. What piece(s) of paper authorize(s) that?
3. Is information entered into your computer system at one point or another?
4. Who is supposed to write something down? What are they supposed to write down? When were they supposed to write it down? To whom are they supposed to give the piece of paper? What is that person supposed to do with it? When are they supposed to pass the piece of paper along?
5. After the paper chase, where is the item physically?

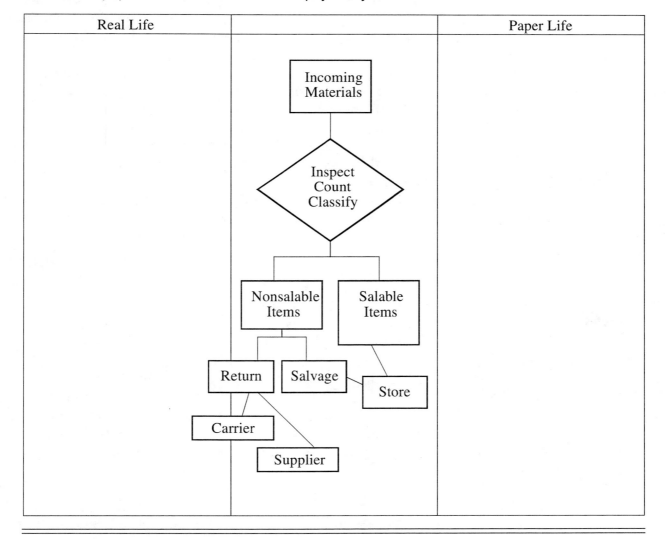

ELECTRONIC DATA INTERCHANGE

Stockkeepers who do not understand how and when an item's paper life is first created within a system become even more confused if there is no hard copy (paper) audit trail they can follow. How could:

- an order be placed
- an order be accepted
- confirmation of the order be given
- shipping instructions be given
- notice of shipping arrangements be given
- a paper life for an item be created in advance of it entering the facility

all without there being any paper copies of these transactions existing? All of these events and more can occur in a paperless environment through electronic data interchange.

Electronic data interchange (*EDI*) occurs when routine business transactions are sent over standard communication lines (telephone lines, for example) between your computer and that of a customer or vendor.

Consider this example of EDI with a vendor. You place an order electronically directly from your computer into the vendor's computer. The vendor's computer then electronically confirms the order and transmits information about the order to the vendor's Shipping and Accounting departments. The vendor's computer also electronically notifies a carrier of the upcoming shipment. The carrier's computer electronically confirms the pickup and provides the vendor with pickup and delivery information. The vendor's computer then notifies your computer of the date, time, and other details of the upcoming delivery. All of this would be accomplished without any human intervention other than the original placement of the order. EDI works in an equivalent manner with customers.

For EDI to work, all system participants must agree to strict rules regarding message content, format, and structure.

An organization's inventory—whether it is sold directly to the customer (as it is for manufacturers, distributors, and retailers) or is linked to a service (as it is for banks, schools, and hospitals)—is a critical aspect of the value all organizations add to their customers.

A key point in managing inventory is to understand how an item's real life and its paper life can exist independently of one another. To comprehend their own systems, managers must be able to trace how both product and information move through the system.

Important issues related to the various types of stock—raw materials, finished product, work in process, and transit inventory—include when and how stock appears in your records. The Uniform Commercial Code's Article

2-319 governs the transfer of title to product and includes terms that spell out possession of transit inventory.

In order to control and manage the items coming into, through, and out of your facility, it is important to understand not only where an item is physically located at any given time, but also how and where the item exists in the inventory accounting system at any given time.

Review Questions

INSTRUCTIONS: *Here is the first set of review questions in this course. Answering the questions following each chapter will give you a chance to check your comprehension of the concepts as they are presented and will reinforce your understanding of them.*

As you can see below, the answer to each numbered question is printed to the side of the question. Before beginning, you should conceal the answers in some way, either by folding the page vertically or by placing a sheet of paper over the answers. Then read and answer each question. Compare your answers with those given. For any questions you answer incorrectly, make an effort to understand why the answer given is the correct one. You may find it helpful to turn back to the appropriate section of the chapter and review the material of which you are unsure. At any rate, be sure you understand all the review questions before going on to the next chapter.

1. Inventory costs generally fall into:
   (a) sales expenditures.
   (b) work in process.
   (c) line during the annual physical inventory.
   (d) ordering costs and holding costs.

   1. (d)

2. EDI is a process whereby:
   (a) routine business transactions are sent over standard communication lines.
   (b) accounting tasks are performed off site.
   (c) delivery schedules are automated.
   (d) the purchasing function is outsourced.

   2. (a)

3. Service and repair stock:
   (a) must never be retained beyond five years from date of purchase.
   (b) are items used to "keep things going."
   (c) should be treated like finished goods for forecasting purposes.
   (d) are often treated like raw materials.

   3. (b)

4. Anticipation stock is:
   (a) inventory en route from one place to another.
   (b) inventory produced to meet demand for an upcoming season.
   (c) a relatively risk-free investment.
   (d) kept at the same level all year.

   4. (b)

Do you have questions? Comments? Need clarification?
Call Educational Services at 1-800-225-3215
or e-mail at ed_svcs@amanet.org.

© American Management Association. All rights reserved.

INVENTORY AS BOTH A TANGIBLE AND AN INTANGIBLE OBJECT   **15**

5. Which article of the Uniform Commercial Code governs the sale   5. (c)
of goods?
  (a) 9
  (b) 1
  (c) 2
  (d) 117

2

Inventory as Money

Learning Objectives

By the end of this chapter, you should be able to:

- Explain how inventory is valued.
- Identify where and why inventory appears on the balance sheet and income statement.
- Calculate various inventory ratios and explain their significance to financial performance.
- Explain the impact of carrying costs on obsolete and slow moving stock.

INTRODUCTION

Why should you care about the financial aspects of inventory?

If for no other reason, you should care about the financial aspects of inventory because top management thinks in terms of dollars—not units. In order to carry on meaningful discussions with management, you must be able to speak in the correct "language."

What do you know about the financial aspects of your inventory right now? Self-Assessment 2–1 will help you take stock of your understanding of some basic accounting concepts.

Self-Assessment 2–1
Basic Understanding of Accounting for Your Inventory

Instructions: Answer each of the following questions by checking "Yes" or "No."

1. Do you know the difference between LIFO and FIFO cost assumption methods?	Yes [ ] No [ ]
2. Do you know your current cost of carrying inventory?	Yes [ ] No [ ]
3. Has your employer given you any of the following three reasons as to why you cannot dispose of your existing, obsolete stock: (a) "I've already paid for it," (b) "We might need it someday," (c) "We might sell it someday"?	Yes [ ] No [ ]
4. Can you calculate the current ratio and the quick ratio and explain their significance to your organization's financial performance?	Yes [ ] No [ ]
5. Do you know what costs should be factored into the valuation of your inventory?	Yes [ ] No [ ]

Even if you do not have a financial background and do not presently have the answers to the questions in Self-Assessment 2–1, it is important to understand and appreciate that inventory information in financial statements can be useful in the operation of your business. A basic understanding of how inventory appears on the balance sheet and its impact on the income statement and cash flow statement will improve your ability to communicate effectively with middle and upper management.

Because inventory is money, it causes management to make decisions. When cash is tight, a controller might insist (with the CEO's backing) that inventory be reduced by 10 percent within a month. Inventory causes management to invest in facilities, people, and equipment to handle and store it.

However, inventory is also a *result* of management decisions. Those decisions include:

- High customer service levels (in traditional thinking, the higher the customer service level, the higher the level of inventory required).
- Tolerance of poor quality (tolerating poor quality and/or unreliable processes requires buffer stocks throughout the company)
- Tolerance of long lead times and long setup times (each of which substantially increases inventory levels)
- Unwillingness to dispose of obsolete or dead inventory
- Traditional approaches, such as EOQ and ROP to inventory management. In contrast, the use of JIT/lean approaches allows a company to reduce inventory while improving quality and customer service.

ACCOUNTING FOR INVENTORIES

As stated in Chapter 1, there are four basic types of inventory:

1. *Raw materials inventory* is made up of goods that will be used in the production of finished products. It includes items like nuts, bolts, flour, and sugar. No value has been added by your company.
2. *Work-in-process inventory (WIP)* consists of materials entered into the production process but not yet completed—subassemblies, for example.
3. *Finished goods inventory* includes completed products waiting to be sold—bar stools, bread, and cookies, for example.
4. *In-transit, or subcontract, inventories* are en route from one place to another.

Most inventory fits into one of these general buckets, yet the amount of each category varies greatly depending on the specifics of your industry and business. For example, the types of inventory found in distribution environments are fundamentally different from those found in manufacturing environments. Distribution businesses tend to carry mostly finished goods for resale, while manufacturing companies tend to have less finished goods and more raw materials and work in process. Given these differences, it is natural that the accounting choices vary between distribution and manufacturing settings.

HOW INVENTORY IS VALUED

In order to assign a cost value to inventory, you must make some assumptions about the cost of inventory on hand. Under the federal income tax laws, a company can only make these assumptions once per fiscal year. Tax treatment is often an organization's chief concern regarding inventory valuation. There are five common inventory valuation methods:

1. *First-in, first-out* or *FIFO* inventory valuation assumes that the first goods purchased are the first to be used or sold regardless of the actual timing of their physical use or sale. This method is most closely tied to actual physical flow of goods in inventory. See Exhibit 2–1.
2. *Last-in, last-out* or *LIFO* inventory valuation assumes that the most recently purchased/acquired goods are the first to be used or sold regardless of the actual timing of their physical use or sale. Since items you have just bought can have different costs than those purchased in the past, this method best matches current costs with current revenues.
3. *Average cost method* of inventory valuation identifies the value of inventory and the cost of goods sold by calculating an average unit cost for all goods available for sale during a given period of time. This valuation method assumes that ending inventory consists of all goods available for sale.

Average Cost = Total Cost of Goods ÷ Total Quantity of Goods
Available for Sale   Available for Sale

4. *Specific cost method* (also *actual cost method*) of inventory valuation assumes that the organization can track the actual cost of an item into, through, and out of the facility. That ability allows you to charge the actual cost of a given item to production or sales. Specific costing is generally used only by companies that have sophisticated computer systems and is ususally reserved for high-value items, such as artwork and custom-made items. This method is substantially more costly than the others.
5. *Standard cost method* of inventory valuation is often used by manufacturing companies to give all of their departments a uniform value for an item throughout a given year. This method is a best-guess approach based on known costs and expenses, such as historical costs and any anticipated changes coming up in the foreseeable future. It is not used to calculate actual net profit or for income tax purposes. Rather, it is a working tool more than a formal accounting approach.

xhibit 2–1

FIFO vs. LIFO vs. Average Cost Method of Inventory Valuation Example

Assume the following inventory events:

- November 5   Purchased 800 widgets at $10.00/unit—Total cost $8,000
- November 7   Purchased 300 widgets at $11.00/unit—Total cost $3,300
- November 8   Purchased 320 widgets at $12.25/unit—Total cost $3,920
- November 10   Sold 750 widgets
- November 14   Sold 460 widgets
- November 15   Purchased 200 widgets at $14.70/unit—Total cost $2,940
- November 18   Sold 220 widgets

BASIC EVENTS

Units Purchased			
Date	# Units	Cost/Unit	Total Cost
11/5	800	$ 10.00	$ 8,000
11/7	300	11.00	3,300
11/8	320	12.25	3,920
11/15	200	14.70	2,940
Total	1,620	N/A	$18,160

Units Sold			
Date	# Units	Cost/Unit	Total Cost
11/10	750	Varies by	
11/14	460	Valuation	
11/18	220	Method	
Total	1,430	N/A	N/A

Exhibit 2–1 continues on next page.

Exhibit 2–1 continued from previous page.

FIFO method of Inventory Valuation:

	Basic Events			FIFO Method of Accounting				
	Units Purchased			Units Sold			Ending Inventory	
Date	# Units	Cost/Unit	Total Cost*	# Units	Cost/Unit	Total Cost*	# Units	Total Cost*
11/5	800	$ 10.00	$ 8,000				800	$ 8,000
11/7	300	11.00	3,300				1,100	11,300
11/8	320	12.25	3,920				1,420	15,220
11/10				750	$ 10.00	$ 7,500	670	7,720
11/14				50	10.00	500	620	7,220
				300	11.00	3,300	320	3,920
				110	12.25	1,348	210	2,572
11/15	200	14.70	2,940				410	5,512
11/18				210	12.25	2,573	200	2,939
				10	14.70	147	190	2,792

*Rounded to nearest whole dollar.

LIFO Method of Inventory Valuation:

	Basic Events			LIFO Method of Accounting				
	Units Purchased			Units Sold			Ending Inventory	
Date	# Units	Cost/Unit	Total Cost*	# Units	Cost/Unit	Total Cost*	# Units	Total Cost*
11/5	800	$ 10.00	$ 8,000				800	$ 8,000
11/7	300	11.00	3,300				1,100	11,300
11/8	320	12.25	3,920				1,420	15,220
11/10				320	$ 12.25	$ 3,920	1,100	11,300
				300	11.00	3,300	800	8,000
				130	10.00	1,300	670	6,700
11/14				460	10.00	4,600	210	2,100
11/15	200	14.70	2,940				410	5,040
11/18				200	14.70	2,940	210	2,100
				20	10.00	200	190	1,900

*Rounded to nearest whole dollar.

Average Cost Method of Inventory Valuation:

$$\text{Average Cost} = \frac{\text{Total Cost of Goods Available for Sale}}{\text{Total Quantity of Goods Available for Sale}}$$

$$= \$18,160 \div 1,620 \text{ units}$$

$$= \$11.21/\text{unit}$$

	Basic Events			Average Cost Method of Accounting				
	Units Purchased			Units Sold			Ending Inventory	
Date	# Units	Cost/Unit	Total Cost*	# Units	Cost/Unit	Total Cost*	# Units	Total Cost*
11/5	800	$ 10.00	$ 8,000				800	$ 8,000
11/7	300	11.00	3,300				1,100	11,300
11/8	320	12.25	3,920				1,420	15,220
11/10				750	$ 11.21	$ 8,407	670	6,812
11/14				460	11.21	5,157	210	1,655
11/15	200	14.70	2,940				410	4,595
11/18				220	11.21	2,466	190	2,129

*Rounded to nearest whole dollar.

Ending Inventory

© American Management Association. All rights reserved.

INVENTORY ON THE BALANCE SHEET

The *balance sheet* shows the financial position of a company on a specific date. It provides details for the basic accounting equation: Assets = Liabilities + Equity. In other words, assets are a company's resources, while liabilities and equity are what pay for those resources.

- Assets represent a company's resources. Assets can be in the form of cash or other items that have monetary value—including inventory. Assets are made up of (a) current assets (assets that are in the form of cash or that are easily convertible to cash within one year, such as accounts receivable, securities, and inventory), (b) longer-term assets, such as investments and fixed assets (property/plant/equipment), or (c) intangible assets (patents, copyrights, and goodwill).
- Liabilities represent amounts owed to creditors (debt, accounts payable, and lease-term obligations).
- Equity represents ownership or rights to the assets of the company (common stock, additional paid-in capital, and retained earnings).

Inventory is typically counted among a company's *current assets* because it can be sold within one year. This information is used to calculate financial ratios that help assess the financial health of the company. (See *Ratio Analyses and What They Mean*, covered later in this chapter.) Note, however, that the balance sheet is not the only place that inventory plays a role in the financial analysis of the company—in fact, inventory shows up on the income statement in the form of *cost of goods sold*.

INVENTORY ON THE INCOME STATEMENT

The *income statement* is a report that identifies a company's revenues (sales), expenses, and resulting profits. While the balance sheet can be described as a snapshot of a company on *a specific date* (June 30, for example), the income statement covers *a given period of time* (June 1–June 30). The *cost of goods* sold is the item on the income statement that reflects the cost of inventory flowing out a business. Exhibit 2–2 illustrates a sample balance sheet and income statement.

The old saying "It costs money to make money" explains the cost of goods sold. You make money by selling inventory. Most accounting systems assume that processing inventory in a manufacturing process "makes" money, because it increases the value. That inventory costs you something. Cost of goods sold (on the income statement) represents the value of goods (inventory) sold during the accounting period. Exhibit 2–3 calculates cost of goods sold.

The value of goods that are *not sold* is represented by the ending inventory amount on the balance sheet, calculated as:

Ending Inventory = Beginning Inventory + Purchases – Cost of Goods Sold

Exhibit 2-2

Sample Balance Sheet and Income Statement

Balance Sheet (assumes FIFO Method of Accounting)

Assets		Liabilities and Equity	
Cash	$5,000	Accounts Payable	$10,000
Accounts Receivable	11,500	Notes Payable	7,500
Inventory (per FIFO method)	2,793	Current Portion of	
Other Current Assets	7,000	Long-Term Debt	3,050
Total Current Assets	26,293	Total Current Liabilities	20,550
Investments	1,800	Long-Term Debt	30,500
Property, Plant, and		Long-Term Lease Obligations	12,250
Equipment, net	53,000	Total Liabilities	$63,300
Deferred charges	1,000		
Patents, Goodwill	1,200	Shareholders' Equity	$19,993
Total Assets	$83,293	Total Liabilities and Equity	$83,293

Income Statement

	FIFO	LIFO	Avg. Cost Method
Revenues	$ 21,582	$21,582	$ 21,582
Less: Cost of Goods Sold	15,367	16,260	16,030
Gross Profit	6,215	5,322	5,552
Less:			
Selling, General, and Administrative Expenses	2,500	2,500	2,500
Depreciation and Amortization Expenses	1,250	1,250	1,250
Goodwill Expense	553	553	553
Profit before Taxes	1,912	1,019	1,249
Less: Federal Income Tax (assume 40%)	765	408	500
After-Tax Income	$ 1,147	$ 611	$ 749

CONCLUSIONS

1. By valuing its inventory under the FIFO method of inventory valuation, this company would have earned an extra $536, or $398 more in after-tax income than under the LIFO or average cost methods of inventory valuation, respectively, due to rising prices. However, taxes would be $357, or $265 higher.
2. By valuing its inventory under the LIFO method of inventory valuation, this company would pay $357, or $92 less in federal income taxes than under the FIFO or average cost methods of inventory valuation, respectively, due to rising prices.
3. If prices fall during an accounting period, FIFO and LIFO have reverse effects on taxes paid and earnings. LIFO would increase earnings and taxes. FIFO would decrease them.

Exhibit 2-3

Calculating Cost of Goods Sold

	FIFO	LIFO	Avg. Cost Method
Cost of Goods Purchased	$18,160	$18,160	$18,160
Minus: Ending Inventory	2,793	1,900	2,130
Cost of Goods Sold	$15,367	$16,260	$16,030

This information is also useful as it can be used to show how a company "officially" accounts for inventory. With it, you can back into the cost of purchases without knowing the actual costs by turning around the equation as follows:

Purchases = Ending Inventory − Beginning Inventory + Cost of Goods Sold

Or, you can figure out the cost of goods sold if you know what your purchase costs are by making the following calculation:

Cost of Goods Sold = Beginning Inventory + Purchases − Ending Inventory

Finally, as you sell or use inventory and take in revenue for it, you subtract the cost of the items from the income. The result is your gross profit.

RATIO ANALYSES AND WHAT THEY MEAN

Is something good or is it bad? To answer that question we often compare one thing to another. That is what a *ratio* is. It is an expression of how many of one item is contained within another.

Ratios can be used in the business world by selecting parts of an organization's finacial statements and comparing one set of financial conditions to another. A company's financial statements summarize key aspects of the business. By reviewing these aspects you can determine that organization's economic well-being. One way of reviewing these financial conditions is to compare one to another by dividing one by the other. For example, if you had $200 cash and $100 worth of debts, you could divide the cash (assets) by the debt (liabilities) getting a ratio of 2 to 1. In other words, you have twice as many assets as you do liabilities.

Ratios are useful tools to explain trends and to summarize business results. Often third parties, such as banks, use ratios to determine a company's creditworthiness. By itself, a ratio holds little meaning. However, when compared to other industry and/or company-specific figures or standards, ratios can be powerful in helping to analyze your company's current and historical results. Companies in the same industry often have similar liquidity ratios or benchmarks, as they often have similar cost structures. Your company's ratios can be compared to:

- Prior period(s)
- Company goals or budget projections
- Companies in your industry
- Companies in other industries
- Companies in different geographic regions

Three ratios are particularly useful when assessing inventory. They are the current ratio, the quick or acid-test ratio, and the inventory turnover ratio.

1. *Current ratio*   The current ratio assesses the organization's overall liquidity and indicates a company's ability to meet its short-term obligations. In other words, it measures whether or not a company will be able to pay its bills. Technically speaking, the current ratio indicates how many dollars of current assets we have for each dollar of current liabilities that we owe. The current ratio is calculated as follows:

Current Ratio = Current Assets ÷ Current Liabilities

Current assets are assets in the form of cash or assets that are easily convertible to cash within one year. They include accounts receivable, securities, and inventory. Current liabilities are liabilities that are due and payable within 12 months, such as accounts payable, notes payable, and the short-term portion of long-term debt.

Standards for the current ratio vary from industry to industry. Companies in service industries that carry little or no inventory typically have current ratios ranging from 1.1 to 1.3—that is, $1.10 to $1.30 in current assets for each dollar of current liabilities. Companies that carry inventory have higher current ratios. Manufacturing companies are included in this latter group and often have current ratios ranging from 1.6 to 2.0; not only do they have inventory in the form of finished goods ready for sale, but they also carry inventory of goods that are not yet ready for sale. Generally speaking, the longer it takes a company to manufacture the inventory and the more inventory it must keep on hand, the higher the current ratio.

What might the current ratio mean? A *low current ratio* may signal that a company has liquidity problems or has trouble meeting its short- and long-term obligations. In other words, the organization might be suffering from a lack of cash flow to cover operating and other expenses. As a result, accounts payable may be building at a faster rate than receivables. Note, however, that this is only an indicator and must be used in conjunction with other factors to determine the overall financial health of an organization. In fact, some companies can sustain lower-than-average current ratios because they move their inventory quickly and/or are quick to collect from their customers and therefore have good cash flow.

A *high current ratio* is not necessarily desirable. It might indicate that the company is holding high-risk inventory or is doing a bad job of managing its

26   FUNDAMENTALS OF INVENTORY MANAGEMENT AND CONTROL

assets. For example, fashion retailers may have costly inventory, but they might also have significant trouble getting rid of the inventory—if the wrong clothing line was selected. This makes it a high-risk company, forcing creditors to require a bigger financial cushion.

If a high current ratio is a result of a very large cash account, it may indicate that the company is not reinvesting its cash appropriately. Even if the current ratio looks fine, other factors must be taken into consideration, as liquidity problems might still exist. Since ratios look at quantity, not quality, it is important to look at what the current assets consist of to determine if they are made up of slow-moving inventory. In order to assess inventory's impact on liquidity, another test of liquidity should be taken into account—the quick ratio (or acid-test) ratio.

2. *Quick ratio or acid-test ratio*   The quick ratio compares the organization's most liquid current assets to its current liabilities. The quick ratio is calculated as follows:

Quick Ratio = (Current Assets − Inventories) ÷ Current Liabilities

Assume that an industry that sells on credit has a quick ratio of at least 0.8. In other words, the company has at least 80¢ in liquid assets (probably in the form of accounts receivable) for every $1 of liabilities. Industries that have significant cash sales (such as grocery stores) tend to be even lower. As with the current ratio, a low quick ratio is an indicator of cash flow problems. A high ratio may indicate poor asset management, as cash may not be properly reinvested or accounts receivable levels may be out of control. An organization's ability to promptly collect its accounts receivable has a significant impact on this ratio. The quicker the collection, the more liquidity the organization has.

3. *Inventory turnover ratio*   The inventory turnover ratio measures, on average, how many times inventory is replaced over a period of time. In its simplest sense, an inventory turn occurs every time an item is received, is used or sold, and is then replaced. If a SKU came in twice during the year, was used/sold, and then replenished, that would be 2 turns per year. If this happened once per month, it would be 12 turns per year.

Inventory turnover is an important measure since the ability to move inventory quickly directly impacts the company's liquidity. Inventory turnover is calculated as follows:

Inventory Turnover Ratio = Cost of Goods Sold ÷ Average Inventory

Essentially, when a product is sold, it is subtracted from inventory and transferred to cost of goods sold. Therefore, this ratio indicates how quickly inventory is moving for accounting purposes. It does not necessarily reflect how many actual physical items were sold from the facility itself. This is true because the cost of goods sold number may include items you sold but never physically handled. For example, items that you purchased and then drop-

© American Management Association. All rights reserved.

shipped directly to your customer's site aren't ever handled within your facility. A more accurate measure of how many times actual physical inventory turned within the site would be:

Actual Physical Inventory Turnover Ratio = Cost of Goods Sold ÷ Average Inventory from Inventory Only

Note that if the inventory has increased or decreased significantly during the year, the average inventory for the year may be skewed and may not accurately reflect the turnover ratio going forward. Also, if the company uses the LIFO method of accounting, the ratio may be inflated because LIFO may undervalue the inventory during times of inflation.

Unlike the current ratio and quick ratio, the inventory turnover ratio does not adhere to a standard range. Organizations with highly perishable products can have inventory turns of 30 times a year or more. And companies in very tight supply chains can have very high inventory turns; some automotive parts manufacturers that sell to the final assembly plants—for example, to Ford, Honda, and Toyota—have 50 turns. Companies that retain large amounts of inventory or that require a long time to build their finished products might have turns of only 2 or 3 times a year. In general, the overall trend in business today is to reduce carrying costs by limiting the amount of inventory in stock at any given time. As a result, both individual inventory turnovers and industry averages in this area have increased in recent years.

It is important to understand, however, that many factors can cause a low inventory turnover ratio. The company may be holding the wrong type of inventory, its quality may be lacking, or it may have sales/marketing issues. Activity 2–1 provides an opportunity for you to calculate the current ratio, quick ratio, and inventory turnover ratio. After completing Activity 2–1, try calculating the same ratios for your organization.

Activity 2–1
Using Ratios

Instructions: Using Exhibit 2–2, calculate the current, quick, and inventory turnover ratios.

1. Assume FIFO method of inventory valuation.
2. Assume that the average inventory value for the period is $5,600.

Current Ratio = Current Assets ÷ Current Liabilities

$$\frac{}{\text{Current Ratio}} = \frac{}{\text{Current Assets}} \div \frac{}{\text{Current Liabilities}}$$

Quick Ratio = (Current Assets − Inventories) ÷ Current Liabilities

$$\frac{}{\text{Quick Ratio}} = \frac{()}{\text{(Current Assets − Inventories)}} \div \frac{}{\text{Current Liabilities}}$$

Activity 2–1 continues on next page.

Activity 2–1 continued from previous page.

Inventory Turnover Ratio = Cost of Goods Sold ÷ Average Inventory

$$\overline{\text{Inventory Turnover Ratio}} = \overline{\text{Cost of Goods Sold}} \div \overline{\text{Average Inventory}}$$

Work with your organization's controller or other financial officer to analyze your own company's ratios. The greater your ability to state ideas in terms meaningful to the decision-makers in your organization, the more persuasive you become.

OBSOLETE STOCK

Any stockkeeper who has had to repeatedly move really slow-moving or outright *dead stock*—stock that cannot be sold—out of the way, or who finds herself hurting for space because obsolete product eats up square foot after square foot, knows that these items "just gotta go."

Self-Assessment 2–2
Your Very Slow-Moving, Obsolete, and Just Plain Dead Stock

Instructions: After reviewing your inventory master list:

1. List those items you consider to be very slow movers, obsolete, or "dead."
2. Write down your thoughts on why those items are still part of your overall inventory.

_____

_____

_____

_____

_____

_____

_____

_____

_____

Self-Assessment 2–2 continues on next page.

© American Management Association. All rights reserved.

Self-Assessment 2–2 continued from previous page.

Why do you believe the above items are still part of your inventory?_____

_____

_____

_____

_____

Why You Have Been Told Not to Dispose of It

Why is the dead stock still in your facility? Here are the four reasons most often given as to why the product can't be disposed of:

1. It's already paid for.
2. We might use it someday.
3. We might sell it someday.
4. We can't write it off; it would hurt our financials.

These explanations seem logical and the idea of throwing away dead stock may be counter-intuitive. Indeed, there are some very real practical problems with simply hauling it off to the dumpster.

Problems with Convincing Decision-Makers That "It's Gotta Go"

Decision-makers often have difficulty disposing of "dead" inventory because it will adversely affect the balance sheet and deplete resources considered to be valuable for lending purposes.

- *Impact of write-off*—Anything that appears as an asset on the balance sheet has an accounting value. This value, consisting of an item's original cost minus depreciation, is called the *book value*. It is irrelevant that the item may actually be worthless to either a customer or as part of a manufacturing process. If it has a one-dollar value on the books, then disposing of dead inventory has an accounting consequence to an organization.

If an organization sells dead inventory that has a monetary value at a deep discount, throws it away, or gives it away to a charity, it will have to immediately write off the book value of those items, which will, of course, have a negative impact on the financial statements.

If your organization resists making extraordinary adjustments to the balance sheet and never or seldom writes off dead inventory, you may have a difficult time convincing any decision-maker to dispose of these items. The decision-maker will simply not be willing to "take the hit on the books."

- *Organization's capital structure*—Almost everyone has heard the expression "Cash is king." The problem for many organizations is that cash flow doesn't always keep up with their needs.

Many organizations raise operating capital by borrowing against their accounts receivable and the book value of the inventory they are carrying.

Accounts receivable are the amounts due from customers resulting from normal sales activities. Depending on the industry, banks will generally lend up to 75 percent of the value of accounts receivable due in 90 days or less.

Bankers will also lend against the book value of inventory. The willingness to lend against this asset is not as straightforward as it is with accounts receivable. The more complex nature of these transactions derives from the fact that in accordance with generally accepted accounting principles inventory should be valued at the *lower* of cost or fair market value. Therefore, dead stock should logically be valued at a fair market value of zero dollars no matter what it originally cost.

In spite of standard accounting practices and even though parts of your inventory have no real market value (and should be valued at zero dollars), bankers will often loan your organization 50 percent to 60 percent of the value of the inventory *as that value is shown on the books.* So, companies will sometimes continue to carry dead stock in order to retain this artificial value on the books. This is an area over which most stockkeepers will not have any direct control. However, the arguments in the following section may overcome the need to keep inventory values artificially high.

Arguments in Favor of Disposing of Dead Stock

Strong arguments can be made in favor of disposing of nonproductive stock. They include recapture of space, efficient utilization of labor and equipment, and reduction of carrying costs associated with having inventory sitting around.

Recapture of Space

In terms of space utilization, there are some simple mathematical facts to keep in mind.

- Multiplying an item's length times its width tells you the amount of square feet the item occupies.
- Multiplying an item's length times its width times its height tells you the amount of cubic feet it occupies.

If you were to calculate the space taken up by dead product, you would gain a powerful argument in favor of disposing of this inventory. To bolster the argument, you may want to ask your organization's financial officer how much the company is paying per square foot for rent. Multiplying the square footage consumed by dead product times the rent per square foot often yields a truly eye-opening dollar amount.

Providing actual numbers to a decision-maker is far more effective than speaking in generalities like, "Dead stock is taking up a lot of space." Pointing out that obsolete stock is "taking up 4,000 square feet" or "represents $2,000 per month in per-square-foot costs" should help you convince your decision-maker that "it's gotta go."

Efficient Utilization of Labor and Machine Resources

Not only does obsolete inventory take up a lot of space, it can also get in the way of workers. Repeatedly moving obsolete product out of the way diminishes efficient use of both labor and machine time.

Too often, in trying to argue against keeping obsolete stock, stockkeepers will state such generalities as, "It takes us a lot of time to move that stuff around." How long is "a lot of time"? Is it an hour a day or four hours per week? Without specific numbers your arguments will sound hollow.

As many business writers have noted, "You cannot control what you do not measure." To get specific time and dollar amounts you need to do the following:

- Every time you or your staff move dead product out of the way, measure the amount of direct labor that goes into that effort for one month. Remember, if two workers are working together to move the items and they work for 15 minutes, that represents 15 minutes times 2, or 30 minutes, of direct labor.
- At the end of the month, divide the total amount of labor hours by 4 to determine a weekly average. To determine the amount of yearly labor involved in moving dead stock, multiply the weekly average times the number of weeks in a year that your company operates.

Once again obtaining base information from your financial officer, multiply the average hourly wage you pay your workers, including benefits, times the annual labor number. The result will make a rather impressive argument as to how the organization can save thousands of dollars per year by disposing of its dead stock.

Reduction of Carrying Costs (The K Factor)

The *K factor* represents the number of pennies per inventory dollar per year a company is spending to house its inventory. It is generally expressed as a percentage. In other words, a K factor of 25 percent means that you are spending 25¢ per inventory dollar per year to house your inventory. A $1 dead item that sits on your shelf for a year would cost you 25¢ that year, a total of 50¢ at the end of the second year, a total of 75¢ at the end of the third year, and so on.

There are two ways of computing the K factor: a traditional method in which you add together various expenses directly related to carrying inventory, and a rough rule-of-thumb method. Exhibit 2–4 illustrates both methods.

Since it always costs something to carry inventory, it is obvious that the longer dead stock remains in your facility, the more it will cost. Two approaches can be used to argue this point effectively.

1. Demonstrate the impact of carrying costs on your existing dead stock. This addresses the we've-already-paid-for-it argument in favor of retaining dead stock. See Exhibit 2–5.
2. Demonstrate that if the product remains in inventory long enough, even selling it at a profit will not recapture your original cost. This addresses

Exhibit 2-4
Methods of Determining the Cost of Carrying Inventory

Traditional Accounting Method		Rule-of-Thumb Method
Warehouse space	$ 130,000	
Taxes	65,000	20% + Prime Lending Rate = K Factor
Insurance	40,000	
Obsolescence/shrinkage	23,000	
Material handling	64,800	
Cost of money invested	200,000	
Total annual costs	$ 522,800	

$$\frac{\text{Total Annual Costs}}{\text{Average Inventory Value}} = \frac{\$522,800}{\$2,000,000} = 26\% \text{ K Factor}$$

the we-might-need-it-someday and we-might-sell-it-someday arguments in favor of retaining dead stock.

In Exhibit 2–5 a percentage is used to indicate the amount of dead stock in the facility. Note, however, that it is always more convincing to a decision-maker if you use actual lists and dollar amounts to demonstrate those items

Exhibit 2-5
Demonstrating the Impact of the K Factor on Existing Dead Stock

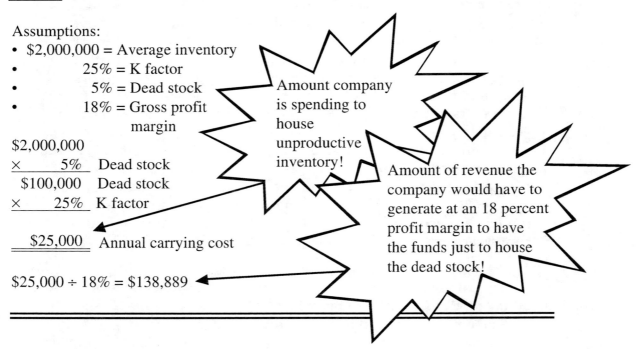

xhibit 2–6
Creating an Inventory Analysis Report Listing Dead Stock

SKU #	Description	Quantity on Hand	Unit Cost	Dollar Value of Product in House	Monthly Usage	Projected Annual Usage	Months Supply on Hand

that are dead instead of a generality like a rough percentage. See Exhibit 2–6 for an example of an effective inventory analysis report.

Exhibit 2–7 demonstrates the negative effect on profit of keeping dead stock. Activity 2–2 allows you to calculate the annual costs of holding dead stock in your organization.

xhibit 2–7
Demonstrating the Impact of the K Factor on Items Sold at a Profit but After Remaining in Stock for Long Periods of Time

Assumptions:

- 720 pairs of earmuffs purchased at $2.25/pair ($1,620 original cost)
- Earmuffs have remained unsold for 2 years
- We hope to sell at a 30% gross profit per pair ($2.93/pair)
- 25% K factor

$1,620 × 25% = $405 per year in carrying cost
$405 ÷ 720 pairs = 56¢ per year, per pair in additional carrying cost expense

Total cost after one year: $2.25 + $0.56 = $2.81/pair (720 pairs × $2.81/pair = $2,023)
Total cost after two years: $2.81 + $0.56 = $3.37/pair (720 pairs × $3.37/pair = $2,426)

Exhibit 2–7 continues on next page.

© American Management Association. All rights reserved.

34   FUNDAMENTALS OF INVENTORY MANAGEMENT AND CONTROL

Exhibit 2–7 continued from previous page.

Costs are going up $0.002 per day ($0.56 ÷ 365 days/yr)
$2.93 = Sales price
− 2.25 = Original cost
$0.68 = Gross profit expected
$0.68 ÷ $0.002 = Breakeven at 340 Days—after 340 days there is no profit at all!

    Original cost: $1,620
    Cost including carrying costs after two years: $2,426
    Revenue from selling earmuffs at $2.93/pair: $2,110 ($2.93/pair × 720 pairs)

Loss on sale made after inventory has been in-house for two years even though sale made at 30 percent gross profit on original cost: $316 ($2,426 − $2,110)

Activity 2–2
Demonstrating the Effect of Carrying Dead Stock

Instructions: Using Exhibit 2–5 as a model, calculate the impact of the K factor on your organization's dead stock.

Assumptions:

- _____ = Average inventory

- _____ % = K factor

- _____ % = Dead stock

- _____ % = Gross profit margin

$
×_____ Dead stock
$ Dead Stock
×_____% K factor

$_____ **Annual carrying cost of holding your dead stock**

$_____ ÷ _____ % = $_____ Amount of sales needed to generate the money needed to carry the dead stock

---

Methods Of Disposal

Various approaches to disposing of dead stock exist.

- Sell it at net price.
- Temporarily raise commissions for salespeople.

© American Management Association. All rights reserved.

- Discount the price.
- Return it to the vendor.
- Donate it.
- Write it off.
- Auction it off.

It is important to remember that when reports or other information flow up a chain of command, the level of detail at each level *decreases.* Generally, each higher level of management wants to see less and less information on which to base decisions. You should resist providing only minimal data in making arguments regarding dead stock. This is a time to let the detail do the talking.

ORDERING COST AND PURCHASING

Although you should only have the minimum amount of inventory required for either production or distribution on hand, be careful not to purchase small quantities over and over again. Buying small amounts frequently leads to excessive replenishment costs (the *R factor*).

Here is a simple example of how an excessive R factor can be created. Assumptions:

- It costs a certain amount of money per line item, per purchase order to buy something. For this example assume $2.59 per line item, per purchase order.
- You purchase 1 million widgits per year.

If you bought all 1 million widgits at one time, the R factor would be $2.59 since there was only one purchase order with one line item on it.

If you bought 250,000 widgits at a time, the R factor would be $10.36 because you would have four purchase orders with one line item each at a cost of $2.59 each.

If you bought 1 million widgits one at a time at an R factor of $2.59, the replenishment cost would be $2,590,000!

Because of the R factor, modern purchasing dictates that you buy larger quantities on fewer purchase orders but have suppliers release items on a prearranged schedule or on demand.

Ultimately, the point at which your cost of carrying inventory matches the cost of purchasing it is the proper economic order quantity of that item. See Chapter 5, *Planning and Replenishment Concepts, Replenishment Costs* for a more detailed discussion of replenishment costs and order quantities.

Organizations can use five common methods for valuing inventory: first-in, first-out, or FIFO; last-in, first-out, or LIFO; the average cost method; the specific cost method (also known as the actual cost method); and the standard cost method. Tax treatment is often a chief concern in relation to inventory valuation.

Although inventory managers may never participate in the preparation of month- or year-end financial statements, it is in their own self-interest to review these statements and think about how the inventory values reflected there impact the operation and how their decisions and actions affect the company's financial results.

Three financial ratios are useful when assessing inventory. They are the current ratio, which assesses the organization's overall liquidity and indicates a company's ability to meet its short-term obligations; the quick, or acid-test, ratio, which compares the organization's most liquid current assets to its current liabilities; and the inventory turnover ratio, which measures, on average, how many times inventory is replaced over a period of time.

Carrying costs on slow-moving stock include warehouse space, taxes, insurance, obsolescence/shrinkage, material handling, and the cost of money invested. If product remains in stock long enough, even selling it at a profit will not recapture the original cost. This information is best conveyed using actual lists and dollar amounts rather than percentages. Remember, "If you can measure it, you can control it."

Review Questions

1. A balance sheet is best described as a report that:
   (a) identifies a company's revenues (sales), expenses, and resulting profits for a given period of time.
   (b) shows the financial position of a company on a specific date.
   (c) shows the relationship between inventory on-hand and on-order.
   (d) identifies the number of items per level and number of tiers of product on a pallet.

   1. (b)

2. An income statement is best described as a report that:
   (a) identifies a company's revenues (sales), expenses, and resulting profits for a given period of time.
   (b) shows the financial position of a company on a specific date.
   (c) shows the relationship between inventory on hand and on order.
   (d) identifies the number of items per level and number of tiers of product on a pallet.

   2. (a)

3. The K factor represents:
   (a) the number of pennies per inventory dollar per year a company is spending to house its inventory.
   (b) anything that appears as an asset on the balance sheet.
   (c) the impact of carrying costs on your dead stock.
   (d) the percentage of operating capital raised by borrowing against the book value of your inventory.

   3. (a)

4. Ratio analyses are financial tools that can be used to compare your company's performance to:
   (a) forecasted results.
   (b) companies in your industry.
   (c) budget projections.
   (d) all of the above.

   4. (d)

5. The average cost method of valuing inventory assumes:
   (a) the organization can track the actual cost of an item into, through, and out of the facility.
   (b) the first goods purchased are the first to be used or sold regardless of the actual timing of their use or sale.
   (c) a uniform value for an item throughout a given year.
   (d) the value of inventory and cost of goods sold can be found by calculating an average unit cost for all goods available for sale during a given period of time.

   5. (d)

Do you have questions? Comments? Need clarification?
Call Educational Services at 1-800-225-3215
or e-mail at ed_svcs@amanet.org.

© American Management Association. All rights reserved.

ANSWERS

Answer to Activity 2–1

Current Ratio = Current Assets ÷ Current Liabilities

1.28 = $26,293 ÷ $20,550

Quick Ratio = (Current Assets – Inventories) ÷ Current Liabilities

1.14 = ($26,293 – $2,793) ÷ $20,550

Inventory Turnover Ratio = Cost of Goods Sold ÷ Average Inventory

2.74 = $15,367 ÷ $5,600

3

Physical Location and Control of Inventory

Learning Objectives

By the end of this chapter, you should be able to:

- Describe the characteristics and space requirements of the most common stock locator systems.
- Plan for efficient stock placement within a facility.
- Set up a working stock addressing and tracking system.

INTRODUCTION

If you can't find an item, you can't count it, fill an order with it, or build a widgit with it. This chapter shows you how to set up a system that allows you to put items where they will do the most good for your organization. Self-Assessment 3–1 helps you to see how well your stock is organized.

 Self-Assessment 3–1
Is Your Stock Well Organized?

Instructions: Answer each of the following questions by checking "Yes" or "No."

1. Do my staff or I stop what we are doing several times each day to do a visual stock status check for someone within our organization?	Yes [ ] No [ ]

Self-Assessment 3–1 continues on next page.

© American Management Association. All rights reserved.

Self-Assessment 3–1 continued from previous page.

2. Do my staff or I often have to "look around" for items that were not where we thought they were?	**Yes [ ] No [ ]**
3. Does my organization report stockouts on product we actually have (because we could not find it at the time it was needed)?	**Yes [ ] No [ ]**

If the answer to any of the above questions is "Yes," then the next question to ask yourself is, "Does my locator system allow me to know where each stock-keeping unit (SKU) is at any given time, and in what quantities?" If you cannot control the location of your product or raw materials from both a physical and a recordkeeping standpoint, then your inventory accuracy will suffer.

To sustain inventory accuracy on an ongoing basis, you must:

1. Formalize the overall locator system used throughout the facility
2. Track the storage and movement of product from
   a. Receipt to storage
   b. Order filling to shipping or to staging at a point of use
3. Maintain timely records of all item storage and movement.

The objective of this chapter is to provide you with a working knowledge of four things.

1. Three key *stock locator systems* (these systems relate to the overall organization of SKUs within a facility and their impact on space planning)
2. Item placement theories dealing with the specific arrangement of product within an area of the warehouse (should the box be over here or over there? for example)
3. Some practical methods of attaching addresses to stock items
4. Tying an item number to its location address.

We begin with common locator systems.

COMMON LOCATOR SYSTEMS

The purpose of a material locator system is to create procedures that allow you to track product movement throughout the facility. Although going by many names, the most common "pure" systems are *memory, fixed,* and *random.* One type of fixed system is the *zone* system. The *combination* approach is a commonly used mixture of the fixed and random systems.

In considering which locator system will work best, you should attempt to:

Minimize	**Maximize**
Use of space	Accessibility of all items
Use of equipment	Protection from damage

Use of labor Ability to locate an item
Administrative costs Flexibility
　　　　　　　　　　Safety

Achieving all of these objectives at the same time is difficult, if not impossible. Often each of these concerns creates conflicts with one or more of the others. For example, you may wish to store all cylinders together in order to utilize the same equipment to handle them or locate them together for ease of getting to and retrieving them. However, if the chemical nature of the contents of these cylinders prohibits them from being stored in the same area, safety and protection of property concerns override other considerations. Exhibit 3–1 provides scenarios in which various valid considerations are in conflict.

The stockkeeper should select a locator system that provides the best solution given the tradeoffs between conflicting objectives. No one system is "right." What is best will depend on considerations such as the following:

- Space available
- Location system (see *Impact On Physical Space* discussions in this chapter.)

---

 xhibit 3–1

Examples of Valid Storage Considerations In Conflict

- Scenario One: *Accessibility Versus Space* Charmax, Inc. wishes to have its entire product as easy to get to as possible for order-filling purposes. It therefore attempted to have a *picking face* (a front-line, visible position from which product may easily be selected) for each item. In order to actually create a picking face for each SKU, Charmax would have to assign a specific location for every product appearing on all of its pick tickets, with no two items placed one on top of another and no item placed behind another. Charmax quickly realized that it lacked sufficient space in its facility to have a specific position for every item it carried.
- Scenario Two: *Use of Labor Versus Protection from Damage* Alana Banana Enterprises wishes to reduce labor hours by putting into place efficient product-handling procedures. Its intent is to develop standard operating procedures so that workers will only handle SKUs four times: once when received, once when stored, once when picked, and once when loaded. However, in order to protect SKUs from bruising, items must be placed into protective cartons for storage. SKUs are not picked in full carton quantities so workers have to remove various quantities at different times from the cartons. Empty cartons must then be stacked, cleaned, restacked, and taken back to the receiving area for reuse. These protective measures add a number of labor-intensive steps to the process.
- Scenario Three: *Ability to Locate an Item Versus Space Utilization* Racquetballers America wants to assign a specific home to each of its products for inventory control purposes; however, it has a small stockroom. Racquetballers realizes that, if it uses a fixed storage location approach, it must assign sufficient space to store the maximum amount of any one of its SKUs that will ever be on hand at one time in that location. If it uses a random location approach where items can be placed one on top of another or behind one another, then it will minimize the space required. Racquetballers decides using its limited space is more important than putting in the extra labor and administration necessary to keep track of where everything is as it moves around the floor.

- Dimensions of product or raw materials stored
- Shape of items
- Weight of items
- Product characteristics, e.g., stackable, toxic, liquid, crushable, etc.
- Storage methods, e.g., floor stacked, racks, carousels, shelving, etc.
- Labor availability
- Equipment, including special attachments, available
- Information systems support

Every company has a limited amount of space available for stock storage. Some locator systems use space more effectively than do others. When choosing your locator system, you need to think carefully about how much space it will use. The following pages show several types of locator systems, and evaluate the strengths and weaknesses of each type.

Memory Systems

Memory systems are solely dependent on human recall. Often they are little more than someone saying, "I think it's over there."

The foundations of this locator system are simplicity, relative freedom from paperwork or data entry, and maximum utilization of all available space. Memory systems depend directly on people and only work if several or all of the conditions listed in Exhibit 3–2 exist at the same time.

Impact on Physical Space—Memory Systems

The most complete space utilization is available through this system. Why? Because no item has a dedicated location that would prevent other SKUs from occupying that same position if it were empty (either side-to-side or up-and-down).

xhibit 3–2

Conditions Under Which Memory Systems Will Work

- Storage locations are limited in number.
- Storage locations are limited in size.
- The variety of items stored in a location is limited.
- The size, shape, or unitization (e.g., palletization, strapping together, banding, etc.) of items allows for easy visual identification and separation of one SKU from another.
- Only one or a very limited number of individuals work within the storage areas.
- Workers within the storage area do not have duties that require them to be away from those locations.
- The basic types of items making up the inventory do not radically change within short time periods.
- There is not a lot of stock movement.

Pros—Memory Systems
- Simple to understand
- Little or no ongoing paper-based or computer-based tracking required
- Full utilization of space
- No requirement for tying a particular stocking location (bin, slot, drawer, rack, bay, spot, etc.) identifier to a specific SKU.
- Meets requirements of single-item facilities—a grain silo, for example

Cons—Memory Systems
- The organization's ability to function must strongly rely on the memory, health, availability, and attitude of a single individual (or a small group of people).
- Significant and immediate decreases in accuracy result from changes in the conditions set out in Exhibit 3–2.
- Once an item is lost to recall, it is lost to the system.

Despite its limitations, a memory system may be as efficient as any other, particularly if there are only a limited number of different SKUs within a small area.

Fixed Location Systems

In a pure *fixed location system* every item has a home and nothing else can live there. Some (not pure) fixed systems allow two or more items to be assigned to the same location, with only those items being stored there.

Impact on Physical Space—Fixed Location Systems

If quantities of any given SKU are large, then its "home" may consist of two or more storage positions. However, all of these positions collectively are the only places where this item may exist within the facility, and no other items may reside there. Basically, everything has a home and nothing else can live there.

Fixed location systems require large amounts of space. There are two reasons for this:

- Honeycombing
- Planning around the largest quantity of an item that will be in the facility at one time

Honeycombing is the warehousing situation where storage space is available but is not fully utilized for one of the causes listed in Exhibit 3–3.

Honeycombing is unavoidable given location system tradeoffs, product shape, and the like. The goal of a careful layout is to minimize how often and to what extent this happens.

Honeycombing occurs both horizontally (side-to-side) and vertically (up-and-down), robbing a facility of both square feet and cubic space, as illustrated in Exhibit 3–4.

Exhibit 3-3
Causes of Honeycombing

Cause	Description
Product shape	Physical characteristics cut down on stackability and prevent use of cubic space or prevent placing one item against another.
Product put-away	Product is not stacked or placed in a uniform manner, causing loss of vertical or horizontal space.
Location system rules	Situation where a location is empty but no other item may be placed there since it is not the second item's assigned home.
Poor housekeeping	Trash, poorly placed desks, etc., force empty space around it.

 Exhibit 3-4
Honeycombing

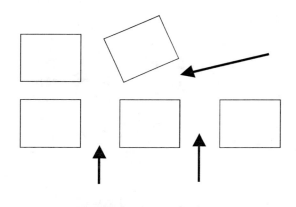
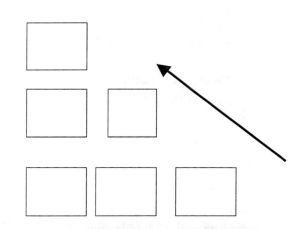

© American Management Association. All rights reserved.

PHYSICAL LOCATION AND CONTROL OF INVENTORY   45

Exhibit 3–5
Determining Impact of Honeycombing—Ratio Method

Determine the impact of honeycombing on your present facility using the following procedure.

1. Count the number of locations you currently have set up to store items, both horizontally and vertically. Include all locations whether full, partially full, or empty.
2. Count the number of empty positions.
3. Divide the number of empty locations by the total number of storage positions you have. The result will be your honeycombing ratio.

$$\text{Honeycombing Ratio} = \frac{\text{Empty Storage Locations}}{\text{Total Storage Locations}}$$

Example

$$\text{Honeycombing Ratio} = \frac{353}{1{,}200} = 0.294, \text{ or about } 30\%$$

That ratio represents the percentage of empty space within the storage portion of your stockroom(s). Determining this ratio provides you with a baseline. If you decide to change your storage philosophy or change your storage mechanisms (from racks to floor stacking, from racks to shelving, etc.), you can then determine the new ratio and measure improvement in space utilization.

There are two simple methods of determining the level of honeycombing within your own facility. One deals with a simple ratio analysis, the other with cubic space. Exhibit 3–5 shows how to use ratio analysis; Exhibit 3–6 shows the cubic footage method.

Exhibit 3–6
Determining Impact of Honeycombing—Cubic Footage Method

Globus, Inc. has 16,000 cubic feet (ft³) of storage space. Globus has a fixed location system and has divided the storeroom into 490 storage locations with the following sizes (and empty locations):

No. of Locations	Ft³	Total Ft³	Empty Locations
400	20	8,000	65
50	50	2,500	15
25	100	2,500	5
15	200	3,000	8
490		16,000	93

The honeycombing ratio on a location basis is:

$$\frac{\text{Empty Spaces}}{\text{Total Spaces}} = \frac{93}{490} = 19\%$$

Exhibit 3–6 continues on next page.

© American Management Association. All rights reserved.

Exhibit 3–6 continued from previous page.

The ratio method is a relatively simple approach to determining a rough estimate of honeycombing. However, the ratio method doesn't account for the fact that storage spaces within a given facility come in various sizes. A more precise method for determining honeycombing is to calculate the amount of unused cubic feet.

The honeycombing ratio on a ft^3 basis is:

$$\frac{\text{Empty Spaces} \times \text{Ft}^3}{\text{Total Ft}^3} = (65 \times 20 \text{ Ft}^3) + (50 \times 15 \text{ Ft}^3) + (5 \times 100 \text{ Ft}^3) + (8 \times 200 \text{ Ft}^3)\backslash 16,000 \text{ Ft}^3$$

$$= \frac{1,300 + 750 + 500 + 1,600}{16,000}$$

$$= \frac{4,150}{16,000}$$

$$= \mathbf{26\%}$$

The other thing that causes the fixed system to require significant space is the necessity of planning around the largest quantity of an item that will be in the facility at one time. Each SKU will have an assigned location or locations. This "home" must be large enough to contain the total cubic space the item will fill up at the time that the largest quantity of that item will be in the facility. In other words, if a thousand cases of widgits are all in the warehouse at the same time, the home of the widgits has to be large enough to hold all one thousand cases. Therefore, the total space required for all items in a fixed system will be the total cubic space of 100 percent of all SKUs as though the maximum quantity of each of them was in the facility at one time. Space planning for an entire inventory in a dedicated location environment is done around a one-year time period. Stated differently, all of the space needed for all of the widgits has to be added to all of the space needed for all of the gidgits, and that space has to be added to all of the room needed for the doodads, and so on. . . .

Pros—Fixed Location Systems

- Immediate knowledge of where all items are located (this system feature dramatically reduces confusion as to where to put it, where to get it, etc., which increases efficiency and productivity, while reducing errors in both stocking and order fulfillment)
- Reduces training time for new hires and temporary workers
- Simplifies and expedites both receiving and stock replenishment because predetermined put-away instructions can be generated
- Allows for controlled routing of order fillers (Exhibit 3–7 provides an example of how a fixed location system can assist an organization in fulfilling an order quickly)
- Allows product to be aligned sequentially (SKU001, SKU002, SKU003, etc.)
- Allows for strong control of individual lots, facilitating *first-in, first-out* (FIFO) control, if that is desired (Lot control can also be accomplished under a random location system; however simpler, more definitive control is possible using the dedicated location concept.)

- Allows product to be positioned close to its ultimate point of use (Product positioning is discussed in the *Item Placement Theories* section of this chapter.)
- Allows product to be placed in a location most suitable to that SKU's size, weight, toxic nature, flammability, or other similar characteristics

Cons—Fixed Location Systems
- These systems contribute to honeycombing within storage areas.
- Space planning must allow for the total cubic volume of all products likely to be in a facility within a defined period of time.
- Dedicated systems are somewhat inflexible. If you have aligned product by sequential numbering and then add a subpart or delete a numbered SKU, then you must move all products to allow for the add-in or collapse your locations to fill in the gap.

Exhibit 3–7
Controlling Order-Filling Operations Through Specific Item Placement

Scenario One: Shawn Michael Irish Linens, Inc. has two sections of select rack on which it randomly places product. This organization uses the *whole order* method of order filling in which a single picker pulls each item on the pick ticket/work order for an entire order, marshaling it together as the order filler travels from storage location to storage location. No planning has gone into item placement. Consequently, heavy items which should be picked first are commingled with light, crushable items that should be selected last. In addition, work orders/pick tickets do not display SKUs to be picked in any particular order. The filler must run up and down the aisle trying to pull product in some semblance of order. Therefore, a typical order run, where product was located in positions 1, 5, 10, 11, 15, and 20, may look like this:

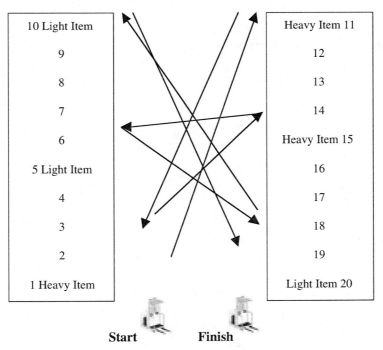

Exhibit 3–7 continues on next page.

© American Management Association. All rights reserved.

Exhibit 3–7 continued from previous page.

Scenario Two: If product were placed into assigned positions, with the heaviest items appearing first, lighter ones last, and the pick ticket routed the filler sequentially, then the pull would look more like this:

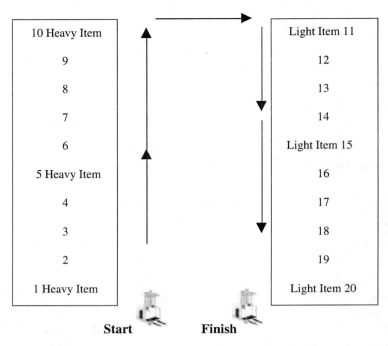

This layout and route will decrease travel time, allow for efficient use of labor, and protect product.

Basically, fixed or dedicated location systems allow for strong control over items without the need to constantly update location records. That control must be counterbalanced by the amount of physical space required by this system.

Zoning Systems

Zoning systems are based on an item's characteristics. As in a fixed system, only items with certain characteristics can live in a particular area. Items with different attributes can't live there.

A SKU's characteristics would cause the item to be placed within a certain area of the stockroom or at a particular level within a section of shelving or rack section. See Exhibit 3–8. For example, irregularly shaped SKUs might be placed in lower levels to ease handling, or all items requiring the use of a forklift for put away or retrieval might be located in a specific area and on pallets.

Impact on Physical Space—Zoning System

As with dedicated systems (see discussion under *Fixed Location Systems* in this chapter), the more you tightly control where a particular item will be stored, the more you contribute to honeycombing or to the need to plan around maximum quantities.

Exhibit 3–8
Examples of zoning system layouts

1. Natural zones created by the nature of the product

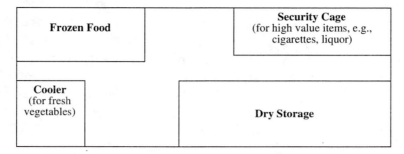

2. Zones created by assigning related types of SKUs to specific areas

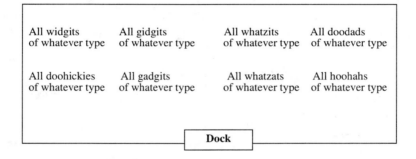

Pros—Zoning Systems
- Zoning allows for the isolation of SKUs according to such characteristics as size, variety, flammability, toxicity, weight, lot control, and private labeling.
- Zoning is flexible in that items can be moved from one zone to another quickly or different zones can be efficiently created.
- Unlike a fixed system, zoning allows for the addition of SKUs within a zone without having to move significant amounts of product to create room within an assigned location or within a sequentially numbered group of items. It also does not require the collapsing of space if an item is deleted.
- Although items are assigned to a general zone, because they do not have a specific position they must reside in, there is no need to plan around 100 percent of any given item's cubic requirements.

Cons—Zoning Systems
- Zoning is not always required for efficient product handling. You may be adding needless administrative complexity by utilizing zoning.
- Zoning may contribute to honeycombing.
- Zoning requires updating of stock movement information.

Basically zoning allows for control of item placement based on whatever characteristics the stockkeeper believes to be important.

Random Location Systems

In a random system nothing has a home, but you know where everything is. Pure random location systems allow for the minimization of space requirements since no item has a fixed home and may be placed wherever there is space. This allows SKUs to be placed above or in front of one another or for multiple items to occupy a single bin/slot/position/rack. The primary characteristic of a random locator system that makes it different from a memory system is that each SKU identifier is tied to whatever location address it is in while it is there. In other words, memory systems tie nothing together, except in the mind of the stockkeeper. Random systems have the flexibility of a memory system coupled with the control of a fixed or zone system. Essentially an item can be placed anywhere so long as its location is accurately noted in a computer database or a manually maintained paper-based card file system. When the item moves, it is deleted from that location. Therefore, a SKU's address is the location it is in while it is there.

Impact on Physical Space—Random Location Systems

Because items may be placed wherever there is space for them, random locator systems provide us with the best use of space and maximum flexibility while still allowing control over where an item can be found.

Planning space around a random locator system is generally based on the cubic space required for the average number of SKUs on hand at any one time. Therefore, in planning space requirements around a random locator system you need to discern from your inventory records what your average inventory levels are and what products are generally present within that average. By multiplying the cubic footage of each of those items by the quantity of each usually on hand, you can determine your space required. See Exhibit 3–9.

Pros—Random Location Systems
- Maximization of space
- Control of where all items are at any given time

Cons—Random Location Systems
- Constant updating of information is necessary to track where each item is at any given time. Updating must be accomplished through manual paper-based recording, bar code scanning, or data-entry-intensive updating. The section *Update Product Moves* in this chapter provides more information regarding maintenance of product location information.
- These systems may be unnecessarily complicated if your organization has a small number of SKUs.

Basically random location systems force a tradeoff between minimization of space and minimization of administration.

Exhibit 3-9

Planning a Storage Area Around a Fixed or a Random Location System

Hammer Company manufactures widgits. It has broken down its bill of materials, the listing of all of the pieces and parts required to build a widget, and has come up with the following list:

SKU #	Description	Container	Dimensions	Total Ft^3	Maximum Expected at One Time	Total Ft^3 Req Fixed System	Total Ft^3 Req Random System
12345	Gidgit	Box	2' × 3' × 1'	6 ft^3	50	300	90
54321	Whazzit	Carton	4' × 4' × 4'	64 ft^3	100	6,400	1,920
67890	Whozzit	Case	3' × 4' × 2'	24 ft^3	25	600	180
09876	Doodad	Box	2' × 3' × 1'	6 ft^3	50	300	90
						7,600	2,280

If Hammer Company were going to store product in fixed positions, it would have to plan around a minimum of 7,600 cubic feet of actual storage space. Although each of these items is required to produce Hammer Company's products, they are not all needed at the same time. On average Hammer only has 30 percent of any of the above items on hand at any one time. If it used a random locator system, it would plan for approximately 2,280 cubic feet of actual storage area.

Combination Systems

Combination systems enable you to assign specific locations to those items requiring special consideration while the bulk of the product mix is randomly located. Very few systems are purely fixed or purely random; most are combination systems.

Combination systems attempt to give you the best features of fixed and random systems. You achieve this by assigning only selected items to fixed homes. Therefore, you only have to plan around the maximum space required for the selected items. For the items not in fixed homes, you can plan around the average quantities you expect to have on a daily, ongoing basis. In other words, you use the fixed system for the selected items and the random system for everything else.

A common application of the combination system approach occurs when certain items constitute an organization's primary product or raw materials line and must be placed as close as possible to a packing/shipping area or to a manufacturing work station. Those items are assigned a fixed position, while the remainder of the product line is randomly positioned elsewhere. See Exhibit 3–10 for typical scenarios for utilizing a combination locator system. Then complete Self-Assessment 3–2.

Exhibit 3-10
Typical Scenarios Involving Combination Location Systems

Scenario One: Barash Foods decided to speed up its order-filling efforts by changing where product was located in relationship to the shipping dock. First it determined which 15 to 20 percent of its product lines showed up on 80 percent of its orders. (See the discussion of Pareto's law under *A-B-C Categorization.*) These items would be assigned to fixed positions close to the point of use (shipping dock), while those items found in only 20 percent of the orders would be randomly stored.

Barash had to decide if these fixed homes would be large enough to hold 100 percent of the cubic space necessary to house a product if the maximum quantity of it were in the facility at one time during the year. The company decided it could not devote that much space per product in the limited area closest to the point of use. It therefore decided to allow for 100 percent of the space needed for one week's worth of product movement for the fixed location SKUs. In other words, while still having to follow the fixed location system rule that space must exist for 100 percent of the cubic space required for the maximum quantity of an item expected during a given time period, it controlled the space and quantity by shortening the time frame. It stored overflow of these "fixed home" items in an overflow area, using random methods.

Random items were stored in accordance with the general rule that random space is planned around the average quantity expected in an area during a defined time period. In this case the time period was one year.

Scenario Two: Charmax Manufacturing is a job shop electronics manufacturer. It manufactures special order items and often will only produce one never-to-be-repeated run of an item. Therefore, some specific raw materials inventories required for any given production run may never be needed in the future. However, the company uses many common electronics components, such as resisters, transistors, and solder, in most of the final assemblies it produces. Its physical plant is very small.

Charmax carefully reviews its master production schedule to determine when various sub-assemblies and final assemblies will be produced. It then analyzes the bill of materials (the recipe of components) for the sub- or final assemblies and orders as many specific-purpose items as possible on a to-be-delivered, just-in-time basis. This holds down the quantity of nonstandard inventory it will have in-house at any one time.

Charmax then establishes fixed positions for working stock, both special order and standard stock items, during a production cycle around the appropriate workstations. Where working stock would consume too much space around a work area, working reserve stock is placed in zone locations close to the workstations. Regular, general-use product such as resisters and transistors is stored in random order.

This combination location system—which is comprised of fixed, zone, and random storage for working, working reserve, and general stock—allows Charmax to maximize its use of space at any given time.

© American Management Association. All rights reserved.

Self-Assessment 3–2

Understanding Your Present Stock Locator System

Instructions: Respond to the questions and issues in the appropriate spaces.
My current locator system is:

Memory   [ ]
Fixed/dedicated [ ]
Random   [ ]
Combination   [ ]

If your system is a memory system, which of the factors described in Exhibit 3–2 that lead to successful use of this type of approach exist at your facility?

_____

_____

If your system is a fixed/dedicated system:

- How much honeycombing do you have? (Use Exhibit 3–6 as a guide to calculate your percentage, both on a location basis and a cubic foot basis

Location: _____ Ft³ _____

- Could your company benefit from implementing a combination system?

_____

_____

- When was the last time your system was reviewed for efficiency and effectiveness? How efficient and effective is your fixed system with respect to product damage, picking costs, and put-away costs?

_____

If your system is a random system:

- Is your random system computerized or manual?

_____

- How efficient and effective is your system? How much work is required to keep all records accurate and timely?

_____

_____

Self-Assessment 3–2 continues on next page.

© American Management Association. All rights reserved.

54 FUNDAMENTALS OF INVENTORY MANAGEMENT AND CONTROL

Self-Assessment 3–2 continued from previous page.

• How accurate is your system? How many labor hours per week does your company spend looking for misplaced items?

_____

_____

If your system is a combination system:

• Was the system designed to be a combination system or did it evolve in an unstructured manner?

_____

_____

• Do you have a listing of items that have been assigned specific homes?   Yes [ ]   No [ ]
• If you have a listing of items within your combination system that have a permanently assigned location, how often do you review and update it?   Monthly [ ]   Annually [ ]   Never [ ]

List three things that are good about your current locator system

1. _____

2. _____

3. _____

List three things about your present system you may wish to change and why.

Locator System Proposed Changes	Justification
1.	
2.	
3.	

It is recommended that you discuss this self-assessment with your supervisor or mentor for an evaluation of your responses.

ITEM PLACEMENT THEORIES

Locator systems provide a broad overview of where SKUs will be found within a facility. Physical control of inventory is enhanced by narrowing the focus of how product should be laid out within any particular locator system. As with locator systems, *item placement theories* (that is, theories of where a par-

© American Management Association. All rights reserved.

ticular item or category of items should be physically positioned) go by many different names. By whatever name, most approaches fall into one of three broad categories: *inventory stratification, family grouping,* and *special considerations.*

Inventory Stratification

Inventory stratification consists of two parts:

1. A-B-C categorization of SKUs
2. Utilization of SKU's unloading/loading ratio

A-B-C Categorization

This item placement approach is based on Pareto's law. In 1907 an Italian sociologist and economist named Vilfredo Pareto (1848–1923) published his belief that 80 to 85 percent of Italy's money was held by only 15 to 20 percent of the country's population. He called the small, wealthy group the "vital few" and everyone else the "trivial many." This ultimately came to be known as the 80–20 rule, or Pareto's law. According to this concept, within any given population of things approximately 20 percent of them have 80 percent of the "value" of all of the items concentrated within them; the other 80 percent have only 20 percent of the value concentrated within them. "Value" can be defined in various ways. For example, if the criterion is money, then 20 percent of all items represent 80 percent of the dollar value of all items. If the criterion is usage rate, then 20 percent of all items represent the 80 percent of the items most often used or sold.

Accordingly, for efficient physical inventory control, using popularity (speed of movement into and through the facility) as the criterion, the most productive overall location for an item is a storage position closest to that item's point of use. SKUs are separated into A-B-C categories, with A representing the most popular, fastest moving items (the "vital few"), B representing the next most active, and C the slow-movers.

Providing product to outside customers is often the chief objective of a distribution environment. Therefore, the point of use would be the shipping dock, with SKUs being assigned in the manner shown in Exhibit 3–11. In a

Exhibit 3–11
A-B-C Placement of SKUs

manufacturing environment, a work station would become the point of use, with the most active, most often required raw materials positioned in near proximity to it.

In order to separate an inventory into A-B-C categories, it is necessary to create a sorted matrix which presents all SKUs in descending order of annual usage and allows for the calculation of those items representing the greatest concentration of value. Exhibit 3–12 represents selected rows of the complete listing of SKUs sorted in this manner shown in Appendix A. Refer to Appendix A as you read about sorting and categorizing inventory.

Exhibit 3–12
Categorization for Item Placement by Popularity*

Line No.	Part No.	Description	Annual Usage	Cumulative Usage	% Total Usage	% Total Items
1	Part 79	Product A	8,673	8,673.00	6.3%	0.3%
2	Part 133	Product B	6,970	15,643.00	11.3%	0.7%
3	Part 290	Product C	5,788	21,431.00	15.5%	1.0%
⋮						
17	Part 70	Product Q	1,896	64,915.00	47.0%	5.7%
18	Part 117	Product R	1,888	66,803.00	48.4%	6.0%
19	Part 134	Product S	1,872	68,675.00	49.7%	6.3%
20	Part 170	Product T	1,687	70,362.00	50.9%	6.7%
21	Part 182	Product U	1,666	72,028.00	52.1%	7.0%
22	Part 28	Product V	1,646	73,674.00	53.3%	7.3%
⋮						
30	Part 278	Product AD	997	82,919.00	60.0%	10.0%
⋮						
93	Part 295	Product CO	325	123,350.00	89.3%	31.0%
94	Part 30	Product CP	325	123,675.00	89.5%	31.3%
95	Part 11	Product CQ	323	123,998.00	89.8%	31.7%
96	Part 192	Product CR	321	124,319.00	90.0%	32.0%
97	Part 96	Product CS	321	124,640.00	90.2%	32.3%
98	Part 40	Product CT	298	124,938.00	90.4%	32.7%
⋮						
272	Part 86	Product JL	6	138,053.00	99.9%	90.7%
273	Part 32	Product JM	6	138,059.00	99.9%	91.0%
274	Part 129	Product JN	5	138,064.00	99.9%	91.3%
275	Part 164	Product JO	5	138,069.00	100.0%	91.7%
276	Part 283	Product JP	5	138,074.00	100.0%	92.0%
277	Part 252	Product JQ	5	138,079.00	100.0%	92.3%
⋮						
298	Part 151	Product KL	—	138,134.00	100.0%	99.3%
299	Part 61	Product KM	—	138,134.00	100.0%	99.7%
300	Part 165	Product KN	—	138,134.00	100.0%	100.0%

*Complete listing shown in Appendix A.

Before attempting to understand how the matrix is mathematically constructed, you first have to explore what information the matrix is presenting. Unless otherwise stated, all references are to Exhibit 3–12.

Here is what the matrix shows.

- Column A is merely a sequential listing of the number of SKUs in the total population. In the example there are 300 items. If an organization had 2,300 SKUs, Column A of its matrix would end with row 2,300.
- Recall that there are two components of Pareto's Law. The first refers to the percentage of all items that a certain number of items represent, and the second represents value that the same grouping of items has as a percentage of the value of all items combined.
  - Column G reflects the first aspect. For example, 30 items represent 10 percent of 300. Therefore, Column G, Row 30 shows 10 percent of all 300 items.
  - Column F reflects the second aspect. For example, the first three items (Rows 1, 2, and 3) of Column A have a combined value (usage rate) of 15.5 percent. That 15.5 percent is shown at Row 3 of Column F. (How the 15.5 percent is arrived at is explained below.)
- After creating the matrix, a review of Column F leads to decisions as to where the cutoff should be for each (A-B-C) category. The decision of where the cutoff points should be is a common sense, intuitive one. In Exhibit 3–12, since 19 of all items represented almost 50 percent of the value of all items (see Row 19, Column F), it seems appropriate to cut off the A category at that number. It would have been just as appropriate to cut it off at Row 20, Column F, which shows 50.9 percent, or at Row 30, with Column F showing 60.0 percent.
- In manufacturing companies, A-B-C calculations usually use annual usage, rather than units, and divide roughly as follows:

	% of items	% of $
A	20	80
B	30	15
C	50	5

And here is how you create the matrix.

- Most application software programs include a report generator module that allows various fields of information, such as SKU identifiers, descriptions, quantities, and the like, to be extracted from the general database and saved in a generically formatted (ASCII)[1] file. This information may then be exported into one of the commonly available spreadsheet programs—for example, Excel® or Lotus 1-2-3®. Rather than undertaking the data entry required to input the information found in Columns B, C, and D, you should use your report generator to obtain this information and then export it into a spreadsheet program.

---

[1]American Standard Code of Information Interchange (ASCII) is the basic 128-character set understood by all computer systems.

- Column **A**—the number of SKUs being analyzed. It is organized in ascending numeric sequence, that is, 1, 2, 3....
- Column **B**—SKU number/identifier.
- Column **C**—SKU description.
- Column **D**—Annual usage quantity of the SKU.
  - In a retail or distribution environment where the inventory comprises finished goods, Column D will contain the immediately preceding 12 months' usage quantities. This is based on the assumption that the product lines will remain relatively unchanged during the upcoming 12-month period. The immediately preceding 12 months' usage rates will reflect any product trends and is more timely than using the immediate past calendar year's rates.
  - In a manufacturing environment, raw materials, components, and sub-assemblies used during the past 12 months may not be required during the upcoming 12 months. Therefore, the data for Column D must be derived from the *master production schedule* (the projection of what is to be built and in what quantities). After determining what will be built and in what quantities, examine the bill-of-materials (BOM), the recipe of what pieces and parts will actually go into the items to be manufactured. The data necessary for Column D is ascertained by multiplying the appropriate items in the BOM times the quantity of items to be built. This calculation is often performed by materials requirements planning (MRP) software.
  - Column D is sorted in descending order, with the highest use item appearing at the top, the most inactive item at the bottom.
  - Column D is the sort field. However, if only Column D were sorted, the information in it would become disassociated from the SKUs the data represents, which information is reflected in Columns B and C. Therefore, the sort range includes columns B, C, and D, so that all related information is sorted together.
- **E**—Cumulative total of Column D.
  - In order to derive the percentage value that a number of items have compared to the value of all items, it is necessary to establish that overall value as well as the value that any given number of items added together may possess. This is what Column E does.
  - Note that the first row of Column E is the same as the first row of Column D. Note that adding together the first 2 rows of Column D results in the second row of Column E. The sum of the first 3 rows of Column D equals the third row of Column E. The sum of the first 17 rows of Column D results in the data in Row 17 of Column E, and so forth....
  - The data shown in Row 300 of Column E reflects the usage value of all 300 items added together. The information on any given row of Column E reflects the value of all of the preceding SKUs added to the value of that specific row's value.
- **F**—This column reflects the second aspect of Pareto's law. It reflects the percentage value that a grouping of items has when compared to the value of all other items.

© American Management Association. All rights reserved.

- Column F is derived by dividing every row of Column E by the last value of Column E. In other words, the first value in Column F (6.3 percent) results from dividing the first row of Column E (8,673) by the last row of Column E (138,134). The value found in Row 2 of Column F is derived by dividing the amount shown in Row 2 of Column E (15,643) by the last row of Column E (138,134). Using arithmetic terminology, each row of Column E acts as a numerator, the last row of Column E is the denominator, and the quotient is found in Column F.
- **G**—This column reflects the first aspect of Pareto's law. Column G shows the cumulative percentage of lines. In other words, 3 is 1% of 300.
  - Column G is derived by dividing every row of Column A by the last number in Column A. In other words, the first value in Column G (0.3%) results from dividing the first row of Column A (1) by the last row of Column A (300). The value found in Row 2 of Column G is derived from dividing the amount shown in row two of Column A (2) by the last row of Column A (300), and so forth.
- After creating the chart, you look down Columns F and G and decide where you want to place the cutoff for categories A, B, and C. Product would then be arranged according to the category in which it appears.
- Appendix B sets out the formulas necessary to create the matrix for 300 SKUs in Microsoft Excel®.

Utilizing a SKU's Unloading/Loading Ratio

Even more efficiency in physical inventory control can be achieved through placing items within the A-B-C zones according to that SKU's unloading to loading (unloading/loading) ratio. The *unloading/loading ratio* reflects the number of trips necessary to bring an item from a receiving point to a storage location compared with the number of trips required to transport it from a storage point to a point of use. If one trip was required to bring in and store a case of product, but 10 trips were required to actually take its contents to a point of use, the unloading/loading ratio would be 1 to 10 (1 : 10). Substantial reductions in handling times can be achieved through application of this principle, which is illustrated in Exhibit 3–13.

The closer the unloading/loading ratio is to 1 : 1 the less it matters where an item is stored within an A-B-C zone because the travel time is the same on either side of the storage location. The more the ratio increases, the more critical it is to place an item closer to its point of use. Assuming 7 productive hours of labor within an 8-hour work shift, a reduction of even 30 seconds in travel time every 5 minutes will result in a timesaving of 42 minutes. See Exhibit 3–14.

Family Grouping

An alternative to the A-B-C approach is the *family grouping/like product approach*. This approach to item placement positions items with similar characteristics together. Theoretically, similar characteristics will lead to a natural grouping of items that will be received/stored/picked/shipped together.

xhibit 3–13
Unloading/Loading Ratio Timesavings

Assumptions:
- One case of photocopying machine paper is brought in and stored.
- One case holds 10 reams.
- Only one ream of paper is used at a time.

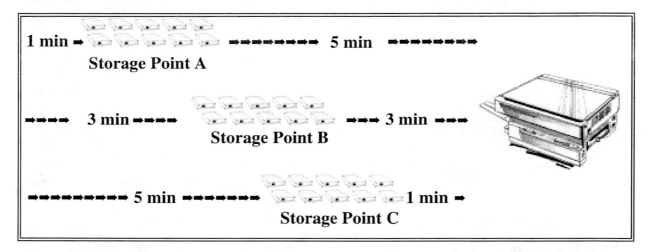

POINT A	POINT B	POINT C
10 items × 1 trip × 1 min = 10 min 10 items × 10 trips × 5 min = 500 min ――――― 510 min	10 items × 1 trip × 3 min = 30 min 10 items × 10 trips × 3 min = 300 min ――――― 330 min 180 min saved over Point A 180/60 = 3 hours saved	10 items × 1 trip × 5 min = 50 min 10 items × 10 trips × 1 min = 100 min ――――― 150 min 360 min saved over Point A 360/60 = 6 hours saved

xhibit 3–14
Practical Effect of Inventory Layout Changes

If a change in procedure, layout, product design, paperwork, or any other factor saved 30 seconds every 5 minutes, how much time would you save each day?

- Assume 7 actual work hours per day
- 60 minutes × 7 hours = 420 minutes
- 420 minutes/5 minutes = 84 segments
- 84 × 30 seconds = 2,560 seconds
- 2,560 seconds/60 seconds = 42 minutes

Saving 30 seconds every 5 minutes saves 42 minutes per day!

© American Management Association. All rights reserved.

Groupings can be based on:

- Like characteristics—for example, widgits with widgits, gidgits with gidgits, and gadgits with gadgits.
- Items that are regularly sold together—for example, parts needed to tune up a car.
- Items that are regularly used together—for example, strap with sports goggles.

Pros—Family Grouping
- Ease of storage and retrieval using similar techniques and equipment
- Ease of recognition of product groupings
- Ease of using zoning location systems

Cons—Family Grouping
- Danger of substituting very similar items for one another—electronics parts, for example
- Danger of properly positioning an active item close to its point of use but consuming valuable space close to that area by housing far less active "family member" items with their popular relative
- Danger of housing an active product with its inactive relatives far from the popular SKU's point-of-use, all for the sake of keeping like items together.
- Danger of confusion when one item can be used in more than one family

Using Inventory Stratification and Family Grouping Together
Effective item placement can often be achieved through tying both the inventory stratification and family grouping approaches together. For example, assume order-filling travel up and down a main travel aisle, moving into picking aisles to select items and then back out to the main aisle to proceed further. Also assume that there are 12 brands of gidgits which are all stored in the same area for purposes of family grouping. Pareto's law indicates that not each brand of gidgits will be as popular as others. Consequently, using both the inventory stratification and family grouping concepts together, the most popular gidgit brands are positioned closer to the main travel aisle and the least popular furthest from it. The end result is a more efficient overall layout.

Special Considerations

A product's characteristics may force us to receive/store/pick/ship it in a particular manner. The product may be extremely heavy or light, toxic or flammable, frozen, odd in shape, or similarly unusual.

Even with items requiring special handling or storage (for example, frozen food stored in a freezer) the inventory stratification and family grouping concepts can and should be employed to ensure efficient inventory layout.

Self-Assessment 3–3
Your Current Item Placement

Instructions: Score your responses in the appropriate spaces on a scale of 0 to 10 as indicated below:

0	1	2	3	4	5	6	7	8	9	10
Never		Almost Never			Sometimes			Almost Always		Always

Current Item Placement:

1. My organization reviews the overall layout of our facility twice each calendar year.
2. My organization assigns a location to an item at the time it is received.
3. My organization locates items in the facility in relationship to those items' point of use.
4. My organization knows where to find any particular SKU at any given time.
5. My organization mixes together both the inventory stratification and the family grouping philosophies of item placement.

Add your scores for each question, then divide your score by 50 to determine the difference between an efficient working environment and one in which you work.

Your score: _____   Ideal score: 50

It is recommended that you discuss Self-Assessment 3–3 with your supervisor or mentor for an evaluation of your responses.

LOCATION ADDRESSES AND SKU IDENTIFIERS

You simply cannot control what you can't find.

Significance

These are the major factors contributing to the success of inventory systems:

- Adequate, appropriate identification markings on SKUs, including both SKU number and stockkeeping unit of measure. These markings allow a worker to quickly and easily identify an item without having to read and translate product descriptions and confusing pack size designations. This ease of recognition reduces errors and the time required for either stock selection or put-away.
- Adequate, appropriate identification markings on bin/slot/floor/rack/drawer/shelf locations. Just like the address on a house, the address of a specific location in the stockroom lets you quickly find the "tenant" or "homeowner" SKU you are looking for.
- Procedures tying any given SKU to the location it is in at any given time. How does the U.S. Postal Service know where to send mail to someone after they have moved? Obviously, the relocated person fills out a change-

of-address form. In much the same manner, you must set up a procedure that tells your system where a product lives, and if it moves—where to.

- Procedures tying a single SKU to multiple locations in which it is stored. If a person has two homes, she lets her friends know both addresses. These friends put that information together in their address books. You must do the same thing for products residing in two or more locations within the building.
- A system for tracking items on a timely basis as they change locations. Whatever format your change-of-address form takes, it has to be filled out and processed quickly.
- Package advertising that does not obscure SKU identifier codes.
- Use of simple marking systems that are easy to read and understand. You should avoid complicated marking systems that are difficult to read, understand, or recall or are conducive to numerical transposition. For example, markings such as "12/24 oz" and "24/12 oz" are quantity-oriented codes employing numbers to describe the quantity and size of the inner packages. However, such numbers are easily reversed or transposed and are not intuitively understood.

Inventory systems with elements of the above have the following results:

- Decreased labor costs related to search time for product. These search-time savings manifest themselves not only when you search for an individual item, but most definitely when product is located in multiple unspecified locations.
- Decreased labor costs associated with searching for appropriate storage locations.
- Avoidance of the need to purchase emergency items that are already in the facility but that cannot be found when required.
- Correct selection of SKUs during order filling.
- Correct selection of pack size(s) during order fulfillment.

All of the above lead to more accurate inventory tracking, less wasted time to correct errors, and increased customer satisfaction.

Keys to Effectively Tying Together SKUs and Location Addresses

In order to keep track of where SKUs are at any given time, it is necessary to do the following:

1. Clearly mark items with a SKU identifier.
2. Clearly mark items with a unit of measure, such as pack size.
3. Clearly mark location addresses on bins/slots/shelves/racks/floor locations/drawers and the like.
4. Tie SKU numbers and location addresses together in either a manual card file system or a computerized database.
5. Update product moves on a real-time basis with bar coding coupled with radio frequency scanners (see Chapter 14, The Basics of Bar Coding) or with stock movement reporting (see *Update Product Moves* in this chapter).

*Clearly Mark Items with a SKU Identifier; Clearly Mark Items
with a Unit of Measure*

Too often managers believe that workers can read a product's markings and packaging and actually understand what they are looking at. The end result of this belief is error after error. To eliminate many of these identification miscues, you need to clearly mark each item with its identifying number and unit of measure. Workers will make far fewer errors matching a number on a box to the same number on a piece of paper than they will trying to match words, abbreviated descriptions, and the like.

The SKU identifier is generally an organization's own internal identifying code for the item rather than a manufacturer's or customer's number for the item. Although the SKU number itself is often adequate for identification purposes, in manufacturing it may be necessary to also include lot and serial numbers to aid in quality control. Lot and serial numbers make it possible to track manufacturing batch, date, location, inspector, and so forth. Exhibit 3–15 reflects various methods of getting items actually labeled or marked.

Markings related to unit of measure (each/pair/dozen/barrel/ounce/pound/cylinder/barrel/case, for example) serve to greatly reduce errors in picking and shipping.

*Clearly Mark Location Addresses on Bins/Slots/Shelves/Racks/
Floor Locations/Drawers*

Just as you could not find a house in a city if its address were not clearly identified, you cannot find a storage location unless its address is clearly marked

---

Exhibit 3–15
Marking SKUs

BY MANUFACTURER
- Manufacturer prints or affixes your plain, human-readable label on the item and/or a bar code label with your coding on the items. Manufacturer obtains labels or you provide them.

AT VENDOR SITE
- Vendor from whom you obtain the product prints or affixes your plain, human-readable label on the items and/or a bar code label with your coding on the items. Manufacturer obtains labels or you provide them.

AT TIME OF RECEIVING
- Everything comes through Receiving; it is a natural node. That convergence allows you the opportunity to affix your plain, human-readable label on the items and/or a bar code label with your coding on the items.
- If you start labeling each incoming item, you can have some product that turns even once during the year marked in this manner, with faster moving items (12 turns a year, for example) all marked within a few weeks. You can then mark the rest at your convenience.

or easily discerned in some other manner. The addressing or location system you choose should have an underlying logic that is easy to understand. Addresses should be as short as possible, yet convey all needed information.

An initial consideration is, should the system be all numeric, all alphabetic ("alpha"), or alphanumeric? In deciding which system to adopt, consider the following:

- All numeric systems require sufficient digit positions to allow for future growth. Because each numeric position only allows for 10 variations (0–9), numeric systems sometimes become too lengthy. In other words, since a single numeric position allows only 10 variations, if you required 100 different variations (for 100 different SKUs) you would need 2 digit positions, representing 00 through 99 (10 × 10). One thousand variations would require three numeric positions, 000 through 999 as shown in Exhibit 3–16, AlphaNumeric Variations.
- Systems that are completely alphabetic allow for 26 variations per position, A through Z (assuming only capitol letters). Two alphas together, AA through ZZ (26 × 26), allows for 676 variations. Three alphas, AAA through ZZZ, allow for 17,576 variations. Although alphas provide numerous variations in a short address, systems that are completely alphabetic—like HFZP—are visually confusing.
- Alphanumeric systems combine the 10 numeric digits with the 26 alphabetic characters, resulting in 36 possible characters for a given position. They often provide for visual differentiation while allowing sufficient variations in a short address.
- Caution: While alphanumeric systems require fewer characters to hold the same number of variations, they are more error prone. For example: Is that a "zero" or a letter "O"? A "one" or the letter "I"? A "two" or the letter "Z"? A "P" or an "R"? A "Q" or an "O"? If you are only dealing with a computer

Exhibit 3–16

Alphanumeric Variations

0 → 9 = 10

00 → 99 = 100   10 × 10 = 100

000 → 999 = 1,000   10 × 10 × 10 = 1,000

A → Z = 26

AA → ZZ = 676   26 × 26 = 676

AAA → ZZZ = 17,576   26 × 26 × 26 = 17,576

system, then characters are "cheap" and you could use only numerics to avoid confusion. However, if part of your system will involve human-readable labels, placards, or markings, where a long string of numbers might present a problem or where you are trying to keep a bar code label short, you might have to balance out the merits of shorter alphanumeric systems against longer pure numeric systems.

Exhibit 3–17 presents some common location addressing systems for racks or shelving.

Exhibit 3–17
Addressing Racks, Drawers, and Shelving

APPROACH	EXPLANATION
Street Address 03A02B02	03 A 02 B 02 Room Aisle Rack Tier Slot (City) (Street) (Building) (Floor) (Apartment) Although this is a lengthy address, an automated storage and retrieval system (AS/RS) detailed required exact spot information for the selector arm to find the desired load.
Rack-Section-Tier-Bin 030342	03 03 4 2 Rack Section Tier Bin A rack section is that portion of the weight-bearing horizontal support between two upright supports.
Room/Bldg-Rack-Bin AA001	A A 001 Rm/Bldg Rack Bin
Rack-Bin AA001	AA 001 Rack Bin These last two systems are short, simple, and easy to remember but do not provide tier information.

Exhibits 3–18 and 3–19 present common location addressing systems for bulk storage.

Exhibit 3–18
Bulk Storage Grid Addressing System

Address: A02C = A   02   C
                 Aisle Cross Aisle Tier

- In bulk storage areas you can utilize a simple grid denoted with placards on walls or on the building's structural supports to find an address on the floor. This is done through two lines bisecting on a flat plain.
- For vertical addresses you triangulate three lines.
- The above is applied geometry (Cartesian coordinates) developed by René Descartes, the famous French mathematician.

Exhibit 3–19
Bulk Storage Quadrant Addressing System

Quadrant addresses are read major to minor. In other words, the northeast corner of the southeast quadrant is written SENE.

Tie SKU Numbers and Location Addresses Together

The placement of identifiers on both product and physical locations creates an infrastructure by which you can track product as it moves. The next step is marrying a SKU number and the location(s) where that item is located. This can be easily accomplished by using a simple 3″ × 5″ card file system (which should be computerized as soon as possible) as illustrated in Exhibit 3–20.

Update Product Moves

A final step in managing inventory is tracking it as it is added to, deleted, or moved. This challenge exists for any organization whether or not the company uses manual tracking, computerized approaches, or bar coding.

The best generally available approach for real-time tracking of items as they move is using bar coding mobile scanners with radio frequency (RF) capability. See Chapter 4, The Basics of Bar Coding.

If RF-capable bar coding is not available, then updating can be accomplished by any of the following methods:

---

 xhibit 3–20

Simple Card File Tracking System

SKU#	QUANT	LOC
SKU 3	135	LOC 1
	87	LOC 2
	965	LOC 3

SKU#	QUANT	LOC
SKU 2	27	LOC 1
	57	LOC 2

SKU#	QUANT	LOC
SKU 1	1235	LOC 1
	187	LOC 2
	187	LOC 3
	543	LOC 4

Cards are marked with all SKU numbers. Cards are indexed in ascending number sequence; that is, put lowest SKU number in the front of the file box and the highest SKU number in the back. All locations and quantities for that specific item are noted. As SKUs are added to, moved, etc., card file information is updated as often as possible. Updates should occur at least twice daily—for example, during the lunch hour and at the end of the workday.

- Portable bar code scanners that capture the information within the scanner mechanism or on a disk in the scanner. The information is then uploaded into the computerized database either through the communications ports on the scanner and computer or by loading the scanner disk into the computer.
- Manually captured, paper-based information (see Exhibit 3–21) is entered into the database through keying (data entry by a human being).
- Manually captured, paper-based information is manually written onto file cards.

No matter what method is used, it is imperative that information relative to inventory additions, deletions, or movement be input into the system as soon as possible. To the greatest extent possible, the *shelf count* (what is actually in the facility) and where it is located should match the *record count* (the amount reflected in the main database records). The longer the time lag between inventory movement and information capture and updating of the record count, the greater the chance for error, lost product, and increased costs.

Organizations should carefully consider specific item placement within an overall location system in order to maximize each SKU's accessibility while being mindful of that item's point-of-use, unloading/loading ratio, relationship to similar items, or characteristics requiring special handling.

Organizations lacking procedures that identify the location of each SKU within the facility suffer from excessive labor costs, "lost" product that makes it necessary to purchase additional items to cover for those on-site but unavailable when required, poor customer service, and general confusion. Controlling product location and movement centers around establishing an overall locator system that

---

E xhibit 3–21
Simple Stock Movement Report

STOCK MOVEMENT REPORT

SKU# _____

DATE _____   QUANT _____

FROM _____   TO _____

effectively reflects the organization's basic inventory nature (that is, finished goods in a retail/distribution environment or raw materials and subassemblies in a manufacturing facility). Often legitimate operational and storage objectives are in conflict with one another, resulting in final location system decisions made on the basis of a series of tradeoffs.

And finally, each item's present location must be identified with that SKU's identifier, with address and quantity changes updated on an ongoing, timely basis.

Review Questions

1. Honeycombing is best described as: 1. (c)
   (a) product unevenly stacked.
   (b) matrix racking or shelving layout.
   (c) empty space in usable storage areas.
   (d) the number of items per level and number of tiers of product on a pallet.

2. Memory location systems are: 2. (b)
   (a) simple and efficient.
   (b) dependent on human recall.
   (c) dependent on updating of location information.
   (d) useful when a large number of different SKUs must be quickly located.

3. Regarding random location systems: 3. (b)
   (a) each item has an assigned home in a random zone.
   (b) an item's home is the location it is in while it is there.
   (c) a SKU's storage location must be planned around the maximum quantity of that item expected to be on-site during a defined time period.
   (d) only certain items may be placed in the bulk storage areas of the facility.

4. In relationship to its unloading/loading ratio, a SKU should be placed closer to its point of use if the ratio is: 4. (a)
   (a) 1:28.
   (b) 1:1.
   (c) 3:15.
   (d) 28:28.

5. Pareto's law holds that: 5. (c)
   (a) 80 percent of all items account for 80 percent of the dollar value of 20 percent of those items.
   (b) 20 percent of all items account for 20 percent of the usage value of 80 percent of those items.
   (c) 20 percent of all items contain 80 percent of the value of those items.
   (d) A fixed locator system is operationally efficient 20 percent of the time for 80 percent of all items.

4

The Basics of Bar Coding

Learning Objectives

By the end of this chapter, you should be able to:

- Explain the differences and use of the most common linear bar code symbologies (languages).
- Inquire intelligently in the marketplace concerning which bar code symbology would be best in your own application.
- Describe basic bar code scanning equipment.
- Plan basic bar code applications within your own organization.

INTRODUCTION

Errors and time increase dramatically the more often a human being is involved in identifying an object, inputting that information into a data base, and then modifying the knowledge to keep track of changes in location, pack size, quantity, and so forth.

 Self-Assessment 4–1
What Do Errors Cost Your Organization?

Instructions: Answer each of the following questions by checking "Yes" or "No."

| 1. Poor handwriting and writing down incorrect numbers and descriptions of items cause at least three identification errors per day at my facility. | Yes [ ]   No [ ] |

Self-Assessment 4–1 continues on next page.

© American Management Association. All rights reserved.

Self-Assessment 4–1 continued from previous page.

2. Incorrect identification of items causes order selectors at my organization to pick at least three incorrect items per day.	Yes [ ] No [ ]
3. During receiving, members of my organization often have to match the descriptions and SKU numbers of incoming items against manual lists or listings on a computer screen.	Yes [ ] No [ ]
4. My organization has to track physical movement of inventory manually within the facility.	Yes [ ] No [ ]

Instructions: For each of the items above where you answered "Yes," estimate the amount of time needed to correct the problem.

Problem	Estimated Time to Correct
1. Poor handwriting and writing down incorrect numbers and descriptions of items cause at least three identification errors per day at my facility.	
2. Incorrect identification of items causes order selectors at my organization to pick at least three incorrect items per day.	
3. During receiving, members of my organization often have to match the descriptions and SKU numbers of incoming items against manual lists or listings on a computer screen.	
4. My organization has to track physical movement of inventory manually within the facility.	

Your own analysis will lead to the conclusion that the less you rely on human intervention to identify items, input information, and track data, the more timely and accurate your records will be. Bar coding is a major tool in capturing critical data quickly and accurately.

The time and dollar savings that would be realized if your organization could eliminate the time and errors you noted above will often pay for a bar coding system. See Exhibit 4–1. The speed of information capture and the accuracy of bar coding are often sufficient reasons to justify the cost of installing bar coding in your operation.

Bar coding is an optical method of achieving automatic identification. It relies on visible or invisible light that is reflected off of a printed pattern. The dark bars or dark areas within the pattern absorb light, and the intervening spaces or areas reflect light. The contrasting absorption and reflection is sensed by a device that "reads" this reflected pattern and decodes the information.

Exhibit 4–1
Data Entry Comparisons Assuming a 12-Character Field

	Key-Entry	OCR	Bar Code
Speed	6 seconds	4 seconds	0.3 seconds to 2 seconds
Error Rate	1 character error in 300 characters entered	1 character error in 10,000 characters entered	1 character error in 15,000 to 36 trillion characters entered

Bar coding is not the only automated method of identifying inventory. Other common techniques include optical character recognition, machine vision, magnetic stripe, surface acoustic wave, and radio frequency tags. The technologies are described in Exhibit 4–2.

Exhibit 4–2
Various Automated Methods of Identifying Inventory

Technology	How It Works	For Your Information
Optical character recognition (OCR)	Numbers, letters, and characters are printed in a predetermined, standard character style or font. Like a bar code, the image is illuminated and the reflection is sensed and decoded.	• Allows for both human and machine readability • 10 characters per inch data density • Slower read rate than bar codes • Higher error rate than bar codes • Very sensitive to print quality
Machine vision	Cameras take pictures of objects, encode them, and send them to a computer for interpretation.	• Very accurate under the right light conditions • Reads at moderate speed • Expensive
Magnetic stripe	A magnetic stripe, like those on credit cards, is encoded with information.	• Proven technology • Readable through grease and dirt • Relatively high density of information—25 to 70 characters per inch • Information can be changed • Must use a contact reader making high speed reading of many items impractical • Not human readable

Exhibit 4–2 continues on next page.

Exhibit 4–2 continued from previous page.

Technology	How It Works	For Your Information
Surface acoustic wave (SAW)	Data is encoded on a chip that is encased in a tag. In response to a radar pulse from a reader with a special antenna, the tag converts the pulse to an ultrasonic acoustic wave. Each tag is uniquely programmed so that the resulting acoustic wave has an amplitude matching the chip's code. The wave is converted back to an electromagnetic signal and sent back to the reader.	• Can be used in highly hazardous environments, e.g., high heat, acid baths, etc. • Can be read up to 6 ft. away • No line of sight required • Physically durable
Radio frequency tag	Data is encoded on a chip that is encased in a tag. In response to a radar pulse from a reader with a special antenna, a transponder in the tag sends a signal to the reader.	• Tags can be programmable or permanently coded • Can be read up to 30 ft. away • No line of sight required • Physically durable, life in excess of 10 years

This text will only deal with one-dimensional, linear bar coding—probably the most commonly used method of automated inventory identification.

Bar code systems generally consist of three components, namely the code itself, the reading device(s), and the printer(s). The objective of this chapter is to provide you with a working knowledge (1) of elements of a bar code symbol; (2) of the fundamentals of the more commonly used linear bar code languages/symbologies in the inventory control world; (3) of printing and scanning (reading) basics; and (4) of some practical bar code applications.

ELEMENTS OF A BAR CODE SYMBOL

Why can you easily read the sentence, "Inventory control is fun"? You can read that sentence because you recognize the alphabet used and understand the rules of grammar and sentence construction utilized. A bar code *symbology*, or language, is very similar in that it has a fixed alphabet made up of various patterns of dark bars and intervening light spaces coupled with rules for how this alphabet is presented.

There are many types of bar codes, not all of which are the linear symbols most commonly found in the inventory control world. For example:

Appearance of common one-dimensional, linear types of bar code patterns:

© American Management Association. All rights reserved.

Appearance of common two-dimensional, matrix and stacked bar code patterns:

Linear bar codes are the most commonly used for general inventory control purposes today.

Structure of a Generic Bar Code Symbol

The entire pattern is called the *symbol*. Each bar or space is called an *element*.

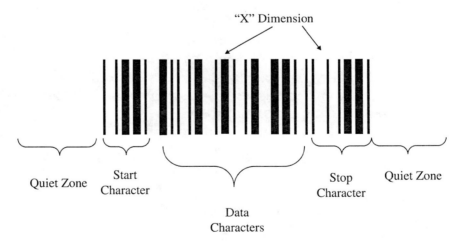

Quiet Zone
Symbols can be read from left to right or right to left. A bar code scanner (reader) must make a number of measurements in order to decode the symbol accurately. The quiet zones on each side of the symbol gives the scanner a starting point from which to start its measurement.

Start and Stop Characters
In order for codes to be read from either direction or top to bottom or bottom to top in a vertically oriented symbol ↕, *start and stop characters* tell the scanner

where the message is commencing. It is customary for the character on the left or at the top of the symbol to be the start character, and the one on the left or bottom to be the stop character.

Data Characters

The *data characters* contain the actual message within the code. These can be letters of the alphabet, numbers, symbols (+, −, /, =, etc.), or a combination of all three.

"X" Dimension

The narrowest bar or space in a bar code is called the "*X*" *dimension*. This width can run from 5 mils to 50 mils. A mil is one-thousandth of an inch.

This is a very important width because it determines how wide each narrow and wide bar or space will be. The narrow bars/spaces are a single "X" in width, while the wide bars/spaces can be two, three, or four "X"s wide. Therefore, an element (a bar or space) can be a single "X" or several "X"s.

The larger the "X" dimension of a symbol, the easier it is to read.

SYMBOLOGIES

Just as there are rules for how an English sentence is structured, for the relationship of upper case to lower case letters, and for punctuation, there are similar rules governing bar codes. These rules are set out in a *symbology*. A symbology controls how information will be encoded in a bar code symbol.

Just as there are different languages—French, English, Spanish, Italian, Russian, Japanese, and Chinese, for example—there are different symbologies. Common symbologies found in the inventory world are Code 39, Code 128, Interleaved 2 of 5, and UPC.

Symbologies are like typefaces with different character sets and separate printing characteristics. Some symbologies only include numbers. Some have numbers, uppercase alphabetics (A–Z), and limited special characters. Others have both upper and lowercase alphabetics (A–Z, a–z), numbers, and a wide range of special characters. Some symbologies only allow for a set number of characters in a pattern, while others allow for variable length messages.

Discrete and Continuous Symbologies

Bar codes can either be discrete or continuous.

Characters in a *discrete* code start with a bar and end with a bar, and have a space between each character. Characters in a *continuous* code start with a bar, end with a space, and have no gap between one character and another. The primary significance of the difference is that a discrete code is easier to print and read, but you can get more characters per inch with a continuous code.

Which of the following is easier to read?

Symbologies   Symbologies   Symbologies   Symbologies

© American Management Association. All rights reserved.

The word on the far left is the most difficult to read but has the greatest amount of information in the smallest amount of space—a good thing on a (bar code) label with limited space available. The word on the far right is the easiest to read, would allow for a more forgiving print job—that is, if the ink spread on the label surface between each letter, we would still be able to read it—but it takes up more space. Discrete symbologies are easier to print and read, but they take up more space.

Symbology Summary

The rules of a particular symbology control the following characteristics:

- *Character set*—which alphabetics, numbers, and special characters are in the symbology
- *Symbology type*—discrete or continuous
- *Number of element widths*—how many different "Xs" there are in the wide bars/spaces
- *Fixed or variable lengths* of characters in a pattern
- *Density*—how many characters can appear per inch

Popular Symbologies Found in the Inventory World

There are dozens of bar code symbologies. Many have failed in the marketplace because a large number of printer and scanner suppliers will not support them. Others are owned by individual companies that control and limit

---

xhibit 4–3

Structural Differences—Discrete Versus Continuous Bar Code Symbologies

DISCRETE SYMBOLOGIES

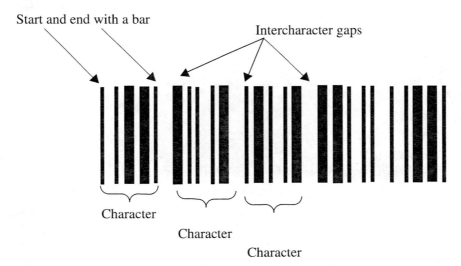

Exhibit 4–3 continues on next page.

Exhibit 4-3 continued from previous page.
CONTINUOUS SYMBOLOGIES

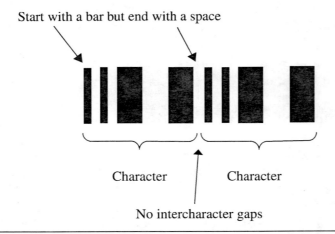

their use. Others like Postnet, which is used by the U.S. Postal Service, have specialized uses. Some are widely supported and accepted in the inventory control world.

Universal Product Code/European Article Numbering System
In dealing with point-of-sale identification of product, as in a grocery or other retail store, the universal product code (UPC) is used in the USA. A very similar code, which will eventually be interchangeable with UPC, is the European article numbering system (EAN).

The UPC symbology is highly structured and controlled; it is only used in general merchandise retailing. It is an all numeric, fixed length (11 characters) symbology. The UPC symbol is physically arranged into two halves. The left half has six numbers that identify the manufacturer or packager. The right half identifies the product. See Exhibit 4-4. You have to license the right to use the UPC from the Uniform Code Council (UCC), an organization created by the grocery industry.

The UPC is not suitable for inventory control use within a warehousing or manufacturing facility where there is a need for variable length messages, alphanumeric coding, flexible identification patterns, or the like.

Code 39
This symbology is the most widely used bar code in nonretail applications. It was first introduced in 1975.

There should be a Code 39 software interface to work with most stockkeepers' existing application software systems. In other words, you should be able to find a Code 39 bar code package that will allow you to continue to use your existing in-house software, numbering systems, and internal procedures.

Code 39 is sometimes referred to as "3 of 9 Code" because three of the nine elements (bars or spaces) making up a Code 39 character are wide and the other six are narrow.

xhibit 4-4

Structure of the Universal Product Code Symbol

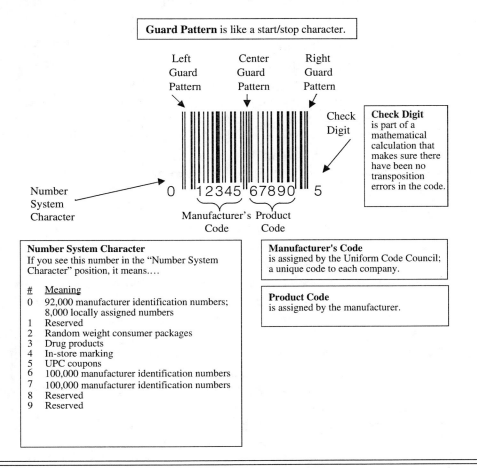

Code 39 was the first alphanumeric symbology developed. Among its most important features are the following:

- It includes the entire alphabet in uppercase letters.
- It allows all numerics, that is, 0 through 9.
- It includes seven special characters: -, ., *, $, /, +, %, and a character representing a blank space.
- It has discrete symbology.
- It allows variable length symbols.
- It allows two messages to be decoded and transmitted as one (*concatenation*).
- It can be printed using a wide variety of technologies.
- Although there are only 43 data characters in the basic Code 39 set, by using certain of the characters as internal codes, it is possible to encode all 128 ASCII (American Standard Code of Information Interchange) characters used by computers. This feature is cumbersome and is not widely used.
- It is self-checking, which means a single printing defect cannot cause an error where one character is mistaken for another.

Code 128

This code, introduced in 1981, is the preferred symbology for most new bar code applications. It is one you should seriously consider if your business is going to enter into the world of bar coding.

This symbology has many desirable features, including the following:

- It uses three start codes to allow the encoding of all 128 ASCII characters without cumbersome procedures. Therefore, you can use the entire alphabet in both upper and lower case, all ten numerics, and all special characters. Each printed character can have one of three meanings.
- It uses high data density, continuous symbology, which takes the least amount of label space for messages of six or more characters.
- It employs a highly readable code with high message integrity.
- It has become one of the two standard bar code symbologies used to identify the contents of corrugated boxes. (The other standard for corrugated shipping boxes is Interleaved 2 of 5 symbology.)
- It allows for concatenation.

Which Symbology Is Right for Your Organization

Each symbology has its strengths and weaknesses. No one "right" bar code language will fit every organization's needs.

A starting point in reviewing appropriate symbologies actually begins with your own industry. Has your industry selected a particular type of symbology? For example, the automotive industry has been using Code 39 since 1980. You can obtain guidance from trade associations in your industry segment.

The reason to start with a symbology accepted by your industry is that you will be able to find direct application software and hardware that has been written or created for the specific requirements of your business. It is the old question, "Why recreate the wheel?"

If no symbology dominates your industry then the real questions become (1) what do you want the system to do for you and (2) how large is your budget?

Self-Assessment 4–2
Determining Your Needs

Instructions: Answer the following questions to the best of your ability leaving the far right column empty. After reading the *Bar Coding Applications* section of this chapter, complete the far right column.

Issue	Current Thoughts	Possible Solutions
My current software has a bar coding module. (*Tip:* Most standard accounting software packages with an inventory module have bar code modules as well.)	Yes [ ] No [ ] Don't know [ ] Need to check with _____ _____	

Self-Assessment 4–2 continues on next page.

Self-Assessment 4–2 continued from previous page.

Issue	Current Thoughts	Possible Solutions
If my current software has a bar coding module, it supports the following symbologies: • UPC • Code 39 • Code 128 • Other (*Tip:* These symbologies are supported by most software packages that have a bar code module.)	Yes [ ] No [ ] Yes [ ] No [ ] Yes [ ] No [ ] Yes [ ] No [ ]	
My industry has adopted a specific symbology as its standard? (*Tip:* Check with your industry's major trade association to obtain this information.)	Yes [ ] No [ ] If so, it is: _____	
Product arrives with my organization's SKU number in both human and machine readable (bar coded) form on the outer container.	Yes [ ] No [ ]	
My order fillers could use bar code technology to pick orders.	Yes [ ] No [ ]	
If I am in manufacturing, my work-in-process could be tracked using bar codes.	Yes [ ] No [ ]	
My organization could use automated item identification to track capital assets.	Yes [ ] No [ ]	
As product is either received or shipped at my facility, its movement could be tracked in a real-time manner.	Yes [ ] No [ ]	
Three identification errors commonly occurring at my facility could be solved with bar coding in my opinion.	1. 2. 3.	
I believe bar coding could save my organization time related to data input in three ways.	1. 2. 3.	

SCANNING BASICS

Something has to read a bar code. That something is a scanner. These electro-optical devices include a means of illuminating the symbol and measuring reflected light.

© American Management Association. All rights reserved.

Exhibit 4-5
Scanner Types

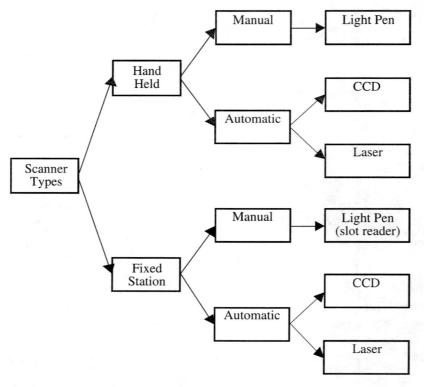

- Light pen (wand scanner)
  - Makes contact with the label or surface on which pattern is printed
  - Inexpensive
  - Durable
  - Can be tied into various decoder types of equipment
- Charge coupled device (CCD)
  - Has a depth of field of several inches so you do not have to make contact with the label or other surface; therefore, can read through shrink-wrap common in warehousing operations
  - Floods symbol with light, and reflectance illuminates photodetectors in the CCD scanner; can read very high bar code densities
  - Moderate cost
- Lasers
  - Project a beam of energy off of a rotating prism or oscillating mirror
  - Depth of field of several feet
  - Expensive but versatile

A scanner projects a tiny spot of light that crosses the bar code symbol and then measures the exact width of the bars and spaces. The measurement is determined by the amount of reflectance off the dark and light bars and spaces. Software in either the scanner or in a separate plug-in device then translates the visual (analog) signal into a digital one that a computer can understand and then decodes the symbology (language) that it is reading and the message contained in the pattern.

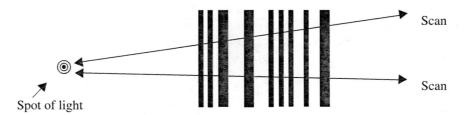

Reflected light is converted from an analog voltage (visual) format to a digital waveform for decoding.

The spot of light must not be larger than the "X" dimension used for that label or you will get misreads.

Scanner might believe that both narrow bars are a single wide element and that the space is merely an ink void printing error.

Scanners must be purchased so that they match the "X" dimension that will be used for printing.

Scanners can either be manual, where the user supplies the scanning motion, or automatic, where the device provides the scanning motion. See Exhibit 4–5.

PRINTING BASICS

Bar code printing can be done by an on-site user or by an off-site third-party vendor. On-site printing generally occurs close to where product is either being received or shipped—its point-of-use.

There are five basic on-site bar code print technologies: direct thermal, thermal transfer, dot matrix impact, ink jet, and laser (xerographic). These technologies are described in Exhibit 4–6.

Exhibit 4–6
Common Bar Code Print Technologies

- *Direct thermal*—Overlapping dots are formed on a heat-sensitive substrate (label or other foundation) by selectively heating elements in a printhead.
- *Thermal transfer*—Same concept as direct thermal except the image is transferred to the substrate from a ribbon that is heated by the elements in the printhead.
- *Dot matrix impact*—A moving printhead, with rows of hammers, creates images through multiple passes over a ribbon.
- *Ink jet*—A fixed printhead sprays tiny droplets of ink onto a substrate.
- *Laser (xerographic)*—A controlled laser beam creates an image on an electrostatically charged, photoconductive drum. The charged areas attract toner particles that are transferred and fused onto the substrate.

Off-site, commercial printers use a wide variety of printing techniques. See Chapter 3, Exhibit 3–15 for a discussion of methods of affixing bar code labels.

BAR CODE APPLICATIONS

It is far more important that you understand what you want to accomplish with bar codes than for you to understand all of the technical aspects of them.

Think of all of the bits and pieces of information you need to know in order to control inventory in a distribution environment. They would include

- Manufacturer
- Supplier
- SKU number
- Description
- Quantity
- Unit of measure
- Pack size
- Ship to address
- Carrier
- Time, date
- Location
- Purchase order identification

All of this information can be bar coded.

Think of all of the information you need to control material in a manufacturing environment. It includes

- Particular bill of materials
- SKU number
- Quantity
- Work order number

- Individual tasks
- Indentification of machine operator
- Scrap
- Time, date
- Which machine
- Routing step
- Location

All of this information can be given a bar code identifier.

Bar code labels and markings can be printed directly on forms, on boxes, on the product itself, or on labels that are then affixed to forms, boxes, items themselves, individual parts of items, and so on.

A quick and easy way to begin using bar codes is through the use of scan boards or menu cards. A scan board or menu card is merely a sheet of paper or heavier card stock that contains information on it in both machine readable (bar code) and human readable (plain alpha numeric text) formats. See Exhibit 4–7 for examples of common scan boards/menu cards.

Exhibit 4–7

Common Types of Bar Code Scan Boards/Menu Cards

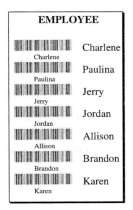

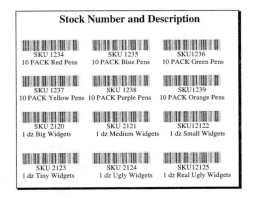

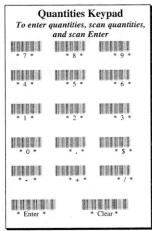

EXAMPLES OF USING BAR CODES

Bar codes facilitate many activities, including receiving and shipping, tracking multiple activities, maintenance programs, and physical inventories.

Receiving/Shipping

1. Employee scans in his or her own identity off an identification badge or scan board.

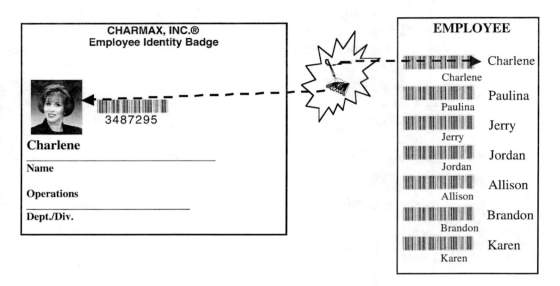

2. Employee scans product code from either items themselves or from scan board.

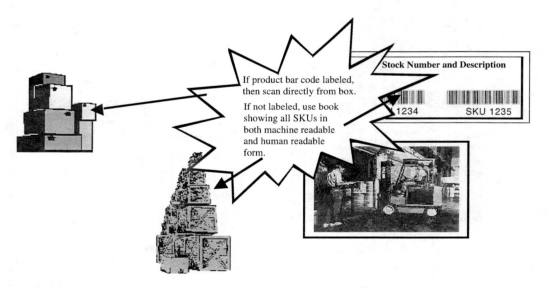

3. Employee scans in quantity.
4. Employee scans in activity—received or shipped, for example.

Tracking Multiple Activities at the Same Time in a Manufacturing Setting

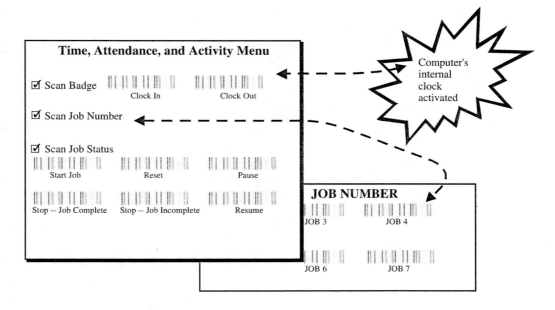

1. Employee scans in his or her identity.
2. Employee scans in either "Clock In" or "Clock Out." This starting/stopping time can be noted by the computer's internal clock. In addition, the computer's internal calendar notes the date.
   a. This information could be automatically routed to accounting for payroll purposes and/or cost accounting.
   b. This information will be captured for the particular job in question. That information can then be used as a part of various variance reports, such as projected starting time versus actual starting time or projected ending time versus actual ending time. See Chapter 6, *Why Inventory Systems Fail and How To Fix Them, Variance Reports.*
3. Employee scans in Job Number.
4. Employee scans in Job Status.
5. When employee scans in "Stop—Job Complete," the system could begin a backflush of all raw materials and components used as part of the job just completed. (See Exhibit 6–1.)

Using Bar Coding as Part of a Maintenance Program

1. Bar codes are assigned to each part of the maintenance procedure and to various parts and engines of the piece of equipment in question.
2. Employee then uses a Time, Attendance, and Activity Menu to track the maintenance tasks.

Bar Coding, Physical Inventory, and Cycle Counting

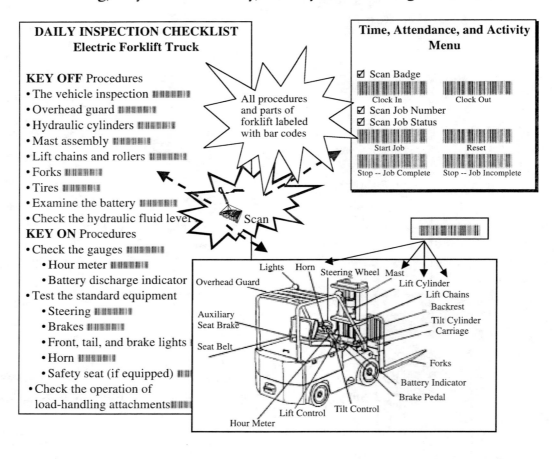

1. Bar code markings in both machine readable and human readable form are placed on both the storage locations (shelves, racks, drawers, bins, etc.) and the product itself.
2. A person (counter) equipped with a portable scanner:
   a. Scans in the identity of the SKU.
   b. Enters the quantity through a keypad on the scanner. The record count and shelf count can be compared in a variety of ways:
      (1) The shelf count as captured by the scanner and counter can be transmitted into the system by way of radio frequency at the time of information capture, or it can be uploaded from the scanner at a later time. The

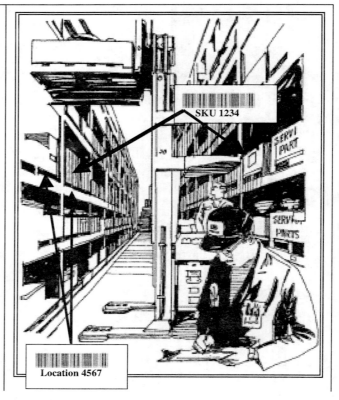

computer system would then generate an exception report of those items where the record and shelf counts did not match.

(2) Scanners are small computers. Thus they can store the record count stored within themselves. As the scanner reads the bar code and the counter enters the quantity information, the scanner could immediately compare the record count and shelf count. If there were a discrepancy, the scanner could alert the counter either through audible tones, flashing lights, or LED displays. The counter could then immediately initiate a recount.

Please return to **Self-Assessment 4–2: Determining Your Needs** and complete the far right column regarding possible bar code applications within your own operation.

Bar code symbology, the set of rules for how the bars and spaces of a bar code language are arranged, dictates how much and what type of data can be displayed within a particular symbol. The language that is most appropriate for your industry will be determined by how much data and in what form that information must be displayed on your goods, inventory, or other materials. Common symbologies found in the inventory world include the universal product code (UPC)/European article numbering system (EAN), code 39, and code 128.

Many industry segments, such as automotive and retail sales, have selected the symbology felt to be most appropriate for their respective needs. It is often more economical and efficient to adopt the symbology commonly found within your own industry segment.

Bar code scanners can be either hand held or automatic; they include light pens, charge coupled devices, and lasers. Printing technologies include direct thermal, thermal transfer, dot matrix impact, ink jet, and laser (xerographic).

In applying bar coding to your system, you are only limited by your imagination—and your wallet. Applications can be simple ones involving scan boards, or they can be complex, utilizing laser scanners, radio frequency, and sophisticated sharing of information throughout the system at the time of information capture.

The Basics of Bar Coding 93

 Review Questions

1. What appears on both sides of a bar code symbol to give the scanner a starting point from which to start its measurements?
   (a) "X" dimension
   (b) A 3 of 9 interleave
   (c) Quiet zones
   (d) An aperture

   1. (c)

2. Bar coding:
   (a) is the only automated method of identifying inventory.
   (b) is a major tool in capturing critical data quickly and accurately.
   (c) relies on optical character recognition to decode information.
   (d) employs magnetic strips and surface wave technology as backups.

   2. (b)

3. Bar codes generally consist of three components:
   (a) the code itself, decoding instructions, and the printer
   (b) the reading device(s), decoding instructions, and the printer
   (c) the code itself, the reading device(s), and the printer(s)
   (d) the code itself, the reading device(s), and decoding instructions.

   3. (c)

4. Scanner types usually found in inventory control environments include:
   (a) light pens, charge coupled devices, and OCR devices.
   (b) light pens, OCR devices, and flatbed scanners.
   (c) charge coupled devices, OCR devices, and lasers.
   (d) light pens, charge coupled devices, and lasers.

   4. (d)

5. The "X" dimension in bar coding is:
   (a) the width of the narrowest line.
   (b) the width of the widest line.
   (c) the ratio between the widths of the narrow line and the wide line.
   (d) the width of the white space between characters.

   5. (a)

Do you have questions? Comments? Need clarification?
Call Educational Services at 1-800-225-3215
or e-mail at ed_svcs@amanet.org.

© American Management Association. All rights reserved.

Planning and Replenishment Concepts

Learning Objectives

By the end of this chapter, you should be able to:

- Identify which planning and replenishment approach(es) apply to your company.
- Comprehend lean and just-in-time approaches to inventory management.
- Calculate replenishment costs.
- Understand the forward-looking nature of materials requirements planning.
- Utilize basic order-point formulas.
- Calculate economic order quantities using simple formulas based on specific variations of the basic EOQ formula.

INTRODUCTION

The objective of this chapter is to provide basic approaches to managing inventory levels and to undertaking stock replenishment. If you implement lean techniques properly, you will have the right item, in the right quantity, at the right time, in the right place.

Self-Assessment 5–1

Do You Have the Right Item, in the Right Quantity, at the Right Time, in the Right Place? Do You Have High Customer Shipment Percentages and Low Inventories?

Instructions: Answer each of the following questions by checking "Yes" or "No."

1. My organization has a very high on-time shipping percentage.	Yes [ ] No [ ]
2. My organization has low inventory levels.	Yes [ ] No [ ]
3. Even though my organization orders the right items, in the right quantities, it often has to slow down production because of a lack of raw materials or parts.	Yes [ ] No [ ]
4. I understand why product arrives in the building in the quantities and timeframes currently being utilized.	Yes [ ] No [ ]

If the answer to Question 1 is "Yes" and your answer to Question 2 is also "Yes," congratulations! However, if your answer to either question is "No," you have a major competitive weakness. Read on.

If the answer to Question 3 is "Yes," then are you ensuring that you not only have the right quantities on hand and on order, but that those items arrive at the right time? Read on. If the answer to Question 4 is "No," read on.

INVENTORY TYPES

In the worlds of distribution, retailing, and replacement parts, an organization deals with finished goods. In the manufacturing world an organization deals with raw materials and subassemblies as well as finished goods. Considerations of what to buy, when to buy it, and in what quantities are dramatically different in these two worlds.

In distribution you are concerned with having the right item, in the right quantity, at the right place. (If you have three distribution centers—New York, Chicago, and Los Angeles—"place" is critical!) Time does not seem to be as important unless you are out of stock. However, traditional formulas used in computing inventory requirements in a distribution environment focus on item and quantity rather than place and time. In manufacturing, you are concerned with having the right item, in the right quantity, at the right time, in the right place.

Demand for finished goods and spare parts for replacements is said to be *independent*, while demand for items in the manufacturing world is said to be *dependent*. Understanding these distinctions will help you apply the right approach to your organization.

Independent demand is influenced by market conditions outside the control of your organization's operations. The demand for the widgets your organization sells will be *independent* of the demand for any other item that you sell.

Your products are independent of one another. Therefore, the penalty for being out of stock is not as severe as in a manufacturing environment.

Dependent demand is related to another item in your own company. The demand for raw materials, parts, and assemblies is *dependent* on the demand for the final product. You would not need the components if you did not also require the finished product. In this environment you must have *all* of the right items, in the right quantities, at the right time in order to complete a finished product. If you are missing only one component, you will not be able to make the finished product. You will have the worst inventory problems: too much inventory *and* high expediting costs *and* poor on-time shipments.

Let's use a chair as an example. The demand for the number of chairs is independent of the demand for the number of bar stools because quantity required is influenced by the demand in the market for each item. The demand for chair legs, seats, or rails is mathematically dependent on the demand for *finished* chairs. Four legs and one seat are required for each chair.

At its simplest, independent demand calls for a *replenishment* approach to inventory management. This approach assumes that market forces will exhibit a somewhat fixed pattern. Therefore, stock is replenished as it is used in order to have items on hand for customers.

Dependent demand calls for a *requirements* approach. When a future need for an assembly or finished item is discovered, then the materials needed to create it are ordered. There is no fixed pattern because an assembly created in the past may never be produced again.

The nature of demand, therefore, leads to different concepts, formulas, and methods of inventory management.

THREE APPROACHES TO REPLENISHING INVENTORY

There are basically three distinct approaches to replenishing inventory:

1. Lean/just-in-time (JIT)
2. Enterprise resource planning (ERP)/manufacturing resources planning (MRP II)
3. Reorder point (ROP)/economic order quantity (EOQ)

They can coexist within a company. Exhibit 5–1 compares the three approaches.

Companies in any industry that apply lean/JIT philosophies and approaches can gain a substantial competitive advantage over those that use either ERP/MRP or ROP/EOQ. The lean advantage over ERP/MRP is shown in Exhibit 5–2.

This study of many manufacturers who had implemented lean/repetitive practices during the prior year showed that inventory dropped approximately 50 percent, while time to ship to customers also decreased by 60 percent. On-time shipments, though not documented in this study, increased substantially, resulting in increased sales.

Exhibit 5–1
Replenishment Approaches

	Lean/JIT	ERP/MRP	ROP/EOQ
Order quantity	Kanban quantity	Period usage or lot size	EOQ
Lead times	Short!	Fixed	Fixed
Trigger	Order point	Future stockout	Order point
Stockouts	Very rare	Uncommon	3–5%
Inventory levels	Very low	Low	Higher
Philosophy	Reduce waste in all places	Integrate information; delay inventory until needed	Minimize ordering and carrying costs

Exhibit 5–2
Lean Advantage over ERP

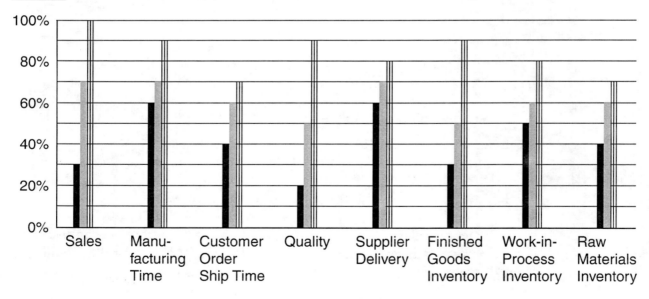

Legend:
— Minimum Improvement
— Mean (Average)
═ Maximum Improvement

Langenwalter, Gary A., *White Paper on Repetitive Methodologies for Manufacturing* (Stow, Mass: Manufacturing Consulting Partners, 1999). Included with permission.

For manufacturers, ERP/MRP has a considerable competitive advantage over ROP/EOQ because it brings in inventory when it is needed, rather than when the bin is running low, and it coordinates information sharing throughout the company.

The most competitive approach for a manufacturer combines lean/JIT approaches and philosophy with ERP integration of information and efficiency.

A Tier 1 automotive supply company experienced the results shown in Exhibit 5–3 when they implemented lean/repetitive practices on top of their existing ERP system.

Since the company was in automotive supply, on-time shipments were very high to start with. However, inventory turns tripled and the materials manager cut her work week from 60 hours to 40.

An instrument (electronics-based) manufacturer achieved the improvements shown in Exhibit 5–4 when they implemented lean.

As they implemented lean, they gained market share because of the dramatic reduction in lead times to customers. They also implemented a program in which suppliers delivered directly to stocking locations on their manufacturing floor.

Finally, a consumer packaged goods manufacturer based in Mexico achieved the results shown in Exhibit 5–5.

Notably, the bulk of the results was achieved in six months.

Lean/JIT

JIT started in Japan in the early 1950s to compensate for the lack of natural resources and space. Taiichi Ohno and its other founders studied Henry

Exhibit 5–3
Lean Improvements in Tier 1 Automotive Supplier

	1992	1997	% Improvement
Inventory turns	15	50	333
On-time ship %	97	99.99	3
Customer order ship time (hrs.)	8	4	50
Sales	$x	$2x	100
Defects (ppm)	50	2	96
Data entry (hrs./week)	y	.25y	75
PO release	hours	1 min	99
Materials Manager workweek (hrs.)	60+	40+	33

Langenwalter, Gary A., *White Paper on Repetitive Methodologies for Manufacturing.* (Stow, Mass.: Manufacturing Consulting Partners, 1999). Included with permission.

xhibit 5-4
Lean Improvements in an Instrument Manufacturer

	1987	1997	% Improvement
Product lead time (weeks)	4–12	2–3	66
On-time supplier delivery	60%	95%	58
Supplier quality	78%	99.8%	28
Ship to stock	0%	84%	8400
Dock cycle time for materials	40	2–3	94

Langenwalter, Gary A., *White Paper on Repetitive Methodologies for Manufacturing* (Stow, Mass.: Manufacturing Consulting Partners, 1999). Included with permission.

Ford's assembly lines and U.S. supermarkets, then applied the best ideas to their own situation to create the Toyota Production System. JIT also included the quality revolution spearheaded in Japan by W. Edwards Deming. It was initially popularized in the U.S. by Bob Hall in the early 1980s (his initial book, *Zero Inventories*, was published in 1983) and was supported by a professional society that he helped create, the Association for Manufacturing Excellence. In the early 1990s, the term *lean* supplanted *JIT* as the focus changed to customer value and the practices spread across many industries outside of manufacturing.

xhibit 5-5
Lean Improvements in International Consumer Packaged Goods Manufacturer

	1994	1996	% Improvement
Manufacturing cycle time (hours)	192	18	91
Quality defects (ppm)	y	.4y	60
Setup time (min.)	240	15	94
Inventory turns	4	7	75
Supplier lead time—direct	90	17	81
materials (days)			
New product introduction (weeks)	26	10	62

Langenwalter, Gary A., *White Paper on Repetitive Methodologies for Manufacturing* (Stow, Mass.: Manufacturing Consulting Partners, 1999). Included with permission.

Lean and JIT share a common philosophy. They try to determine what customers (both internal and external) want and provide it for them, meeting 100 percent of the customers' quality and on-time delivery standards. They ask, "What is the minimum amount of all resources and time that we can consume to meet our customer's needs?" Then they view all other activities as not adding value ("non-value-added") and consider them wastes to be eliminated. JIT identifies seven wastes:

1. Overproduction—making more than is needed at this very moment
2. Waiting—waiting time for any resource (material, human, capital)
3. Transportation—moving materials (or people), both inside the company and throughout the supply chain
4. Processing—why make this item at all? Is it being made the most efficient and effective way?
5. Inventory—except for the item being worked on (or being given to a customer, in the case of distribution) at this very moment, inventory is waste
6. Motion—any motions more than absolutely required to add value in the customer's eyes
7. Defects—any defective product (or service) has three costs: (1) making it the first time, (2) doing whatever it takes to correct the mistake, and (3) trying to repair the long-term damage to customer relationship and trust.

One approach to understanding value-added and non-value-added is to "staple yourself to an order"—to follow an order (either customer order or work order or purchase order) through your entire organization. Record every step that actually occurs—the person doing the step, how long it takes, and what date and time it start and stops. Then ask yourself how that step could be made more efficient, combined with others, or entirely eliminated. Exhibit 5–6 gives an example of this. Notice the level of detail; it is the details that expose non-value-added activities! Notice also that a full day is required to actually order the widgets after the stock clerk initially discovers the need and "only" one-half day to get the widgets from the receiving dock to the stockroom. Some companies can take two weeks to move items from receiving dock to the stockroom! You can compare each step in Exhibit 5–6 with the seven types of waste listed above. Finally, notice that in this example there were no "defects"—no quality problems of the incoming widgets, no price discrepancies on the supplier invoice, and no data entry errors throughout the process. You can use the blank chart in Activity 5–1 to track an order in your own company. It is recommended that you discuss this with your supervisor or mentor for an evaluation of your responses.

Exhibit 5–6
Staple Yourself to an Order

Date	Start Time	Stop Time	Activity Time	Person	Activity	Value Add?
June 3	8:30 a.m.	8:33 a.m.	3	Stock clerk	Opens reserve bin for widgets; takes reorder card; places reorder card in interoffice mail	N
June 3	11:00 a.m.	11:15 a.m.	15	Mail clerk	Takes mail to mail room	N
June 3	1:00 p.m.	1:03 p.m.	3	Mail clerk	Delivers mail to purchasing	N
June 3	2:12 p.m.	2:13 p.m.	1	Buyer	Opens mail envelope	N
June 3	3:14 p.m.	3:17 p.m.	3	Buyer	Calls supplier sales rep; leaves message	N
June 3	4:45 p.m.	4:47 p.m.	2	Supplier	Calls buyer; leaves message	N
June 4	8:38 a.m.	8:42 a.m.	4	Buyer	Calls supplier; places order	N?
June 4	8:42 a.m.	8:47 a.m.	5	Buyer	Enters order details into computer; places reorder card in interoffice mail for stockroom	N
June 4	11:00 a.m.	11:15 a.m.	15	Mail clerk	Takes mail to mail room	N
June 4	1:00 p.m.	1:03 p.m.	3	Mail clerk	Delivers mail to stockroom	N
June 4	2:16 p.m.	2:19 p.m.	3	Stock clerk	Opens mail envelope; places reorder card in "incoming orders" box	N
June 9	7:45 a.m.	8:00 a.m.	15	Receiving clerk	Receives widgets on dock; compares to order; inspects for visible damage; puts on "incoming" shelf	N
June 9	10:38 a.m.	10:48 a.m.	10	Receiving clerk	Enters receiving transaction into computer; prints "move ticket" and tapes to box; files packing slip; places box of widgets on "outgoing" shelf	N
June 9	12:07 p.m.	12:45 a.m.	38	Material handler	Picks up widgets (and several other boxes); makes rounds in factory; delivers to stockroom	Y?

Exhibit 5–6 continues on next page.

© American Management Association. All rights reserved.

Exhibit 5–6 continued from previous page.

Date	Start Time	Stop Time	Activity Time	Person	Activity	Value Add?
June 9	2:07 p.m.	2:18 p.m.	11	Stock clerk	Opens box of widgets; prints copy of receiving report; counts and inspects widgets; pulls reorder card from file; enters receipt into computer	N
June 9	2:18 p.m.	2:33 p.m.	15	Stock clerk	Puts widgets away in stockroom; counts 300 widgets, creates new "reserve bin"; places reorder card with reserve bin	N
June 21	9:38 a.m.	9:42 a.m.	4	AP clerk	Receives vendor invoice for widgets; enters into computer	N
July 2	9:00 p.m.	9:05 p.m.	5	Computer	Prints list of proposed checks in accounting office (automatically runs at night)	N
July 3	10:53 a.m.	10:57 a.m.	4	Controller	Scans proposed checks list; approves with changes	Y?
July 3	2:04 p.m.	2:15 p.m.	11	AP clerk	Prints AP checks; attaches each to paperwork; takes bundle to controller	N
July 3	3:17 p.m.	3:20 p.m.	3	Controller	Signs AP checks	N
July 3	3:38 p.m.	3:45 p.m.	7	AP clerk	Places signed checks in envelopes; files paperwork	N
July 3	4:10 p.m.	4:15 p.m.	5	Mail clerk	Picks up outgoing mail in accounting; takes to mailroom; places in outgoing U.S. mail tub	N
July 3	4:30 p.m.	5:00 p.m.	30	Mail clerk	Takes outgoing U.S. mail to post office	N
Total			215			

Activity 5–1
Staple Yourself to an Order

Instructions: Complete the following worksheet.

Date	Start Time	Stop Time	Activity Time	Person	Activity	Value Add?

© American Management Association. All rights reserved.

You can see how a company that starts eliminating these wastes will quickly gain a substantial competitive advantage by supplying superior products and services, more quickly, and at lower cost. And since lean is a process and philosophy, rather than a one-time program, even after the competition starts to react, the leader continues to improve, maintaining the lead.

Lean thinking has six key steps (Womack and Jones, 1996, flyleaf):

1. Define value in the eyes of the customer
2. Line up all the value-creating activities
3. Along a value stream
4. Make the value flow smoothly
5. At the pull of the customer
6. In pursuit of perfection

Lean and JIT emphasize *pull*—nothing happens until a customer "pulls," or consumes a product, with a specific demand. As soon as that product moves into the customer's hands, the lean system replaces it with an identical product, which waits to be consumed. Except for building buffer inventory for seasonal demand (for example, snow blowers or back-to-school supplies), a lean system builds only what the customer is buying, at the speed at which the customer buys it. This is in direct conflict with traditional inventory planning philosophies, supported by ERP/MRP and ROP/EOQ, which acquire, build, and store inventories in the hope that customers will buy them some day and to insure that there are a few extras on hand just in case some products are defective.

Pull systems can be tailored to fit your unique environment. In the simplest pull system, the supplier and the customer are physically right next to each other, with one unit of product resting in a designated storage place (on a table, for example) between them. Each time the customer takes ("pulls") a unit, the supplier processes another and places it in the storage space. Note that the supplier does *not* build ahead; the supplier only builds after the customer takes a unit!

But when the supplier cannot see the customer's storage space, another signal must be arranged. This signal is frequently some sort of *kanban*, which means "visible record." Typical types of kanbans include an empty container (which can only carry a specific item), a laminated card (an example is shown in Exhibit 5–7), or a similar signaling device. The purpose is to let the supplier know that the customer has just used a unit/container and needs to be replenished. Other methods include a light being turned on, a sound such as a buzzer or beep, or even, "Hey, Charlie—I need another widget!"

Replenishment planning in a lean/JIT system, then, is merely replenishing a specified quantity each time a signal arrives from the customer. A customer can be either internal (the next operation in a manufacturing company) or external (a distribution center or final customer).

Except where the supplier and customer are tightly coupled, a system must have at least two kanbans for each item, and probably more than that, depending on the length of the resupply chain and the length of resupply

xhibit 5–7
Laminated Kanban Card Example

Process (From)	Storage Location	27-A-3		Process (To)
Oak Ave Shipping Post Wave Solder	Part No.	392756-01		Oak Ave. Receiving Post Assembly WC 30
	Descrip.	**Circuit Board**		
	Container Type	C100	Cards Issued	
	Container Qty.	**100**	3/7	

time. Each container is one kanban. The quantity of item per kanban container is not that important, but it should be identical. The number of kanbans can be computed as follows:[1]

$$\text{Number of Kanbans} = \frac{\text{Daily Output} \times (\text{Lead Time} + \text{Safety Margin})}{\text{Quantity per Kanban}}$$

Inventory management in a lean system consists of determining the quantity per kanban and the number of kanbans in the system. Multiplying the two quantities together yields the total quantity of that item that will be in your company. You control inventory by adding or subtracting kanbans. For example, if you are just starting to use kanbans with a process that is not in tight control, you will deliberately include more kanbans to create a safety margin to insure that you will always delight your customer.

A pull system tightly couples the supplier to the customer. Whatever the customer buys is exactly what the supplier makes—no more, no less. When the customer is not buying as much, the supplier has its people doing other things, such as training, or maintaining machines, or whatever—but they are *not* allowed to make inventory!

While the pull system seems so simple and so obvious on the surface, it revolutionizes the entire productive system. It rests on several assumptions:

1. You will always delight the customer—your company will do whatever it takes to insure that you deliver what the customer wants when the customer wants it.
2. Each item will be good—because a defective item will shut down the process until it can be replaced.
   a. All processes are kept under control, so they can only produce good parts. This usually requires starting a quality improvement effort, such as Total Quality Management or Six Sigma.
   b. All supplied parts meet quality specifications.

---

[1] For a more rigorous discussion, see http://www.toyotaproductionsystem.net/

c. The workplace is clean, orderly, and safe. Most companies start a 5-S program to accomplish this.
3. The supplier can keep pace with the demand rate of the customer.
   a. This requires that the supplier can produce exactly what the customer wants, with an acceptably short lead time. This usually means reducing setup times to almost nothing.
   b. This also implies cross-training of workers, so they can successfully make whichever product the customer is actually buying.
   c. All items required for successful operation are at the supplier's place when needed. This includes machinery, tooling, raw materials, and all other items.
4. Top management understands that workers will not be producing items at all times. If customer demand has slacked off, workers will be performing other tasks, and this is the way it should be.
5. Workers are expected to observe what is happening and suggest (and implement) improvements to the process.

These assumptions sound completely unrealistic to a person or company that is new to this approach. In one respect, they are. But wise companies start the process of continuous improvement, addressing whichever of these items is most important, then the next, then the next, and so on. These companies understand that they will never "arrive"; they know that they can always improve. They also understand that each improvement provides another incremental competitive edge, which is much more difficult to duplicate than a product innovation or a marketing strategy. If you have doubts, you can reread the results at the beginning of this chapter.

In a lean environment, inventory flows (whenever possible) directly from the receiving area to the point of use. There it is placed so that the next time it is touched, it is adding value to the customer. Incoming inspection, incoming counting, and intermediate storage are all non-value-added activities, so they are slowly eliminated by eliminating the business reasons that required them.

ERP/MRP II

ERP (enterprise resources planning) and ERP II have their roots in *MRP (materials requirements planning)* and *MRP II (manufacturing resources planning)*. The relationship between them is shown in Exhibit 5–8. While MRP had been conceived in the early 1900s, it was impractical because of the huge number of calculations—multiplying, adding, subtracting. This changed as computing power increased in speed and decreased in cost in the late 1960s, and the first primitive MRP programs were created. MRP looks at the company from the point of view of an expediter based in the stockroom. Its purpose is to predict materials shortages in time to fill them (as reflected in its name). Its two major conceptual improvements over reorder point (ROP) are:

1. Time-phasing—MRP understands the timing of future stock movements (ROP does not)
2. Dependent demand

Exhibit 5-8
MRP, MRP II, ERP, and ERP II Functionality Comparison

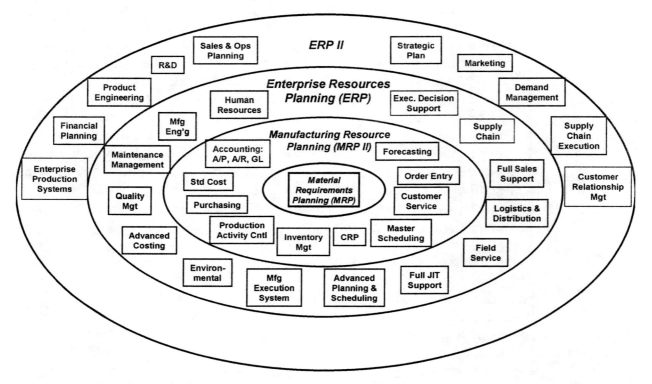

Langenwalter, Gary A., *Enterprise Resources Planning and Beyond: Integrating Your **Entire** Organization* (Boca Raton: St. Lucie Press, 2000). Included with permission.

Time Phasing

MRP is very similar to planning how you are going to pay future bills out of your checkbook. You start with your current balance, add paychecks and other income in the proper time period, and subtract bills when you will pay them, keeping an eye on the running balance. MRP is designed to compute how many of each item your company will need each day, then plan to have the items in the stockroom on time. If there will be enough stock on hand when a future demand is scheduled to leave the stockroom, fine. If not, it tries to expedite existing orders (make the due dates sooner). If there are none of the items, it "orders" (plans a new order) to cover the projected shortage. If the item is purchased, that's all it has to do. If the item is manufactured, MRP has to make sure that there will be enough components on hand to build the quantity required. So it "explodes" the order quantity. It multiplies the order quantity by the quantity per item using the bill of materials (BOM) to create requirements for each of the components. In the example below, one kitchen chair needs four legs, one back, three rungs, and so on.

Conversely, if MRP discovers that there are existing orders that won't be needed, it recommends canceling those orders. MRP repeats this process for each item that it is planning until it has completed all items. It then issues reports to Purchasing and the shop floor, telling them what to reschedule, what to buy, and what to make.

A *bill of materials* (*BOM*) is the list or recipe, of components, raw materials, assemblies, and the like, that go into a manufactured item. It is frequently shown in the manner of an organization chart, as shown in Exhibit 5–9.

Notice that an item (glue) can appear more than once. Notice also that the BOM continues expanding downward until every item is purchased.

In the 1970s and 1980s, MRP programs used a horizontal planning grid, with each column representing one week. This is illustrated in Exhibit 5–10.

Let's see how MRP works. First we'll look at the rows.

- *Timing Row*—OH means *on hand*, in the stockroom, today. The other columns are future periods, which could be days or weeks.

Exhibit 5–9
BOM for a Chair

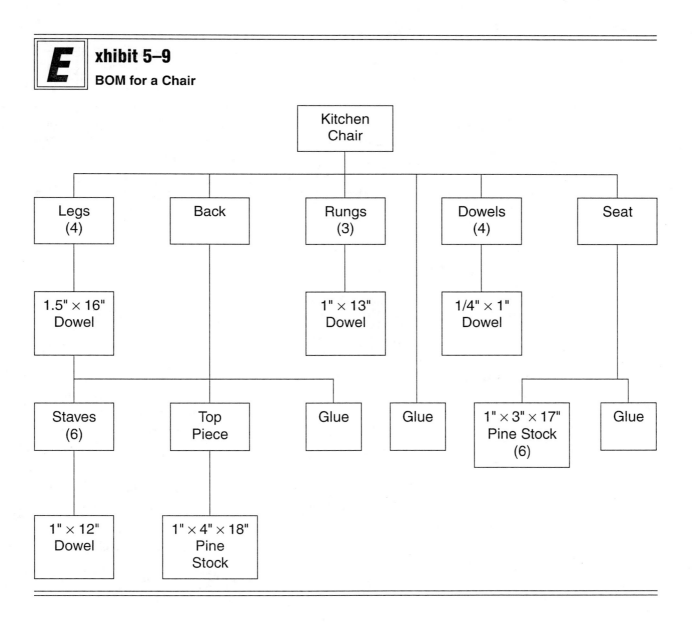

Exhibit 5–10
MRP Planning Grid

Item 3549—Chair Leg

	OH	1	2	3	4	5	6
Gross Requirements		56	36	72	40	60	44
Scheduled Receipts		48					
Projected Available	75						
Net Requirements							
Planned Order Receipt							
Planned Order Release							

- *Gross Requirements*—total amount needed in that period, no matter whether they are already in the stockroom or on order. Requirements decrease inventory; they represent future issues from the stockroom.
- *Scheduled Receipts*—amount already on order (with suppliers or in your plant), which will replenish the stockroom in a given period. Receipts increase inventory.
- *Projected Available*—projected on-hand in the stockroom, if all events (receipts and requirements) occur as planned.
- *Net Requirements*—projected shortage for that week, after all scheduled receipts have been factored in. This must be filled by a planned order receipt or the shortage will indeed occur.
- *Planned Order Receipt*—This is the quantity MRP expects to receive from the new order it is planning. This number must equal or exceed the Net Requirements. It might exceed it due to lot sizing rules (for example, order a minimum of x, order in multiples of y).
- *Planned Order Release*—This is the order quantity that MRP puts on the planned Work Order or the Purchase Requisition. For work orders, this number can be greater than the Planned Order Receipt because of anticipated scrap.

MRP can also use a vertical format, with one line per event (individual outgoing or incoming transaction). The vertical format offers a much greater level of detail to the planner.

Dependent Demand

Manufacturing companies have two types of demand for their items: independent and dependent. This concept underpins MRP logic; without it, the logic would not work. It can also be applied outside of manufacturing companies; indeed, it can be profitably applied throughout a supply chain.

Independent demand is independent of the internal actions of the company; it arrives from an external customer. For a chair manufacturer, independent demand is the customer order for chairs. It is also the customer demand for replacement parts (rungs, replaceable padded seats, and so forth).

Dependent demand depends on a company's internal actions; it is for an internal customer (another production process). Dependent demand is usually created by the master production schedule. For a chair manufacturer, if the master production schedule has scheduled the production of 10 chairs on July 15, that production order creates dependent demand for 40 legs, 10 seats, 40 rungs, 10 backs, and so on, based on the bill of materials for the model of chair being produced. And if each of the backs has 5 slats, the production order for 10 backs will produce dependent demand for 50 slats. Dependent demand supports the company's plan blindly; it does not concern itself with the question, "Are customers going to actually buy these purple chairs with yellow slats and green seats and pink stripes on the legs?" It assumes that marketing and salespeople understand the market and customers; the function of dependent demand is to meet the commitment for finished goods, on schedule.

The total demand for an item is the sum of all independent demand **plus** all dependent demand. For a PC manufacturer such as Dell Computer, the total demand for DVD/CD drives is the sum of two things:

- Independent demand
  - DVD/CD drives ordered directly by customers
  - Service/replacement requirements (for computers being repaired by Dell)
- Dependent demand
  - Computers being assembled by Dell

This concept caused a huge breakthrough in materials planning in the 1970s because it dramatically improved the accuracy of forecasting future demand for components, which was the largest problem for manufacturing companies before MRP. A company could now calculate, with relatively high accuracy, the demand for its components in advance of their use and could, therefore, insure that they would all be available when needed. It only had to forecast independent demand, which was a relatively small percentage of the total demand for component parts. This is why manufacturers experienced a substantial improvement in on-time shipments, while simultaneously reducing inventory, when they implemented an MRP system for the first time.

Supply chain practices, which apply to any company that manages inventory, also take advantage of this concept. *Independent* demand means demand that the company cannot accurately compute in advance; it implies lack of visibility. Supply chain concepts and practices deliberately increase a supplier's ability to see a customer's actual usage, and even the customer's customers', by transmitting usage data back into the supply chain. As an example, companies that sell to large retailers do not just get orders from the

112   FUNDAMENTALS OF INVENTORY MANAGEMENT AND CONTROL

retailers' distribution centers (DCs). The retailer has the supplier manage the inventory levels at the retailer's distribution centers, sending them actual data every night about shipments from the DC. This enables a supplier to see what is occurring in the marketplace as it happens, rather than reacting to a very large "surprise" order from a customer. The customers and suppliers both win, because the level of inventory can be permanently reduced (thereby reducing cost) while maintaining or increasing the service levels. Many industries have adopted and are currently improving their supply chain practices. Between 1996 and 2000, inventories, as a percentage of gross sales, dropped 27 percent in the automotive supply chain, 36 percent in consumer electronics, 17 percent in pharmaceuticals, and 16 percent in retail (Langenwalter, 2000, p. 49).

Supply chain concepts, properly applied, can create a large competitive advantage. The companies with the best supply chain practices had 46 percent lower total supply chain costs (as a percentage of their gross revenues), 48 percent less inventory (in days of supply), 64 percent cash-to-cash cycle time, 16 percent better on-time delivery to customer request date, and 85 percent better flexibility to respond to increased demand (Langenwalter, 2000, p. 49).

MRP Planning Process

When MRP starts planning to produce a part, the only data that it has are the first two rows (gross requirements and scheduled receipts) plus on-hand inventory. All other cells are blank, as shown in Exhibit 5–10. So MRP computes the Projected Available for the first period by adding scheduled receipts to current on-hand and subtracting gross requirements. MRP notices that the Projected Available at the end of period 1 is high, and that it would be above 0 even if the projected receipt could be delayed to period 2. So it recommends rescheduling out the 48 until period 2, as shown in Exhibit 5–11. The Projected Available at the end of period 1 is now missing the originally scheduled incoming quantity of 48. MRP repeats the logic for period 2, finishing with 31.

In period 3, however, subtracting the gross requirements of 72 from the on-hand quantity of 31 leaves a projected shortage of 41 (shown in Net Requirements). Assuming that you buy these chair legs four dozen at a time, the planned order receipt is for 48, leaving 7 in the stockroom at the end of the period. It only takes one period to get chair legs, so you have to release the purchase order to your supplier in period 2 in order to get it in period 3, as shown in Exhibit 5–11.

That's all there is to it. The difference with MRP is that it can plan to receive as many more items as it needs, in the time period when it needs them. This is sort of like having a rich uncle, who will cover all your overdrafts as long as you give him three weeks' notice.

One more detail, however. If your company manufactures the chair legs, rather than buying them from the outside, the Planned Order Release quantities become Gross Requirements for those chair legs, with identical quantities and periods. In this example, there would be gross requirements for 48 legs in periods 2, 3, 4, and 5. Other models of chairs that use the same legs

© American Management Association. All rights reserved.

Exhibit 5-11
MRP Planning Grid

Item 3549—Chair Leg

	OH	1	2	3	4	5	6
Gross Requirements		56	36	72	40	60	44
Scheduled Receipts			*48*				
Projected Available	75	19	31	7	15	3	7
Net Requirements				41	33	45	41
Planned Order Receipt				48	48	48	48
Planned Order Release			48	48	48	48	

would also create gross requirements. When MRP "plans" the chair legs, to spot and prevent future stockouts of the chair legs, it will have all gross requirements from all chairs in which the legs are used. Therefore, it will be able to plan to have enough of the right components on hand, and plan enough work orders, to avoid stockouts.

MRP as a planning tool quickly evolved into closed-loop MRP II, which added purchasing (for maintaining purchase orders), shop floor control (which has since evolved into production activity control, manufacturing execution systems, and enterprise production systems), customer order management, forecasting, master production scheduling, inventory management (for raw materials, WIP, and finished goods), and general accounting and cost accounting. With these functions, MRP II swept the industrial world in the 1970s and into the 1980s. MRP II actually integrated these functions into one database, so that anyone in the company could get accurate and timely information to make better decisions. Companies reduced inventories and improved on-time shipments to customers; their salespeople finally had timely information to offer their customers. Purchasing could project how much of a family of items they needed to buy for the next six months or year, so they could place blanket purchase orders. Exhibit 5-12 shows how the modules of an MRP II system integrate.

Through the years, MRP II software manufacturers kept adding new features and new modules. By the late 1980s, the functionality of MRP II had increased to such an extent that people started using a new term to describe it: *enterprise resources planning (ERP)*. ERP was capable of handling the largest multiplant, multinational companies. See Exhibit 5-13.

By the late 1990s, the same software programs had expanded sufficiently that the industry coined another new name: ERP II. *ERP II* software is highly complex; the most complete packages have upwards of 75 million lines of

Exhibit 5-12
MRP II—The Closed Loop

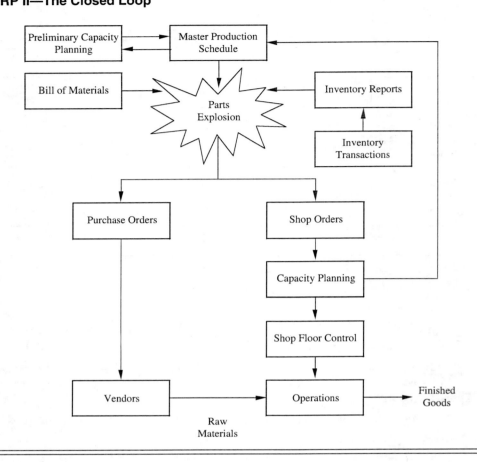

code! The heart of an ERP II system is its integration of the various departments and functions. ERP II systems have two basic objectives:

1. Integrating all information inside a manufacturing company and with its customers and suppliers
2. Empowering each individual throughout a company to make the best possible business decisions by having all relevant information available to that person

Each of the modules in an ERP II system was initially, and still could be, stand-alone; the power of ERP is in the integration, in the arrows. The problem with stand-alone functions is the lack of automated integration with the rest of the business; this requires people to somehow keep the function coordinated and to override its suggestions because it cannot "see" outside its own small area. When manufacturing companies migrate to ERP from ROP/EOQ, they normally achieve a 25 percent reduction in inventory, increased on-time shipments, reduced shipping costs, and reduced costs for raw materials. This is because ROP/EOQ assumes no information

Exhibit 5-13
ERP Flow Chart

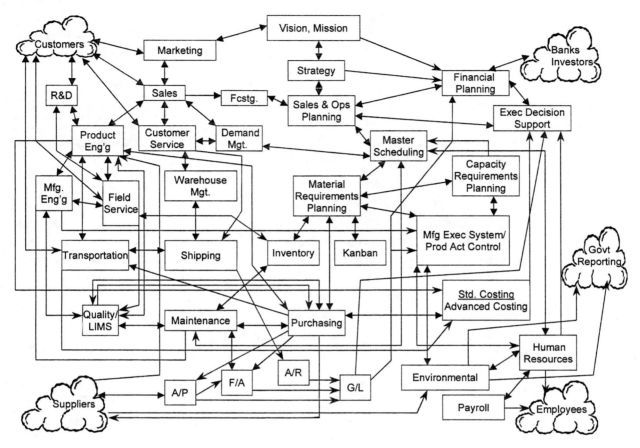

Langenwalter, Gary A., *Enterprise Resources Planning and Beyond: Integrating Your **Entire** Organization* (Boca Raton, St. Lucie Press). Included with permission.

about future requirements for a given component; it uses statistical methods based on past consumption. ROP/EOQ is poorly suited for manufacturing inventories for two reasons:

1. It ignores changes in bills of materials. Suppose that Purchasing receives a message from the inventory control system on June 25 that the reorder point on Circuit Board #2843 has been reached. So they contact the supplier and buy another year's supply (due to quantity discounts for larger purchases and because this is a special-order item—they don't stock it). However, Engineering has put through an engineering change that replaces Circuit Board #2843, effective July 1, with Turbo Circuit Board #2975, which has been a smash hit with customers. So the entire order of #2843 will eventually be written off and thrown away.

2. It assumes that a stockout of one item does not affect the demand for others (dependent demand). But that is not true! An automobile has thousands of individual components, assembled into various groupings. A

finished automobile requires *all of them*, not just most of them. Can you imagine seeing the following sign, neatly printed, inside a car at a showroom: "Due to unforeseen high demand, the brake pedal was not available at the time of manufacture. As soon as it becomes available, we will send it to you. You can bring this car back to the dealer, who will install it for you. We apologize for any inconvenience that this might cause you and assure you of our commitment to providing the highest quality automobiles for your driving experience."

Actually, ROP systems are guaranteed to cause high frustration, stockouts, and high inventory because they are based on service levels. Exhibit 5–14 shows the percentage of all parts being available simultaneously (which is required for assembly!) in an ROP system:

Although ERP is an excellent way for manufacturers to plan, communicate, and integrate, it has several drawbacks:

1. It is data-intensive. All data must be entered quickly and accurately because the system makes recommendations based on the data it has. Some people have quipped that MRP stands for "more ridiculous paperwork."

Exhibit 5–14
Probability of Having All Items Available at the Same Time

	Service Level		
Number of components	90%	95%	98%
5	59	77	90
10	35	60	82
15	21	46	74
20	12	36	67
50	1	8	36

Oden, Howard W., Gary A. Langenwalter, and Raymond Lucier, *Handbook of Material and Capacity Requirements Planning* (New York, McGraw-Hill, 1993, p. 61). Included with permission.

Even with a 98 percent service level for each component (which requires considerable inventory investment), one-third of the time an assembly order that requires 20 components will experience a stockout. And it will "always" be with a different part! Even worse, if the controller has declared that 98 percent service level requires too much inventory and you have cut back to 95 percent, a 20-item assembly will have a stockout two-thirds of the time! So you'll have 19 components, a broken schedule, expediting from the supplier (or a work order in your shop), air shipment to your customer, and lots of management time to solve this crisis.

PLANNING AND REPLENISHMENT CONCEPTS **117**

2. It assumes fixed lead times.
3. It assumes infinite capacity (unless you are including an advanced planning and scheduling module).
4. In spite of all the data, most ERP systems cannot answer the customer's fundamental question, "When can you ship my order?" unless you will be shipping from stock.
5. It can be difficult to implement and maintain.

In spite of these drawbacks, ERP is usually the best way to insure timely and widespread communication throughout a company. Like democracy, it might have its flaws, but it's far better than the other alternatives.

Reorder Point/EOQ

Reorder point/EOQ systems trade off two costs: the cost of ordering, and the cost of carrying. They do not focus on reducing cost (for example, by minimizing ordering and manufacturing setup and restocking costs). In addition, they do not assume any other information (such as pending changes in demand, in BOM, or in scrap rates).

Replenishment Costs

As discussed in Chapter 2, Inventory As Money, every day that an item remains in your stockroom it costs you money in the form of a carrying cost (K factor). If you take that concept to its ultimate extreme, it would make sense only to buy items exactly when you need them. Multiple smaller quantity purchases of the same item certainly hold down your carrying costs. However, it increases your cost of replenishment—the expenses associated with buying things—unless you itemize them as non-value-added costs.

It costs money to acquire things. That sounds absurdly simple when you first read it; however, the total cost of obtaining a product exceeds the actual price paid for an item. Expenses related to replenishment include staff salaries, rent, and other overhead expenses attributable to replenishment. See Exhibit 5–15.

In fact, the more often you buy, the greater your internal costs. For example, if you purchased one million widgets all at the same time, your *replenishment cost* (*R factor*) would be the cost per line item, per purchase order (PO).

- If the per line, per PO cost is $12.25, then your cost to buy all one million at one time would be $12.25.
- If you were to buy the same one million widgets 250,000 at a time, then your R factor would be $12.25 times four (four POs with one line item each), or $49.00.
- If you purchased the widgets one at a time, the cost would be one million times $12.25, or $12.25 million.

There is a substantial difference between buying and replenishing. Buying requires the Purchasing department to reach an agreement (usually through a purchase order) with a supplier. Some organizations, for example

© American Management Association. All rights reserved.

Exhibit 5-15
Calculating the R Factor

The cost of replenishment is calculated on a per-item, per-order basis because it takes virtually the same amount of effort to receive a line item, to inspect it (when required), to move it to the stocking location, and to pay the supplier, no matter the quantity on the line item. Therefore, assuming the R factor is $12.25 per line item, per order, if there is a single line item on an order, the replenishment cost is $12.25. If there are two line items, it's $25.50. If there are three line items, it's $36.75

Annual cost of replenishment activities:	
Receiving department labor/salaries	$205,000
Receiving department overhead (rent, utilities, equipment allocation, etc.)	249,000
Receiving inspection labor/salaries (a percentage of Inspection department)	64,500
Receiving inspection overhead	86,000
Material handling labor/salaries (a percentage of Material handling department)	98,000
Material handling overhead	131,000
Accounts payable labor/salaries (part of the Accounting department budget)	65,000
Accounts payable overhead	81,000
Total Annual Costs of Replenishment	**$979,500**
Number of purchase orders created per year for stock (assume):	10,000
Average number of different stock items per order (assume):	× 8
Total number of times stock items were ordered:	80,000

$$\frac{\text{Total Annual Costs}}{\text{Total Times Stock Items Were Ordered}} = \text{R factor} \rightarrow \frac{\$979,500}{80,000} = \boxed{\$12.25 = \text{R factor}}$$

defense contractors, require their Purchasing departments to get three written quotes before they can issue a purchase order.

Replenishing does not need to involve Purchasing. If Purchasing has created a blanket purchase order, a stock clerk can directly notify the supplier when an item needs replenishing. Replenishing does, however, involve transportation, receiving stock, putting stock away, and paying the supplier. Lean and supply chain concepts focus on minimizing replenishment costs.

You may have noticed that the R factor excludes the cost of purchasing. That's because many companies now place blanket orders (quite often for an entire year). For those items, the replenishment signals do not even have to involve Purchasing; they can go directly from a computer system (or a stock clerk) to the supplier.

Planning and Replenishment Concepts 119

Order size versus frequency of purchase shifts the cost burden from the K factor to the R factor and vice versa. In other words:

- If you buy smaller quantities more often, your replenishment costs go up—or your R factor increases.
- If you buy larger quantities less often, you have a higher inventory level for a longer period of time so your carrying costs go up—or your K factor increases.

In a perfect world the K factor and the R factor would be equal. Although this is difficult to achieve, an organization attempting to have the correct amount of product at the overall lowest cost will strive for that balance.

Activity 5–2
Balancing Carrying and Replenishment Costs

Instructions: The Charmax Co. has asked you to arbitrate a dispute that has arisen between the purchasing and warehouse managers. Examine this situation and propose some solutions.

Charmax's receiving ends at 5:00 pm. At 4:45 pm a 40-foot trailer is backed up to the dock. The doors are opened to reveal three levels of floor-stacked boxes extending from floor to ceiling, back to front.

Joe, the warehouse manager, realizes that it will take four workers at least two hours to hand unload the trailer. Virtually all of that time will be on an overtime basis.

Joe reviews the truck's manifest and determines what items on the trailer are needed for delivery tomorrow morning. He discovers that there are only three boxes on the trailer that are truly required for tomorrow's business. He asks Tracy, the truck driver, if he helped to load the trailer. Tracy replies that he did. Joe asks if Tracy remembers where those three boxes are. With a smile, Tracy replies that they are located in the nose of the trailer.

Joe decides not to incur the overtime. He will have the trailer unloaded in the morning.

Betty, the sales manager, hears that the three items will not be shipped to Acme, a large and important customer. She storms into the warehouse and demands that the trailer be unloaded. Joe explains the overtime situation. Betty replies that Joe should have scheduled the trailer to arrive earlier in the day. Joe replies that the buyer, Bill, handles traffic management as part of the purchase of the product. Betty angrily says she doesn't much care. Joe had told her that the product would be here today for delivery tomorrow. "You promised me," Betty says, "so that's what I promised the customer. Now unload the trailer." Joe reluctantly does so.

Later, Joe confronts Bill and demands that the product be brought in palletized or unitized or in some other manner so it can be unloaded quickly. Joe argues that since internal handling is a major component in computing the cost of carrying inventory, unitization will help cut Charmax's costs.

Bill responds that he has to buy the product as he is buying it now. He argues that to palletize the product would increase the costs per unit of product. He also points out that since the product already extends to the top of the trailer, that the added height of three levels of pallets at approximately 4 inches each, would force him to buy less per order so that it will all fit on a trailer. Therefore, he will have to buy less and buy it more often driving up his replenishment costs.

Ill-will and stalemate result.

Activity 5–2 continues on next page.

120   FUNDAMENTALS OF INVENTORY MANAGEMENT AND CONTROL

Activity 5–2 continued from previous page.

What arguments can be made in favor of Joe's position?

_____

_____

_____

_____

What arguments can be made in favor of Bill's position?

_____

_____

_____

What solution(s) can you offer?

_____

_____

_____

_____

_____

_____

Suggested solutions are found at the end of the chapter.

Independent Demand Inventory

Order point formulas are based on some relatively simple concepts. Order point formulas are used to determine how much of a given item needs to be ordered where there is independent demand. In these formulas a *reorder point* (*ROP*) is set for each item. The ROP is the lowest quantity of an item you will have on hand and on order before you reorder.

Let's look at a simple min-max inventory system to see how these formulas work. Imagine that all of a particular SKU are kept in a single bin. Without a reorder point, the entire batch would be used up without any order being placed. The organization would then be unable to sell or use that item during whatever time frame was required to order and bring in the SKU—the lead time. It would make sense, therefore, to adopt a two-bin system with Bin 1 containing working stock and Bin 2 containing working

© American Management Association. All rights reserved.

reserve. The amount of product in Bin 2 would be equal to the usage rate during that item's lead time.

In a two-bin system, if all goes as it should, then immediately upon using the first item from Bin 2 you would reorder a quantity equal to both bins. As you use the last item in Bin 2 the order arrives and you refill both bins. This assumes that lead time is exact, there are no vendor stockouts or backorders, and that there are never any defects. These assumptions are, of course, often false. Therefore, a true order-point system is a three-bin system, with the third bin containing safety stock.

Bin 3, safety stock, buffers the company against the "real world" by providing additional stock, just in case the supplier does not deliver in time, or customers order more than we thought, or we discover defects, or.... Because safety stock calculations can be relatively complex, some companies apply the A-B-C principle.

- A (expensive items): Monitor stock levels closely; compute safety stock with mathematical formulas.
- B (moderate items): Apply decent rules of thumb (e.g., x weeks' supply, or y% of EOQ.
- C (inexpensive items): Have enough safety stock so you don't run out.

Your company can decide the service levels that it wants to provide its customers in terms of percentage of stock availability when the customer wants to buy. Perfect service would be 100 percent; however, the inventory levels required to support perfect service are unaffordable for most distribution and manufacturing companies. The tradeoffs between inventory and service level are shown in Exhibit 5–16.

In Exhibit 5–16 Safety Factor is the factor by which you multiply the Mean Absolute Deviation (MAD) to determine safety stock levels. MAD is relatively easy to calculate, especially using a computer system. Take the

Exhibit 5–16
Inventory Level Versus Service Level

Service Level %	Stockout Probability %	Safety Factor (× MAD)
90.00	10.00	1.60
95.00	5.00	2.06
98.00	2.00	2.56
99.00	1.00	2.91
99.86	0.14	3.75
99.99	0.01	5.00

© American Management Association. All rights reserved.

average sales of an item over a number of periods (for example, 12 months), then calculate the difference between the average and each month's sales, *ignoring* the plus or minus sign. Add all the differences and divide by the number of periods. Exhibit 5–17 shows the calculations.

In this example, if we want to provide a 99 percent service level to our customers, we have to have a safety stock of 415 × 2.91, or 1,208 packs of batteries!

The formulas used here assume that the replenishment lead time is one period—in this case, one month. If the lead time on batteries is actually a month, a high level of safety stock will indeed be required. However, retailers, distributors, and manufacturers all intuitively understand that the risk of stockout drops as the lead time decreases. Thus, if the lead time is one day, the safety stock level can be dramatically reduced. Mathematically, it reduces by the square root of the lead time (Oden, Langenwalter, and Lucier, 1993, pp. 55–57). In this example, the safety stock would drop by the square root of 30, or approximately 5.5, from 1,208 to 1,208/5.5, or 220.

Exhibit 5–17
Calculating MAD AA Alkaline Batteries, 8-Pack

Month	Sales	Difference
January	1,820	111
February	1,633	298
March	1,585	346
April	1,447	484
May	1,274	657
June	1,729	202
July	1,848	83
August	1,773	158
September	2,464	533
October	2,257	326
November	1,779	152
December	3,562	1,631
Total	23,171	4,981
Average	*1,931*	*415*

Safety stock also assumes that we cannot accurately predict the ups and downs—that every sale is a surprise. However, retailers understand that batteries sell more in September (back to school with new calculators, portable radios, and the like), October (Halloween and fire alarm battery replacement month), and December (Christmas toys). So it is not necessary to carry all the safety stock that the formula suggests if you understand why demand fluctuates and can plan accordingly.

Bins for safety stock can be mathematically created or can reflect actual physical separation of items in the stockroom. A simple formula for determining the ROP reflects these concepts.

$$(\text{Usage} \times \text{Lead Time}) + \text{Safety Stock} = \text{ROP}$$

In the above formula lead time is shown as a percentage of a month, as follows:

1 week = 0.25 = 25%	4 weeks = 1.00 = 100%
2 weeks = 0.50 = 50%	5 weeks = 1.25 = 125%
3 weeks = 0.75 = 75%	6 weeks = 1.50 = 150%

Let's look at a few examples.

Example 1 makes the following assumptions:

- Usage rate of 1,200 items per month
- Lead time of 3 weeks
- MAD of 220
- Service level of 98 percent

The step-by-step calculation follows this procedure:

- Calculate weekly usage. Assume a 4-week month. 1,200 items ÷ 4 weeks = 300 items per week; therefore Bin 1 or working stock should contain at least 300 items.
- Calculate working reserve. Given 3 weeks of lead time, working reserve should be 1,200 items × 0.75 = 900 items.
- Calculate safety stock. 98% service level ⇒ 2.56 × MAD (220) ⇒ 563
- Calculate ROP: (1,200 items × 0.75) + 536 items = 1,463 items

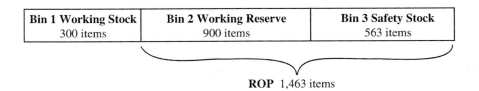

Example 2 makes the following assumptions:

- Usage rate of 1,200 items per month
- Lead time of 1 week

- MAD of 220
- Service level of 98 percent

The step-by-step calculation follows this procedure:

- Calculate weekly usage. Assume a 4-week month. 1,200 items ÷ 4 weeks = 300 items per week; therefore Bin 1 or working stock should contain at least 300 items.
- Calculate working reserve. Given 1 week of lead time, working reserve should be 1,200 items × 0.25 = 300 items
- Calculate safety stock: use same calculation as in Example 1, times the square root of ¼ because the lead time of 1 week is ¼ the demand period, 1 month. The square root of ¼ is ½. So safety stock is 563 ÷ 2 or 282.
- Calculate ROP: (1,200 items × 0.25) + 282 items = 582 items

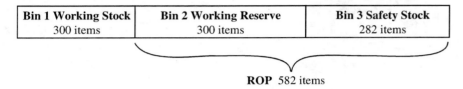

The ROP is the *minimum* (min) in a *minimum-maximum (min-max) inventory control system*. You will not let your stock level fall below a certain minimum nor will you have items on hand or on order above a specified maximum. In order to compute the maximum in these systems, you must first determine how often you will place orders. This time period is called the *review cycle*. The review cycle is the length of time between reviews of when you wish to order product. Here is the formula to determine the review cycle:

$$\frac{\text{Total Quantity Purchased from Vendor for a Year}}{\text{Economic Order Quantity}} = \text{Review Cycle}$$

The unit of measure reflecting total purchases from a vendor can be dollars, pieces, pounds, units, or any other useful measure. The economic order quantity (EOQ) is discussed in the next section.

Let's first look at one example.

$$\frac{200{,}000}{5{,}000} = 40 \text{ reviews per year}$$

Dividing 40 reviews by 52 weeks yields a review roughly every 1.3 weeks. When the review actually occurs will also depend on factors such as seasonality.

The maximum in these systems is also represented by a simple formula.

ROP + Usage During the Review Cycle = Maximum

Let's look at two examples. In the first example, assume the following

- Usage rate of 1,200 items per month
- Review cycle every 1.3 weeks
- ROP equals 1,463 items

$$\frac{1{,}200 \text{ items}}{4 \text{ weeks}} = 300 \text{ items used per week}$$

$$300 \text{ items} \times 1.3 \text{ weeks} = 390 \text{ items used during review cycle}$$

$$1{,}463 \text{ items} + 390 \text{ items} = 1{,}853 \text{ items max}$$

In the second example, assume the following:

- Usage rate of 1,200 items per month
- Review cycle every 1.3 weeks
- ROP equals 582 items

$$\frac{1{,}200 \text{ items}}{4 \text{ weeks}} = 300 \text{ used per week}$$

$$300 \text{ items} \times 1.3 \text{ weeks} = 390 \text{ used during review cycle}$$

$$582 \text{ items} + 390 \text{ items} = 972 \text{ items max}$$

By setting a min-max for each item in your inventory, you can create a simple method of ordering products having independent demand. As you set the min-max, notice the effect of lead time on inventory!

Economic Order Quantity (EOQ) Formula

In 1915, F. W. Harris of General Electric developed the *economic order quantity* (*EOQ*) formula to help stockkeepers determine how much product to buy.

To calculate EOQ, assume the following:

A = Total usage value of SKU per year
K = Carrying cost (the K factor)
R = Replenishment cost (the R factor)
P = Price per unit

Here is the basic formula.

$$EOQ = \sqrt{\frac{2AR}{P^2K}}$$

This formula and its variations allow you to determine the following:

- The optimal quantity to order
- When an item should be ordered
- Total cost
- Average inventory level
- How much should be ordered each time
- Maximum inventory level

The EOQ model is based on several assumptions.

- The demand rate is constant (no variations), recurring, and known.
- Carrying cost and ordering cost are independent of the quantity ordered (no discounts).
- Lead time is constant and known. Therefore, the ordering times given result in new orders arriving exactly when the inventory level reaches zero.

- The model looks at each item independently. There is no linkage between items.
- Orders arrive in a single batch (there are no vendor stockouts or backorders).

Here is a simple example of the basic formula:

$A = \$36,000$
$K = 15\%$
$R = \$75$
$P = \$25$

$$EOQ = \sqrt{\frac{2AR}{P^2K}} = \sqrt{\frac{2(\$36,000)(\$75)}{(\$25)^2(0.15)}} = \sqrt{\frac{5,475,000}{93.75}} = \sqrt{58,400}$$
$$= 242 \text{ units per order}$$

Mathematicians have developed variations of the basic formula. See Exhibit 5–18 for additional formulas. However, none of the calculations reflect the real world. All of these formulas assume that the values in the formulas are accurate. But most companies cannot accurately compute the true cost of carrying inventory or the true cost of replenishing one item. Those estimates can be 25 to 50 percent high or low in a typical company.

Additionally, for many items, the EOQ curve produced by the formula resembles a shallow bowl rather than a V. Thus, an inventory planner can increase or decrease the EOQ quantity by 25 percent or even 50 percent without substantially affecting total cost.

---

xhibit 5–18
Variations of the Basic EOQ Formula

Assume:

A = Total value of SKU per year	= $36,000
K = Carrying cost (the K factor)	= 15%
R = Replenishment cost (the R factor)	= $75
P = Price per unit	= $25

Optimum Number of Orders per Year =

$$\sqrt{\frac{AK}{2R}} = \sqrt{\frac{(\$36,000)(0.15)}{2(\$75)}} = \sqrt{\frac{5,475}{150}} = \sqrt{36.5} = 6.4 \cong 6 \text{ orders/year}$$

Optimum Number of Dollars per Order =

$$\sqrt{\frac{2AR}{K}} = \sqrt{\frac{2(\$36,000)(\$75)}{0.15}} = \sqrt{\frac{5,475,000}{0.15}} = \sqrt{36,500,000} \cong \$6,041.52$$

Exhibit 5–19
Screen Shot

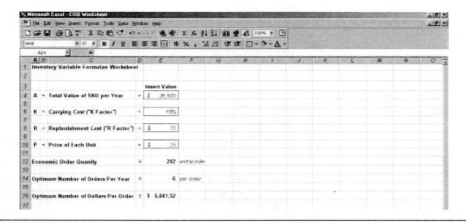

Setting Up an EOQ Worksheet in Microsoft® Excel®
Here's a tip... once you set up a permanent worksheet in Microsoft® Excel® or any similar spreadsheet program, you will be able to quickly calculate important EOQ information simply by entering variable values for *A, K, R,* and *P* under the Insert Value column.

Based on the cell placement as noted below, you can calculate each quantity by entering the following formulas:

Economic Order Quantity → type: =SQRT((2*E4*E8)/((E10^2)*E6))
Optimum Number of Orders per Year → type: =SQRT((E4*E6)/(2*E8))
Optimum Number of Dollars per Order → type: =SQRT((2*E4*E8)/E6)

Exhibit 5–20
Screen Shot II

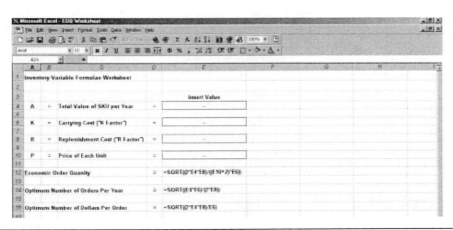

Exhibit 5–19 illustrates the worksheet setup, including the formulas you need to input.

Exhibit 5–20 illustrates a completed worksheet. Values were entered for the variables *A, K, R,* and *P.* The worksheet then updated itself as the formulas were already input.

In determining the best planning and replenishment approaches for an organization, the distinctions between independent and dependent demand are critical. Independent demand, seen in the distribution, retailing, and replacement sectors, calls for a replenishment approach to inventory management. Dependent demand, seen in the manufacturing sector, calls for a requirements approach to managing inventory.

Lean philosophies apply equally to manufacturing and nonmanufacturing sectors. Lean/JIT approaches to inventory management share a common philosophy, based on determining the wants of both external and internal customers and meeting 100 percent of the customer's quality and on-time delivery standards. There is a common focus on eliminating waste and non-value-added activities and an emphasis on continuous improvement.

When calculating replenishment costs, managers must take into account the total cost of obtaining product. Expenses related to replenishment include salaries and overhead for receiving, inspection, material handling, and accounts payable. Internal costs increase with the frequency of replenishment purchases.

The purpose of materials requirements planning (MRP) is to predict materials shortages in time to fill them. MPR is designed to compute how many of each item a company will need each day and plan to have that item in the stockroom on time. Time phasing and dependent demand are two of the conceptual improvements it offers.

Managers use order-point formulas to determine how much of a given item needs to be ordered when there is independent demand. These formulas, in which a reorder point (ROP) is set for each item, are based on minimum-maximum inventory concepts.

Simple formulas based on specific variations of the basic economic order quantity (EOQ) allow managers to determine several key factors when planning how much product to buy, including optimal quantity to order, when to order, total cost, average inventory level, how much to order each time, and maximum inventory level. While many companies cannot accurately compute the true cost of carrying inventory or replenishing an item, the EOQ curve produced by the formula allows for variations of up to 50 percent without substantially affecting total cost.

For individuals not directly involved in purchasing, successful inventory control doesn't so much flow from actually using the various formulas, but rather from understanding what outcomes are supposed to result from their use.

PLANNING AND REPLENISHMENT CONCEPTS   129

 Review Questions

1. Independent demand is best described as: 1. (c)
   (a) erratic purchasing of inventory.
   (b) the need for one item because of its relationship to another item.
   (c) demand for items as a result of market conditions outside the control of your organization's operations.
   (d) demand for items outside of their normal review cycle.

2. Lean manufacturing results in: 2. (a)
   (a) right item, right quantity, right place, right time.
   (b) right item, right quantity, right place.
   (c) right item, right quantity.
   (d) larger inventory levels.

3. The reorder point is: 3. (c)
   (a) the point in time when a product review is undertaken.
   (b) the largest quantity of an item you will have on hand or on order.
   (c) the lowest quantity of an item you will have on hand or on order before you reorder.
   (d) the lowest quantity at which you can obtain a discount from a vendor.

4. The bill of materials is: 4. (b)
   (a) another name for a purchase order.
   (b) the recipe of raw materials and subassemblies that make up a finished product.
   (c) the schedule of what will be built, when, and in what quantities.
   (d) an accounts payable concept.

5. Lean and JIT systems regard inventory in excess of current   5. (c)
   production and R&D needs to be:
   (a) safety stock.
   (b) FIFO inventory.
   (c) waste.
   (d) part of the kanban system.

Do you have questions? Comments? Need clarification?
Call Educational Services at 1-800-225-3215
or e-mail at ed_svcs@amanet.org.

© American Management Association. All rights reserved.

Answers

Suggested Solutions for Activity 5–2

1. Joe and Bill should coordinate traffic management so that loads match the labor, equipment, time resources, and constraints of the organization. By lowering handling costs, the company will reduce overall carrying costs.

2. Both Joe and Bill need to specifically determine their respective costs.
    (a) Joe can determine the handling portion of the K factor by:
        (1) Determining the average time it takes to unload a trailer by hand.
        (2) Multiplying the average hand unloading time times the number of trailers during the year.
        (3) Multiplying the total hand unloading time times the average hourly labor rate being paid to warehouse personnel.
        (4) Determining the average time it would take to unload unitized loads.
        (5) Multiplying the average unitized unloading time times the number of trailers during the year.
        (6) Multiplying the total unitized unloading time times the average hourly labor rate being paid to warehouse personnel.
        (7) Comparing the annual labor costs involved for hand unloading to the annual labor costs of unitized unloading to determine the total dollar savings.
    (b) Bill can determine his added replenishment costs associated with smaller loads purchased more often.
    (c) A fair comparison can then be made as to which alternative is the most advantageous for the overall organization.

3. Alternatives meeting the needs of both parties might be developed. For example, if slip-sheets (thin cardboard or plywood sheets the same length and width as a pallet) were used, Bill might be able to overcome the size of load and volume problem, while Joe could automate the unloading process.

6

Why Inventory Systems Fail and How To Fix Them

focus

Learning Objectives

By the end of this chapter, you should be able to:

- Understand root causes of why inventory systems fail.
- Use various formulas to measure the effectiveness of your own inventory system.
- Design and utilize a number of charts, including run and flow charts, to uncover operational dysfunctions within your own organization.
- Understand how to use various cycle counting techniques to correct inventory system problems.

INTRODUCTION

The objective of this chapter is to provide you with an understanding of the nature of inventory accuracy and the working tools to "fix" your inventory system. If all items are moving through a properly operating system, then it doesn't matter what the characteristics of a SKU are—expensive item, inexpensive item, fast mover, slow mover, long lead time, or critical—the *shelf count* of the item (actual balance-on-hand stock levels) and *record count* (how many your records say are supposed to be here) will match.

Self-Assessment 6–1
Why Accurate Inventory Records Are Important

Instructions: List eight potential consequences of inaccurate records.

1. _____
2. _____
3. _____
4. _____
5. _____
6. _____
7. _____
8. _____

Suggested answers are found at the end of the chapter.

The traditional method of determining if actual balance on hand stock levels match book/record levels is to take an annual physical inventory. As a method of correcting inventory accuracy problems, this costly and time-consuming effort is riddled with deficiencies. Why? Consider the following:

- *Accuracy is often defined in dollars rather than actual physical units.* As discussed in Chapter 1, Inventory As Both a Tangible and an Intangible Object, the dollar value of product does not reflect exactly what items are in house. For example, imagine you sent out a thousand cases of peaches to a customer rather than the thousand cases of pears actually requested. An annual inventory would reflect an overall dollar value roughly equal to whatever it would have been even if the correct item had been shipped. Therefore, our shelf count is a thousand over for one SKU and a thousand under for another with no discrepancy in accuracy *if accuracy is measured in dollars.* (However, APICS, the society of materials management, defines accuracy in terms of SKUs only. For more information, you can visit their web site: *www.apics.org.*)
- *Products are misidentified.* As discussed in Chapter 3, Physical Location and Control of Inventory, product within a facility is misidentified for a variety of reasons. During annual inventories misidentification often occurs because inexperienced counters assisting with the effort do not recognize items, misunderstand package descriptions, and so on.
- *Units of measure are misidentified.* Incorrect quantities are often written down during annual inventories because counters simply do not understand a SKU's pack size, pack size descriptions, or abbreviations on packaging.

- *Discrepancies are "adjusted away."* Perhaps the greatest problem with using the annual inventory as a method for establishing accuracy is that it provides no method for backtracking through physical and paper transactions to determine why an item's shelf count and its record count do not agree—a 12-month time period is simply too long an audit trail. Consequently, if the reason for a discrepancy cannot be immediately found during the inventory, an adjustment is made without ever correcting the underlying cause of the error.

At the end of an annual inventory, after all of the adjustments have been made, and after the lights have been turned off, you have an inventory shelf and record count that agree. At least they agree until the next morning when the same system that spawned the discrepancies found during the effort reasserts itself and a new group of errors is born.

Albert Einstein, the famous physicist, once said, "A problem stated is a problem half-solved." Modern business writers like Peter Drucker have expressed a similar view: "A problem analyzed is a problem half-solved." The sentiment expressed in these sayings, that reviewing the nature of inventory problems is a key step in solving them, provides you with a good starting point for resolving your own inventory-related issues. Consider the example case in the next section.

INVENTORY SYSTEM FAILURES— EXAMPLE CASE

The following paragraphs have been numbered for ease of reference.

1. Big Hammer, Inc. both manufactures and distributes widgets. Manufacturing occurs at its Los Angeles, California, plant. It distributes from two separate locations. One of these locations is in Kansas City, Missouri, and has been part of Big Hammer for many years. The other location is in New York, New York, and is the surviving portion of Paulex Co., a distribution company, just purchased by Big Hammer.

2. Marc, Big Hammer's president, has just reviewed operating reports from all three locations and is upset. It seems that the inventory accuracy level at all three locations is off. The end result is delayed production, too much inventory, and poor customer service. In addition, department heads in all three locations clash with one another. In order to get everything straightened out he hires the consulting firm of Alana, Eric, and Shawn.

3. Alana goes to Kansas City. Eric goes to New York. Shawn goes to Los Angeles.

4. The trio immediately discovers that New York is using a different software system than Los Angeles and Kansas City. In addition, the Los Angeles/Kansas City software was designed for distribution, not manufacturing. However, some modifications have been made to the Los Angeles/Kansas City software to help with manufacturing applications.

134 FUNDAMENTALS OF INVENTORY MANAGEMENT AND CONTROL

5. The New York system allocates inventory on a real-time basis. In other words, as a pick ticket is generated for an item, the quantity in question is allocated to a specific order and is not available for any other customer—its paper life ceases.

6. The Los Angeles/Kansas City system is a batch system. Items are relieved from stock at the time the system is updated. This usually occurs once per day when billing is done. A modification to the system backflushes[1] some items out of stock during the manufacturing cycle.

7. Eric wanders around the New York location and observes the following:

8. Sales people, customer service personnel, clerical staff, and others freely roam through all stockrooms. He notices that some nonstockroom personnel fill their own orders, grab samples for customers, and put things back into the facility that they have previously removed.

9. He observes that some of these individuals document their actions immediately, while others document nothing, and others turn in necessary paperwork—later.

10. Eric observes Sally, a salesperson peering intently into her computer screen. He hears her utter an oath and declare out loud, "I just saw a whole bunch of SKU #1234 out there a little while ago." She then creates a manual invoice within the software system, prints it, walks out to the stockroom, fills the order she has just created, delivers it to customer Acme Widgets of the World, and later drops the signed delivery copy on the accounts receivables clerk's desk.

11. Eric observes an angry exchange between the warehouse manager and the accounting manager of the New York location. They were arguing over a negative stock balance for SKU #1234.

12. He also observes Sally angrily telling the warehouse manager that one of her customers, Widgets, Gidgets, Gadgets and Such, was shorted 10 widgets on an order it received "just a little while ago."

13. Alana has also observed some interesting things in Kansas City.

14. She has observed two different order fillers attempting to fill orders for the same item—from the same empty shelf.

15. At 5 p.m. one evening she was standing behind Carmen, the company's billing clerk. Carmen's in-box contained several inches of delivery slips ready for processing. Carmen got up and began to make preparations to go home. Alana asked her what she was doing. Carmen replied, "It's 5 p.m., I'm going home."

    Alana said, "But you still have a lot of work in your inbox."

    "So what, I'll work on it tomorrow," Carmen indignantly responded.

    "But you'll mess up the warehouse if you don't get those slips processed tonight," Alana stated.

---

[1] *Backflushing* refers to a software technique where raw materials and other components going into a particular subassembly or final product are relieved from stock when that subassembly/product is completed. If a seat and a leg assembly go into a stool, then on completion of the stool these items are deleted from inventory. Until the backflush occurs the respective parts, subassemblies, etc., remain in the record count. Contrast this to having each item relieved from stock as it is removed from the shelf for production purposes. Backflushing reduces the time and effort involved in tracking individual inventory transactions.

© American Management Association. All rights reserved.

Angrily, Carmen stated, "I work in Accounting. I don't work in the warehouse."

Alana asked, "How long would it take you to do those?"

Carmen glanced at her inbox and replied, "About 30 minutes."

"Please stay and get them done," Alana cajoled.

"I couldn't even if I wanted to," Carmen said. "I'm not allowed any overtime."

Bill, one of Carmen's coworkers chimes in and says, "Why can't you get your work done during the day?"

Furious, Carmen turns on Bill and says, "Hey, you sort and distribute the mail every morning, run photocopies of all incoming checks while fighting with people over our one copy machine, and prepare and go out to make the daily deposit like I do, and, then let's see if you can get your stuff done."

16. Hanging around the warehouse, Alana observed that receiving was done on a manual basis—and that there wasn't always a copy of a purchase order in the warehouse to support incoming loads.

She noticed on several occasions that when the receiving staff did not have all appropriate paperwork for an item, they would simply put it away or move it off to the side. Then later, or the next day, they would hunt down all of the appropriate documentation and turn everything in to the data entry people for entry into the system.

Like Eric, she also observed nonstockroom individuals filling their own orders.

17. She also observed a curious exchange between Franklin, the accounting manager, and Carmen, the billing clerk.

While attempting to create an invoice for an item, Carmen's computer screen flashed an error message indicating that she was trying to bill for something that had a zero stock balance in the system. The software would not let her bill for an item it did not reflect as being available for sale.

Carmen called Franklin over. She showed him the signed delivery slip indicating that the item had, in fact, been delivered.

Franklin stated, "Those people in the warehouse can't get anything right." He then proceeded to manually override the system and entered the SKU (SKU #4567) and quantity in question (10). Franklin then directed Carmen to try again. The invoice was created without any further problems.

Midmorning of the next day the stock records began to show that there were 10 of SKU #4567 in the facility. A telemarketing sales person sold 10 SKU #4567s that afternoon. A pick ticket was generated for the order. The order filler could not find any of SKU #4567 in the warehouse. A stock adjustment form is processed to take these 10 items out of stock.

18. Alana overhears a telephone conversation between Carmen and a customer. The customer wants to return five SKU #9876's and wants to ensure that she is not charged for them. Carmen notes the information, prepares a pickup slip, and issues a credit to the customer's account.

Later that day a salesperson sells five SKU #9876s. A pick ticket was generated for the order. The order filler could not find any of SKU #9876s in the warehouse. A stock adjustment form was processed to take these five items out of stock.

19. Meanwhile, Shawn has been talking to Ichiro, the inventory control clerk in Los Angeles. Ichiro is frustrated. He works hard at his job but can't seem to track work in process. Consequently, he is never sure how much of any particular item the company has available for production purposes.

20. Shawn observes a worker disassembling a subassembly. He asks the worker what he is doing. The worker replies that there is a rush order that they lack all of the raw materials for, so they are disassembling some less important assemblies to cannibalize the required parts.

    Shawn asks if the products being disassembled are from other orders. The worker replies that they are. Shawn asks about any paperwork that was generated to support whatever it is the worker is doing. The worker replies that he doesn't know.

Activity 6–1 and Self-Assessment 6–2
Analyzing What Is Actually Happening

Instructions: Use the paragraph numbers for the scenarios presented in the **example case** as references.

1. a. Write down all of the system-related problems you recognized and the causes of those problems.
2. b. Write down all of these problems you recognize as occurring within your own organization.

Paragraph	Problems Identified	Problems Identified at Your Facility

Additional copies of this chart are provided for your use in Appendix B.

© American Management Association. All rights reserved.

WHY INVENTORY SYSTEMS FAIL AND HOW TO FIX THEM **137**

Here is our discussion of the problems presented in the example case.

Events

1. Big Hammer, Inc. both manufactures and distributes widgets. Manufacturing occurs at its Los Angeles, California plant. It distributes from two separate locations. One of these locations is in Kansas City, Missouri, and has been part of Big Hammer for many years. The other location is in New York, New York, and is the surviving portion of Paulex Co., a distribution company, just purchased by Big Hammer.

Problem Identification and Discussion

Any organization having several locations must clearly identify the answers to the "who, what, when, where, why, and how" questions—who is doing what, when are they doing it, where are they doing it, why are they doing it, and how are they doing it—if it hopes to coordinate the flow of materials and information between and among its separate departments. See the *Tools with Which to Uncover System Dysfunctions* section of this chapter for further insights into this problem.

2. Marc, Big Hammer's president, has just reviewed operating reports from all three locations and is upset. It seems that the inventory accuracy level at all three locations is off. The end result is delayed production, too much inventory, and poor customer service. In addition, department heads in all three locations clash with one another. In order to get everything straightened out he hires the consulting firm of Alana, Eric, and Shawn.

Although consultants are helpful in most instances, you should be able to resolve many system problems your organization may be currently experiencing by applying the concepts contained in this chapter.

3. Alana goes to Kansas City. Eric goes to New York. Shawn goes to Los Angeles.

4. The trio immediately discovers that New York is using a different software system than Los Angeles and Kansas City. In addition, the Los Angeles/Kansas City software was designed for distribution, not manufacturing. However, some modifications have been made to the Los Angeles/Kansas City software to help with manufacturing applications.

Trying to integrate different software systems is always difficult. Once again, any organization hoping to achieve such integration must clearly lay out the timing and sequencing of the information flow within the system.

In addition, the demand patterns for items in a distribution world and those in a manufacturing environment are radically different. See Chapter 5, *Planning and Replenishment Concepts, Inventory Types*. Purchasing patterns for finished goods and spare parts in a distribution environment are based on past usage patterns. See Chapter 5, *Planning and Replenishment Concepts, Independent Demand Inventory*. Purchasing patterns for the raw materials

© American Management Association. All rights reserved.

and subassemblies used in manufacturing are based on the master production schedule. See Chapter 5, *Planning and Replenishment Concepts, Dependent Demand Inventory*.) Different concepts and formulas are used for each type of inventory and, therefore, software designed for one or the other or specifically written for a combination environment should be used whenever possible.

5. The New York system allocates inventory on a real-time basis. In other words, as a pick ticket is generated for an item, the quantity in question is allocated to a specific order and is not available for any other customer—its paper life ceases.

Since the items on the pick ticket were immediately allocated[2] to that order (see Chapter 1, *Inventory as Both a Tangible and an Intangible Object*), those SKUs will actually be sitting on the shelves but won't appear as "available" for customer orders.

Somewhere in the software files is the information: total items on hand, items allocated, and items actually available for sale or use. The problem is that *not everyone in the organization has access to this information!* If (a) staff members are allowed to fill their own orders, and (b) they do not understand how to check the then-current stock records and see a lower number of items than are actually sitting in plain view, then (c) they will stop believing in the record count, will only believe their eyes, and will raid product allocated for other orders.

6. The Los Angeles/Kansas City system is a batch system. Items are relieved from stock at the time the system is updated. This usually occurs once per day when billing is done. A modification to the system backflushes some items out of stock during the manufacturing cycle.

The most significant issue created by batch software systems is that items are physically gone from the shelves/building but still appear in the record count until the system is updated. The longer the length of time between physical movement and record updates, the greater the discrepancies between the shelf count and the record count.

Backflushing works well *if* the backflush occurs at each level of the bill of materials. This will be covered as part of the discussion of paragraph 19.

---

[2]*Allocation* refers to an item being tied to a specific order. *Relieving* an item refers to it actually being removed from stock in terms of both its paper life and its real life.

7. Eric wanders around the New York location and observes the following:
8. Sales people, customer service personnel, clerical staff, and others freely roam through all stockrooms. He notices that some nonstockroom personnel fill their own orders, grab samples for customers, and put things back into the facility that they have previously removed.

9. He observes that some of these individuals document their actions immediately, while others document nothing, and others turn in necessary paperwork—later.

10. Eric observes Sally, a salesperson, peering intently into her computer screen. He hears her utter an oath and declare out loud, "I just saw a whole bunch of SKU #1234 out there a little while ago." She then creates a manual invoice within the software system, prints it, walks out to the stockroom, fills the order she has just created, delivers it to customer Acme Widgets of the World, and later drops the signed delivery

Any organization hoping to continuously have its shelf count match its record count simply must stop all unauthorized personnel from touching anything in a stockroom or warehouse. And, authorized personnel must have a paper- or computer-based document before placing anything into or removing anything from storage areas. These points cannot be overstated. They are imperative for inventory accuracy.

Documentation created after something has been placed into or removed from a facility creates all sorts of problems. For example:

a. If an item is physically removed without a document deleting it from inventory, then salespeople, production schedulers, and others will believe that the item is still available for sale or use. They will then generate pick tickets for its selection. Order fillers will then waste their time looking for items that do not exist. The order fillers will then generate adjustment forms leading to the items being removed from inventory. Eventually, when the original documentation goes through the system, these same items are removed from inventory—again. Your shelf count and record count are now almost hopelessly out of balance.

b. If an item is placed into the stockroom without accompanying paperwork, then the subject SKU is unavailable for sale or use—since no one knows it's there. And again, your shelf count and record count are out of balance.

Paragraph 10 is an example of someone who does not understand how it is possible to have a stock record (in the computer or hard paper copy) that reflects a stock balance lower than the actual number of items on the shelves. Recall that the discrepancy is due to the time period between the physical movement of product and the entry of data into the system.

140 FUNDAMENTALS OF INVENTORY MANAGEMENT AND CONTROL

copy on the accounts receivables clerk's desk.

11. Eric observes an angry exchange between the warehouse manager and the accounting manager of the New York location. They were arguing over a negative stock balance for SKU #1234.

Since this is a real-time system, when Sally created a manual pick ticket she caused the system to allocate and delete the subject SKU. If the stock balance was zero when Sally did this, her actions have caused the balance to go into a negative.

As discussed at Paragraph 17, Sally's actions have also created the potential for a much different problem in an entirely different department of the organization. By forcing a manual invoice through the system and dropping off a delivery slip for billing, Sally has created the potential for a billing clerk to try to create an invoice for product which the system has never received into itself. Many accounting programs will not let an invoice be created for product which has never been received.

12. He also observes Sally angrily telling the warehouse manager that one of her customers, Widgets, Gidgets, Gadgets and Such, was shorted 10 widgets on an order it received "just a little while ago."

13. Alana has also observed some interesting things in Kansas City.

14. She has observed two different order fillers attempting to fill orders for the same item—from the same empty shelf.

In Paragraph 10 it should be obvious that the product Sally took had already been allocated to a different customer (Customer #1) than the one she was taking care of at that time (Customer #2). Sally's actions caused her to raid Customer 1's order, causing a stockout for one of her own customers—Customer 1.

It is common in batch systems that are only updated once per day, and in which there is no way to easily check (without going to look) as to the true availability of an item, for multiple orders to be written against the same items. This also creates the danger of multiple adjustments adding to the overall confusion.

15. At 5 p.m. one evening she was standing behind Carmen, the company's billing clerk. Carmen's in-box contained several inches of delivery slips ready for processing. Carmen got up and began to make preparations to go home. Alana asked her what she was doing. Carmen replied, "It's 5 p.m., I'm going home."

Alana said, "But you still have a lot of work in your inbox."

A number of issues are raised by Paragraph 15.
a. The morning following a incident like the one described will find everyone in the company who deals with inventory— sales, accounting, production scheduling, customer service, and purchasing—making decisions on information they believe is current as of the night before when the system was updated. The reality is that the information is no more current than

© American Management Association. All rights reserved.

"So what, I'll work on it tomorrow," Carmen indignantly responded.

"But you'll mess up the warehouse if you don't get those slips processed tonight," Alana stated.

Angrily, Carmen stated, "I work in accounting. I don't work in the warehouse."

Alana asked, "How long would it take you to do those?"

Carmen glanced at her inbox and replied, "About 30 minutes."

"Please stay and get them done," Alana cajoled.

"I couldn't even if I wanted to," Carmen said. "I'm not allowed any overtime."

Bill, one of Carmen's coworkers chimes in and says, "Why can't you get your work done during the day?"

Furious, Carmen turns on Bill and says, "Hey, you sort and distribute the mail every morning, run photocopies of all incoming checks while fighting with people over our one copy machine, and prepare and go out to make the daily deposit like I do, and, then let's see if you can get your stuff done."

16. Hanging around the warehouse, Alana observed that receiving was done on a manual basis—and that there wasn't always a copy of a Purchase Order in the warehouse to support incoming loads.

She noticed on several occasions that when the receiving staff did not have all appropriate paperwork for an item, they would simply put it away or move it off to the side. Then later, or the next day, they would hunt down all of the appropriate documentation and turn everything in to the data entry people for entry into the system.

Like Eric, she also observed non-stockroom individuals filling their own orders.

the last time Carmen made it to the bottom of the in-box. If she hasn't made it to the bottom of her box in several days, then the company's records and operations are really suffering.

The problem is made worse by the fact that roughly 20 percent of the inventory will represent 80 percent of the most important items. See Chapter 3, *Physical Location and Control of Inventory, A-B-C Categorization.* Not only does shelf count not match record count, but they don't match regarding some of the most important items.

b. Another problem revealed by the incident is that the organization does not recognize the importance of getting all receiving and shipping into and out of the building on both a real-life and paper-life basis every day. This is indicated by those duties assigned to Carmen that prevent her from completing her inventory-related tasks on a daily basis. Although these duties are important, they should be performed by someone whose actions do not have such a ripple effect throughout the entire organization.

Virtually every organization has a purchase order system. And, in virtually every organization anyone with the authority to buy something is repeatedly told to have a Purchase Order for everything. In spite of those facts, in many organizations product comes in daily without any supporting documentation. This causes confusion, results in inefficient receiving operations, and separates an item's real life from its paper life. See Chapter 1, *Inventory as Both a Tangible and an Intangible Object.* There should be either a hard copy or a record of the Purchase Order in the computer system available to Receiving for all items that arrive at the stockroom.

When an item's real life becomes separated from its paper life, people begin to ship or

142   FUNDAMENTALS OF INVENTORY MANAGEMENT AND CONTROL

use product that has not been received and to put away product that has not been received, so that no one knows it is available for sale or use. This separation creates an environment where inventory clerks and accounting personnel are making adjustment after adjustment to the record count.

17. She also observed a curious exchange between Franklin, the accounting manager, and Carmen, the billing clerk.

While attempting to create an invoice for an item, Carmen's computer screen flashed an error message indicating that she was trying to bill for something that had a zero stock balance in the system. The software would not let her bill for an item it did not reflect as being available for sale.

Carmen called Franklin over. She showed him the signed delivery slip indicating that the item had, in fact, been delivered.

Franklin stated, "Those people in the warehouse can't get anything right." He then proceeded to manually override the system and entered the SKU (SKU #4567) and quantity in question (10). Franklin then directed Carmen to try again. The invoice was created without any further problems.

Midmorning of the next day the stock records began to show that there were 10 of SKU #4567 in the facility. A telemarketing sales person sold 10 SKU #4567s that afternoon. A pick ticket was generated for the order. The order filler could not find any of SKU #4567 in the warehouse. A stock adjustment form was processed to take these 10 items out of stock.

From Paragraph 16, it appears here in Paragraph 17 that someone delivered an item which had not as yet gone through the paperwork receiving cycle. Then when Carmen tried to bill for it, the software would not let her.

Instead of researching what had actually happened, Franklin overrode the system and put in a quantity of 10. Carmen's billing then deleted the 10 items.

When the receiving paperwork finally made it through the system, it created a quantity of 10 items that were no longer in the building. These 10 phantom items were then sold—maybe more than once.

When the 10 items could not be found, additional paperwork had to be initiated to delete the SKUs from the system.

All of the above issues are caused, in part, by a lack of understanding on the part of various staff members of how the timing and sequencing of the system works.

18. Alana overhears a telephone conversation between Carmen and a customer. The customer wants to return five SKU #9876s and wants to ensure that she is not charged for them. Carmen notes the information, prepares a pickup slip, and issues a credit to the customer's account.

Although application software systems vary widely in how items are accounted for, many systems place an item back into stock (in the data base) when a credit is issued against that item. By issuing a credit, Carmen caused the (primitive) software system to place the five SKUs back into stock—

© American Management Association. All rights reserved.

Later that day a salesperson sells five SKU #9876s. A pick ticket was generated for the order. The order filler could not find any of SKU #9876s in the warehouse. A stock adjustment form was processed to take these five items out of stock.

even though they had not, as yet, been returned to the building. More sophisticated systems understand the difference between a credit and the physical receipt of returned goods and do not update stock on hand until the goods are actually received.

Again, a lack of understanding regarding timing and sequencing of software and events causes terrible dysfunctions to stockroom operations.

19. Meanwhile, Shawn has been talking to Ichiro, the inventory control clerk in Los Angeles. Ichiro is frustrated. He works hard at his job but can't seem to track work in process. Consequently, he is never sure how much of any particular item the company has available for production purposes.

As indicated in Paragraph 4, a key problem Ichiro faces is that the company is using two separate methods of relieving items from stock. One method is batch, while the other is a backflush of some items. Recall that *backflushing* refers to a software technique by which raw materials and other components going into a particular subassembly or final product are relieved from stock when that subassembly or product is completed. Exhibit 6–1 illustrates backflushing.

As indicated in the discussion of Paragraph 6, if a batch system is not updated with some degree of frequency, it is difficult to understand what is available without actually looking. This problem can be overcome through software modules that advise the stockkeeper of those SKUs that have gone into completed orders. This report shows a running total for each SKU that has been drawn down that day. Once the system is updated, a new report begins.

20. Shawn observes a worker disassembling a subassembly. He asks the worker what he is doing. The worker replies that there is a rush order that they lack all of the raw materials for, so they are disassembling some less important assemblies to cannibalize the required parts.

Shawn asks if the products being disassembled are from other orders. The worker replies that they are. Shawn asks about any paperwork that was generated to support whatever it is the

The real issue here is the waste of labor and time in disassembly of completed items, resulting in unsaleable inventory. Building inventory only when needed, in accordance with lean/JIT practices, precludes this type of waste.

© American Management Association. All rights reserved.

worker is doing. The worker replies that he doesn't know.

xhibit 6-1
Backflushing

Although computer systems can backflush more than one level down on the bill of materials, for the purposes of this example, assume a backflush of only a single level down. If the backflush occurs when Level 1 is completed, then SKUs 0021 and 9876 are deleted from the stock record. SKUs 3435, 3436, and 3474 would have been issued by a normal pick list transaction as their work order started.

Although perpetual computer systems backflush more than one level down on the bill of materials, for the purposes of this example, assume a backflush of only a single level down. If the backflush does not occur until Level 1 is completed, then only SKUs 0021 and 9876 are deleted from the stock record. SKUs 3435, 3436, and 3474 would still remain "in stock" even though they were consumed in producing SKU 1234.

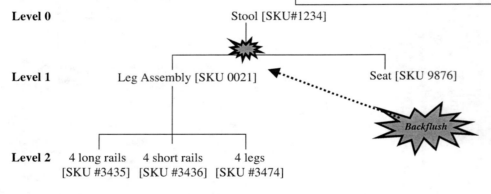

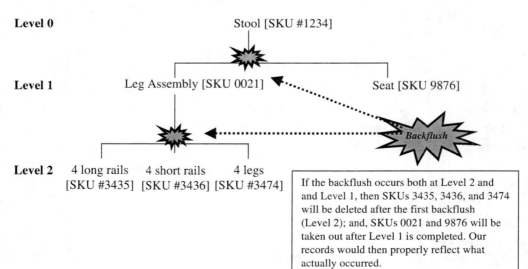

If the backflush occurs both at Level 2 and and Level 1, then SKUs 3435, 3436, and 3474 will be deleted after the first backflush (Level 2); and, SKUs 0021 and 9876 will be taken out after Level 1 is completed. Our records would then properly reflect what actually occurred.

Activity 6–2 and Self-Assessment 6–3
Analyzing What Is Actually Happening, Revisited

Instructions: After reviewing the discussion of the example case, return to the notes your wrote in Activity 6–1 and Self-Assessment 6–2. While they are fresh in your mind, add any final thoughts you may now have regarding problems and solutions for your own organization.

METRICS

"You can't control what you don't measure" Peter Drucker

Before doing *anything* toward establishing methods to discover, analyze, and fix any discrepancies between actual on-hand stock levels and database record levels, you should take a snapshot of where you are *now*. You should develop two sets of numbers related to (a) inventory record accuracy (IRA) and (b) fill rate.

IRA is a reflection of how well your shelf count and record count match. In other words, do your stock records accurately reflect what is actually in the stockroom?

Fill rate is a reflection of how effective your inventory is. Did you have what you needed when you needed it?

Inventory Record Accuracy

We will examine three issues that affect inventory record accuracy—test counting, tolerances, and the impact of tolerances on adjustments.

Test Counting

A quick, accurate method of establishing your current IRA is to perform a test count, as follows:

- Select 100 SKUs that represent a cross-section of all items. In other words, select all sorts of items—fast movers, slow movers, expensive items, inexpensive items, those with both long and short acquisition lead times, and so on.
- Count all 100 in all locations where they are located. Measure accuracy by considering actual units on the floor—not dollar value.
- Divide the number of accurate counts by the total number of counts. Accurate counts are those where the record count and the shelf count exactly match.
- Quotient is your inventory record accuracy. See Exhibit 6–2.

Tolerances

How accurate does accuracy have to be? You may think, at first, that *accurate* means that your stock records match your shelf counts 100 percent of the time. Consider, however, your feelings about counting a large container of nails.

xhibit 6-2

Test Counting to Establish Inventory Record Accuracy

$$\frac{\text{Accurate Counts}}{\text{Total Counts}} = \text{Inventory Record Accuracy} \quad \frac{87}{100} = 0.87 = 87\% \text{ IRA}$$

Would you count a large container of nails by actually counting each nail individually? It is more probable that you would (a) weigh out one pound of nails, (b) count the number of nails in a pound, (c) weigh all of the nails, and (d) then compute the total number of nails by multiplying the number of nails in a pound by the number of pounds of nails in the container. Will your computation capture the exact number of nails in the container? Probably not. Do you really care? Probably not. Why? Because of the nature of the SKU in question. In this case nails are low cost, easy to acquire, and hard to count individually. Therefore, you would probably be willing to accept some percentage of tolerance in your numbers. If you were within ±5 percent of a perfect match between the record count and the shelf count, would you be satisfied? Probably so. Would you be equally satisfied applying the same approach to a large container of diamonds? Of course not.

Many organizations allow a variance or *tolerance* in considering IRA. That is, they allow the plus-minus percentage of accuracy they find acceptable. These tolerances can be set using dollars, actual units, or some combination of the two. Most accountants use dollars. Stockkeepers should use actual units—either it's here or it isn't.

Few organizations accept a tolerance of greater than ±5 percent on any item. In other words, 5 percent should be the highest variance from a 100 percent accuracy level that you will accept for any item no matter what its characteristics.

If you will accept tolerances, they must be set for each item or category of item with great care. Consider the following factors:

- Dollar value—the higher the dollar value, the more accuracy you will demand.
- Usage rate—Usage rate can actually be argued two ways:
  - The higher the usage rate, the lower the tolerance level argument: If you are using a large quantity of an item, you will always want to know how much is available so there is never a stockout.
  - The lower the usage rate, the lower the tolerance level argument: If an item is not moving very quickly, then why should there be any discrepancy between shelf and record count? A low variance percentage for a slow moving item will alert everyone to a problem quickly as opposed to waiting for a crisis. This argument assumes that if there are stockouts on faster-moving products then the situation will alert everyone anyway.
- Lead time—The longer the lead time, the lower the tolerance level. A long lead time requires more working reserve and safety stock. See Chapter 5, *Planning and Replenishment Concepts.*

- Criticality—Some items are critical for reasons other than dollar value, usage rate, or lead time. A safety equipment company may only sell a few biohazard cleanup suits per year, but when they are needed, they are needed immediately.
- Combination of the above.

 Activity 6–3

Considering Tolerances

Instructions: Read the following scenario and discuss who is right—Melvin or Sarah.

Melvin, president of Megawatts, Inc., doesn't believe in allowing any tolerances in his inventory levels. His friend, Sarah, president of Bright Lights Co., does.

A cross-section of 100 items was counted in each of these companies' facilities.

The actual stock count on 87 SKUs in each facility matched the respective companies' stock records.

Bright Lights allowed a variance of ±2% on 5 of the 13 items that were not 100% accurate. The count of these 5 fell within their respective tolerances.

$$\text{Megawatts: } \frac{87}{100} = 87\% \text{ accuracy} \qquad \text{Bright Lights: } \frac{92}{100} = 92\% \text{ accuracy}$$

Melvin argues that Sarah's higher IRA level is artificial and doesn't really reflect accuracy.

Who is right—Melvin or Sarah?

_____
_____
_____
_____
_____

Using 10 items from your own inventory, set a tolerance and discuss why you set that tolerance level.

Items From Your Own Inventory	Tolerance Percent 0%–5%	Reasons for Tolerance Level

Impact of Tolerances on Adjustments

Once you have set tolerances, you should not make adjustments to your records when a discrepancy between shelf and record counts falls within the variance allowed. If an item does fall outside of the tolerance range you would hunt down the reason for the discrepancy and adjust the record, if necessary. See Exhibit 6–3.

Fill Rates

Although matching shelf count to record count is one way of measuring inventory, it does not indicate whether you have the items you need when

Exhibit 6–3
Tolerances and Adjustments

Assume that a count was made of 10 SKUs, with the following results:

SKU #	Record Count	Actual Count	% Deviation	% Tolerance ±	HIT/MISS
1	1,200	1,128	−6%	2%	M
2	2,217	2,106	−5%	5%	H
3	317	304	−4%	5%	H
4	8,947	8,679	−3%	2%	M
5	100	98	−2%	5%	H
6	567	561	−1%	2%	H
7	100	100	0%	0%	H
8	1,367	1,381	+1%	0%	M
9	1,432	1,461	+2%	2%	H
10	185	191	+3%	5%	H

SKUs 1, 4, and 8 fell outside their tolerances. For example, if the count for SKU 1 had fallen within the range of 1,176 to 1,224, ±2% of the record count, then it would have been a hit. It was not; therefore, you would investigate why the discrepancies exist and adjust your records if necessary.

All of the other SKUs fell within their tolerances; however, only SKU 7 was exactly correct. You would nevertheless not make any adjustments to any SKUs where there was a hit. The variance percentages you set should allow you a comfortable range in which you can tolerate some up or down differences. Often pluses and minuses cancel one another out over time.

© American Management Association. All rights reserved.

you need them. Simple fill rate calculations achieve that objective. The *fill rate* looks at the qualitative nature of your inventory efforts.

Fill Rate Formulas
Here is the simple fill rate formula:

$$\text{Fill Rate} = \frac{\text{Items Shipped on a Given Day}}{\text{Items Ordered for Shipment on a Given Day}} \quad \frac{417 \text{ Items Shipped}}{447 \text{ Items Ordered}} = 0.93 = 93\% \text{ Fill Rate}$$

The above indicates that you had 93 percent of the items you needed on the day they were required.

The fill rate can reflect the availability of a single item or a grouping of items.

Here is the formula for stockouts per day.

$$\text{Stockout \%} = \frac{\text{Number of Orders Shipped with at Least One Item Incomplete}}{\text{Total Number of Orders Shipped}} \quad \frac{34}{200} = 0.17 = 17\%$$

This indicates that you were unable to send out complete orders 17 percent of the time on that day. Stated more positively, you were able to send complete orders out 83 percent of the time.

Activity 6–4
Creating Fill Rate Formulas

Instructions: Using the fill rate and stockouts per day formulas as models, determine the fill rate and stockout rates for your own organization.

TOOLS WITH WHICH TO UNCOVER SYSTEM DYSFUNCTIONS

To solve problems, you need to engage in:

- Fact-finding—What is happening now?
- Problem finding—What is wrong with what is going on?
- Solution finding—How can we fix what is wrong?

So far this chapter has focused on (a) beginning to analyze inventory problems in an intellectual, intuitive, "gut feel" manner, and (b) developing some measurements with which to understand your current level of inventory accuracy and availability. This is part of fact-finding.

Another way of determining what is actually happening at your facility is to create a number of charts.

Charts by their very nature allow you to analyze things; however, you need to guard against "paralysis by analysis." If everything is equally important, then nothing is important. In other words, you should only chart things that are really important to controlling inventory items, trends, operational undertakings, and the like.

Run Charts

Run charts allow you to measure a variable that changes over time.

A run chart is an *x-y* axis chart with the unit of measure appearing on the vertical *y*-axis, and the time frame running along the horizontal *x*-axis. The unit of measure can be anything you wish to track, including stockouts, errors, labor hours, pieces, pounds, and gallons. The time frame can also be whatever you desire it to be—seconds, minutes, hours, days, weeks, months, or years. See Exhibit 6–4.

---

xhibit 6–4

Run Charts

The first chart shows trend analysis.

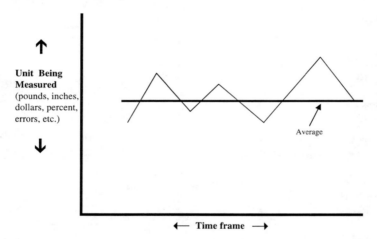

The second chart indicates that you can set an upper and lower control limit on the chart that will alert you to a pending crisis before it occurs.

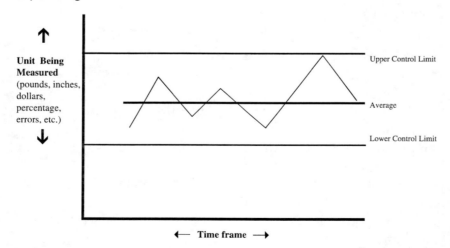

Flow Charts

Flow charts allow you to analyze the sequence of a set of events. They show the interdependence of events or which events are going on at the same time as others. Exhibit 6–5 shows a flow chart.

Flow charts are easier to understand than written procedures.
Caution:

- You do not have to use traditional flow chart symbols. However, with regard to those symbols you do use, be consistent or you will confuse yourself and others. Provide a key to symbols.
- Have version control. If flow charts are not revised as procedures change, they are worthless.

Variance Reports

Variance reports compare an expectation with what actually occurred.

Variance reports can be based on any factor necessary for tracking an expectation. Some factors are dollars, labor, consumption rates, lines/pieces per hour, and trucks per day. Exhibit 6–6 shows a variance report.

CYCLE COUNTING

After becoming familiar with your system by utilizing the techniques described in this chapter, you should be ready to adopt a systematical approach to "fixing" whatever might be causing discrepancies between your shelf and record counts. The most systematic method of solving inventory problems and enjoying a consistently high IRA is cycle counting. *Cycle counting* is simply counting a small cross-section of your inventory frequently. Cycle counting should be done daily.

This continuous counting leads to the discovery of discrepancies soon after they arise. By catching an error quickly, you can backtrack through both

Exhibit 6–5
A Flow Chart

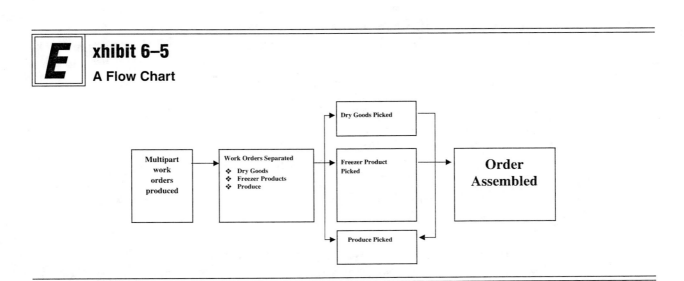

Exhibit 6–6
Variance Report

Variance Report

Description	Projected	Actual	Variance Amount	Variance Percent
Total				

the paperwork and the stock movement of the item(s) to determine why that SKU's paper life became separated from its real life. Once you identify the cause of the error, you can eliminate it. Cycle counting's purpose is to identify and eliminate the causes of inventory record errors, which differs from the purpose of an annual physical inventory.

Since cycle counting is a continuous process, as one cause of error after another is eliminated, the system begins to operate more and more smoothly. Eventually all items move through a series of procedures that work.

Cycle counting differs from an annual inventory in several ways:

- The objective of the annual physical inventory is to produce a financial valuation of the inventory on a given day.
- Every item must be counted as part of the annual inventory.
- The 12-month-long audit trail of the annual physical inventory is too long for any serious effort to be made at uncovering why an error occurred or even when—did it happen yesterday, last month, 10 months ago?

Cycle counting has a number of specific objectives.

- Discover discrepancies soon after they occur
- Identify causes of errors
- Correct conditions causing errors
- Make continuous process improvement
- Achieve a minimum of 95 percent accuracy on *all* items
- Correctly state inventory assets
- Eliminate annual inventory

Most accounting firms will allow an organization to stop taking annual physical inventories once the company has established a mature cycle counting program. Generally a company will cycle count for at least 12 months. Then, an annual physical inventory is taken and the numbers from the annual inventory are compared with the cycle count figures. If they match, then in the future the accounting firm will merely test count once per year for valuation purposes.

Cycle Count Methodologies

There are a number of cycle count methodologies.

- Control group
- Location audit
- Random selection
- Diminishing population
- Product categories
- A-B-C categorization

A key point to remember is that no matter what cycle count methodology you eventually choose to follow, when you first begin and your inventory record accuracy is low you *will not* count a large number of items per day. This is because it will take time to recount, review paperwork, talk to people, and do all of the other things necessary to determine why an item's record count and shelf count do not match. Why count 50 items a day if you can only count and reconcile 10 of them? Any cycle count methodology will assist you in achieving high levels of IRA; however, not every method works in every company setting. Let's look at an example to see why.

- You wish to cycle count each item 4 times per year.
- You can cycle count 200 days per year. (4 days/week × 50 weeks = 200 count days)
- There are 10,000 SKUs.
- Three cycle counters work 7 hours per day.
- Company A has 10,000 items that are unitized and in single locations within the stockroom.
- It takes Company A an average of 2 minutes to count an item.
- Company B has 10,000 items that are not unitized, would have to be counted in "onesy-twosy," and each item is found in multiple locations throughout the facility.
- It takes Company B an average of 5 minutes to count an item.

Exhibit 6–7 shows how these differences affect cycle counting time.

Treating all items equally and counting them four times per year may work for Company A; however, it seems like an unreasonable burden for Company B. (Issues such as who will count, when they should count, and how many people should count will be covered as part of this cycle count discussion.)

You should select a method that fits your own organization's resources and inventory types.

Exhibit 6–7
Cycle Counting: Two Examples

Company A	Company B
10,000 SKUs × 4 counts/year = 40,000 counts	10,000 SKUs × 4 counts/year = 40,000 counts
40,000 counts ÷ 200 days = 200 counts/day	40,000 counts ÷ 200 days = 200 counts/day
200 counts/day × 2 minutes = 400 minutes	200 counts/day × 5 minutes = 1,000 minutes
400 minutes ÷ 60 minutes = 7 hours/day	1,000 minutes ÷ 60 minutes = 17 hours/day
7 hrs/day ÷ 3 counters = 2.33 hours/day each	17 hrs/day ÷ 3 counters = 6 hrs/day each

Control Group Cycle Counting Method

No matter which method you eventually decide to use, always start with a small-scale counting test run. By using a control group approach, you will be able to do the following:

1. Immediately identify significant system problems, such as unrestricted access to the stockroom and major timing problems related to when product is moved and when records of the move are updated.
2. Develop an understanding of the who, what, when, where, why, and how of the way your system actually works.
3. When you first begin cycle counting you will probably make adjustments only to find that you made a mistake. It is much simpler to correct errors related to only a few SKUs rather than to hundreds of them.

You can institute the following control group procedure:

- ☑ Select 100 items as a control group. *Important:* The SKUs selected must be a true cross-section of the entire population of items they represent. You must include some expensive items, some inexpensive, some fast movers, some slow, some with a long lead time, and so forth.
- ☑ Count only 10 items per day. Use a control group count tracking sheet like the one shown in Exhibit 6–8.
- ☑ Count for 100 days.
- ☑ Stats: 10 × 100 = 1,000 counts.
- ☑ "Cycle" is 10 days.
- ☑ Each item counted 10 times during test.

Because you have tracked the same items over and over again, at the conclusion of your control group cycle count you should be able to eliminate major systems problems and have a good understanding of how your overall inventory system is working.

© American Management Association. All rights reserved.

Exhibit 6–8
Control Group Count Tracking Sheet

	SKU #	Description	1	2	3	4	5	6	7	8	9	10
1	BD79	Widget	✓	✓								
2	QD455	Gidget	✓	✓								
3	XD110	Gadget	✓	✓								
4	PD418	Thing-a-ma-jig	✓	✓								
5	AC123	Doohickey	✓	✓								
6	ZG23	Receiver	✓	✓								
97	HG786	Receiver Mount	✓									
98	LK951	Miniplexer	✓									
99	LK236	Multiplexer	✓									
100	DK47	Radome	✓									

The control group approach should only be used as a starting point and not as an ongoing cycle count method. The reason for this is that the control group is not statistically large enough to actually represent your entire inventory.

Now you are ready to select a cycle count method that bests suits your own organization's needs.

Location Audit Cycle Counting Method

In this approach you divide the stockroom(s) up in some logical method—rooms, racks, bins, and the like. See Exhibit 6–9. Then on each counting day you count the SKUs found in those areas.

All items are treated equally. In other words, selection of those items included on that day's count is based solely on the item being located in the area counted. No other characteristics (cost or usage rate, for example) are considered.

The length of the cycle depends on how many areas are to be counted. For example, if you were counting by rack, one rack per day, and there were 45 racks, then the entire cycle would be 45 days. You would then start over again.

The location audit approach has two significant benefits:

1. This approach does not require detailed record keeping of whether or not you have counted a specific item or the exact number of times you have counted it. It is administratively simple to follow.

Exhibit 6–9
Dividing a Stock into Geographic Areas for a Location Audit Cycle Count

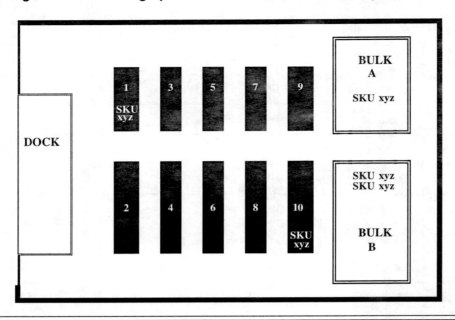

2. This approach serves as a double audit: you are checking the quantity of an item at the same time you are checking to make sure that it is in the right location in your facility. Product that has been misplaced can be "discovered" sooner than with the annual inventory through the use of this method.

Two separate approaches are possible regarding how much of any selected SKU gets counted.

1. Only count the SKU in the location being cycle counted that day.
   Example: Count only the quantity of SKU xyz in Rack 1 (see Exhibit 6–6). Item xyz located in Rack 10 and in both bulk storage areas are ignored.
   This first approach requires a higher level of sophistication within your own inventory control system. Your system must allow you to identify not only how much of an item you have, but also each location it is located in, and how much of it is in each location. See Chapter 3, *Physical Location and Control of Inventory.*
2. Count the selected SKU in all places where it may be located throughout the facility.
   Example: Quantities of SKU xyz counted in Racks 1 and 10, and in both bulk areas.

Activity 6–5

Considering the Location Audit Cycle Count Method

Instructions: Answer the following questions:

1. In either approach the warehouse will be counted wall-to-wall during the cycle. Does this mean that *all* items in the stockroom during the cycle will be counted? YES [ ] NO [ ]
2. If not, why not?

_____

_____

_____

3. Does it matter if every item in the stockroom is counted during a location audit cycle? YES [ ] NO [ ]
4. If not, why not?

_____

_____

_____

Suggested solutions to Activity 6–5 are found at the end of the chapter.

Random Selection Cycle Counting Method

This is probably the easiest form of cycle counting. Because the items selected for counting are totally random, the SKUs selected will, over time, be a true cross-section of the entire population of items they represent: some expensive items, some inexpensive, some fast movers, some slow movers, some with a long lead time, and so on.

The cycle is generally one year, with most SKUs being counted during that time frame. For example,

- 10,000 total SKUs
- 200 counting days
- 50 items/day counted   (10,000 ÷ 200 = 50)

All items are treated equally. Product characteristics like dollar value and usage rate are ignored.

Diminishing Population Cycle Counting Method

This is a versatile approach. It can be used as a stand-alone procedure or used as part of the product category or A-B-C approaches discussed earlier in this chapter.

The basic concept is simple.

1. Count each item in a defined population before counting any item over again.

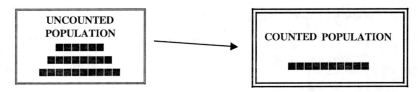

2. Then you begin the count all over again.

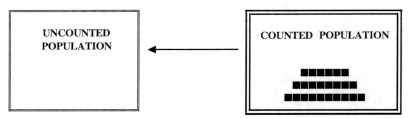

The diminishing population technique ensures all items in the population are counted at least once per cycle.

The number of times the total population is counted during a year depends on the total number of items and how many days you are willing to count. The larger the number of items counted per day, the more cycles can be completed during the year. Exhibit 6–10 provides three examples.

Product Categories Cycle Counting Method

To this point in our cycle count discussion we have ignored an item's characteristics. In the product categories approach the organization decides on what categories it wishes to place SKUs into based on some characteristic(s), such as manufacturer or type of use (the "criteria").

 xhibit 6–10
Diminishing Population Cycle Counting

Example 1	Example 2	Example 3
900 total SKUs	900 total SKUs	900 total SKUs
200 counting days in cycle	100 counting days in cycle	50 counting days in cycle
900 ÷ 200 = 4.5 > 5 items/day	2 cycles per year	4 cycles per year
1,000 total counts/year	900 ÷ 100 = 9 items/day	900 ÷ 50 = 18 items/day
	1,800 total counts/year	3,600 total counts/year

Items matching the criteria are counted on the basis of either: a single event (for example only items whose balance-on-hand equals zero) or using the diminishing population technique for each separate category (for example, all of the widgets this week, all of the gadgets next week, all of the gidgets the week after). The number of items to be counted can vary or be set by the number of items in the group divided by the number of days in the cycle as shown in Exhibit 6–10.

Cycle can be a single day or a defined number of times per year.

Single Criterion
You should be careful of using single event characteristics in defining categories. Exhibit 6–11 shows the benefits and problems associated with using a single criterion.

Using the Diminishing Population Technique with Product Categories
- Define the criteria by which each SKU will be placed into a category.
- Decide the sequence in which categories will be counted—for example, all

Exhibit 6–11
Single-Criterion Cycle Counting

Criterion	Benefits	Problems
Only count items on the day when a purchase order for that item is created	• It ensures that the correct quantity is being ordered. • It allows for count when stock is at a low level, making it easier to count.	• Only the fastest moving items receive attention. Expensive but slower-use items might be ignored until there is a crisis. • A true cross section of all types of SKUs won't be represented until a large part of the year has passed and until purchase orders for most items have been written and released. • It ignores completely items that are not ordered during a given year; for example, where the quantity on hand exceeds the use for the entire year.
Only cycle count items at zero or negative balance.	• Negative balaces should always trigger a count. • Items at zero should be easy to verify.	• Neither of these is statistically significant. • Both fail to represent a cross section of all items.

160   FUNDAMENTALS OF INVENTORY MANAGEMENT AND CONTROL

of manufacturer X's products this week, all of manufacturer Y's products next week.
- Divide the number of SKUs in the category by the number of days to determine how many must be counted per day. See Exhibit 6–10.
- Move to the next category.

The product categories method of cycle counting involves a great deal of administration but provides you with more detailed information and audit trails, making it much easier to trace what you have actually done during a cycle count.

A-B-C Analysis Cycle Counting Method

Most accountants prefer organizations to cycle count by breaking their inventory up into A-B-C classifications. Items *are not* treated equally. Based on classification, A items will be counted more frequently than the B items and the B items will be counted more frequently than the C.

The classifications are based on Pareto's law, the 80-20 Rule. See Chapter 3, *Physical Location and Control of Inventory, Inventory Stratification,* for a discussion of Pareto's law and of how to determine which SKUs go into which categories.

For cycle counting purposes classifications are determined by "value" (annual usage times cost), money, annual usage, or some combination of the three (for example value, plus making a few very expensive items A items).

Step-By-Step Implementation of the A-B-C Cycle Count Method
1. Perform Pareto analysis of SKUs utilizing desired criteria.
2. Assign SKUs to A-B-C categories
3. Decide the count frequency of each category. See *Determining A-B-C Count Frequency* in this chapter.
4. Multiply the respective number of SKUs per category by the desired frequency to establish total counts. Cycle is assumed to be one year. See Exhibit 6–12.
5. Divide total counts by the number of count days—for example, 200 days per year—to determine number of items to be counted each day. See Exhibit 6–12.
6. Ask yourself, Is this a reasonable number of daily items? If "Yes," proceed. If "No," change the frequencies and recalculate until a reasonable daily total is established.
7. Determine how many items from each category will be counted each day, as illustrated in Exhibit 6–13.
   a. Divide the number of annual counts within each category by the total (annual) number of counts. This establishes the percentage of counts represented by the respective categories when compared to the total counts.
   b. Multiply the A, B, and C percentage of the total by the number of items to be counted daily. This establishes the quantity of each category to be counted each day.

© American Management Association. All rights reserved.

xhibit 6-12
Determining Count Frequency and Number of Items to Count per Day

Class	No. of Items	Count Frequency	Total Counts
A	275	× 12	3,300
B	525	× 4	2,100
C	1,700	× 2	3,400

Total counts for the year	8,800
Count days	÷ 200
Items to count per day	44

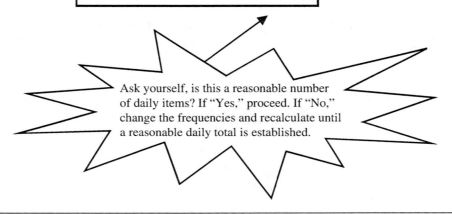

Ask yourself, is this a reasonable number of daily items? If "Yes," proceed. If "No," change the frequencies and recalculate until a reasonable daily total is established.

xhibit 6-13
Determining How Many Items from Each Category Will Be Counted Each Day

The number of counts per year is taken from Exhibit 6-12.

Category	Annual Counts		Count Days/Year		SKUs to Be Counted Each Day
A	3,300	÷	200	=	16.5 => 17
B	2,100	÷	200	=	10.5 => 11
C	3,400	÷	200	=	17

© American Management Association. All rights reserved.

8. Count each category the desired number of times using the diminishing population or random technique with the category.

Determining A-B-C Count Frequency
You can determine count frequency in the following manner:

☑ Decide the count frequency of each category. You can count the respective categories the number of times you desire. There is no rule of thumb. You may want to count A items 12 times per year, B items 4 times per year, and C items 2 times per year. Or you may wish to count A items 4 times per year, B items 2 times per year, and C items once per year.
☑ Multiply the respective number of SKUs per category by the desired frequency to establish total counts. Cycle is assumed to be one year.
☑ Divide total counts by the number of count days (for example, 200 days per year) to determine number of items to be counted each day.

Determining How Many Items from Each Category Will Be Counted Each Day
Use the following method to determine the daily count numbers:

☑ Divide the number of annual counts within each category by the total (annual) number of counts. This establishes the percentage of counts represented by the respective categories when compared to the total counts, as shown in Exhibit 6–13.
☑ Multiply the A, B, and C percentage of the total by the number of items to be counted daily. This establishes the quantity of each category to be counted each day.

Count each category the desired number of times using the diminishing population or random selection technique.

When to Count
The ideal time during the day to cycle count would be when there is no movement of paper or product. You may, therefore, want to count at these times:

- End of the business day
- Prior to the start of the day
- Over the weekend
- During the slowest shift

Another alternative is to create a cycle counting cutoff during a regular business day by using time-of-day. To use this approach you would do the following:

1. Create a list of items to be cycle counted the next day.
2. Distribute the list to Shipping, Receiving, the stock put-away workers, order fillers, and data entry clerks.

3. Have Receiving, Shipping, the stock put-away workers, order fillers, and computer update activities all note the time of day they interacted and actually dealt with any of the items on your list.
4. You now have the ability to audit back into any time frame during the day. For example:
   a. You cycle count widgets at 1:00 p.m. using a stock status report generated at 11:30 a.m.
   b. You find that there are 10 fewer widgets on the shelves than the stock status shows.
   c. You review all of the paper work from these different departments.
   d. Receiving's paperwork shows that 10 widgets were received at 10:30 a.m.; this transaction updated the computer "on-hand balance."
   e. There is no paperwork from the stock put-away workers indicating that the widgets were ever moved into stock.
   f. The missing widgets are sitting out in the dock area. Your record count matches what you have in house.

Who Should Count

If there are four hours of counting involved in cycle counting all items on any given day, should you have a single person count for four hours and then begin any necessary reconciliations—or—does it make more sense to have four people count for one hour each and then let the inventory control clerk have the rest of the day to correct any problems? It makes sense to spread the raw counting portion of the cycle count among a group of people. This will allow the inventory control clerk to devote more hours of each day to actually fixing the system as opposed to spending each day counting boxes.

The failure of inventory control systems is often due to a lack of understanding by individuals in different departments of the unintended consequences of their actions. A review of which individuals are supposed to write something down, what they are supposed to write down, who receives the information, what that person is supposed to do with the information, and the sequencing and overall timing of these events often reveals that respective departments are using different units of measure to define inventory. Some use dollars, while others use actual physical units. In addition, seemingly simple issues like the timing of when an item is entered into the computer system or who is allowed to actually see various items of information can cause severe misunderstandings and inventory inaccuracies.

To measure the effectiveness of your inventory system, develop two sets of numbers: your inventory record accuracy (IRA) and your fill rate. The IRA indicates how well your shelf count and your record count match—in other words, do your stock records accurately reflect what is actually in the stockroom? Your fill rate reflects how effectively your inventory meets the needs of your business—in other words, did you have what you needed when you needed it?

As part of the fact-finding process required to solve inventory management problems, designing and using charts can help determine what is actually happening at a facility. Commonly used charts include run charts, flow charts, and variance reports.

A number of techniques are available to solve inventory problems. Cycle counting is the most systematic of these methods. Its purpose is to eliminate the causes of inventory record errors.

Review Questions

1. Cycle counting involves:
   (a) counting a cross-section of your inventory frequently.
   (b) counting everything in your facility at least twice per calendar or fiscal year.
   (c) determining a fair valuation of your inventory value at least once per fiscal year.
   (d) counting all of the bicycle parts in your facility.

2. Flow charts:
   (a) allow you to analyze the sequence of a set of events.
   (b) allow you to determine trends.
   (c) allow you to compare a projected value against an actual one.
   (d) are reports that identify the number of items per level and number of tiers of product on a flow-through rack.

3. Run charts:
   (a) allow you to analyze the sequence of a set of events.
   (b) allow you to determine trends.
   (c) allow you to compare a projected value against an actual one.
   (d) are reports that identify the number of items per level and number of tiers of product on a flow-through rack.

4. The diminishing population method of cycle counting involves:
   (a) counting each item in a classification before you count any item again.
   (b) randomly selecting items for counting while ensuring the SKUs represent a true cross-section.
   (c) choosing items based on characteristics, then counting on the basis of a single zero-stock event or a series of zero-stock events.
   (d) using Pareto's 80-20 rule to identify which items to count and how frequently to count them.

5. Fill rates indicate:
   (a) how much of a particular SKU you have in stock at the end of a calendar month.
   (b) the quantitative nature of your inventory.
   (c) if you had what you needed when you needed it.
   (d) the ratio of accurate shelf counts to record counts.

1. (a)

2. (a)

3. (b)

4. (a)

5. (c)

ANSWERS

Suggested Answers for Self-Assessment 6–1

1. Lost sales
2. Late delivery
3. Shortages
4. Excessive expediting
5. Excess stock
6. Low productivity
7. Missed production
8. Valuation problems

Solutions to Activity 6–5

1 and 2. Not all items in the stockroom during the cycle will be counted because items will arrive into and leave from areas already counted or to be counted during the cycle. In other words, SKUs will be coming in behind you and moving away from in front of you as you go through the count.

3 and 4. It does not matter that all items are not counted during any particular cycle because of the large number of items that are counted during that cycle. Remember that in cycle counting you are interested in looking at the *system*, not at individual SKUs within the system. Whether or not a SKU's shelf and record counts match is merely a way of determining if the system is actually working. Therefore, as long as you count a reasonable number of the total items in the stockroom, you will accomplish the cycle count objective.

Appendix A—Inventory

A	B	C	D	E	F	G
Line No.	Part No.	Description	Annual Usage	Cumulative Usage	% Total Usage	% Total Items
1	Part 79	Product A	8,673	8,673	6.3%	0.3%
2	Part 133	Product B	6,970	15,643	11.3%	0.7%
3	Part 290	Product C	5,788	21,431	15.5%	1.0%
4	Part 65	Product D	5,690	27,121	19.6%	1.3%
5	Part 111	Product E	4,899	32,020	23.2%	1.7%
6	Part 195	Product F	3,669	35,689	25.8%	2.0%
7	Part 139	Product G	3,364	39,053	28.3%	2.3%
8	Part 131	Product H	3,250	42,303	30.6%	2.7%
9	Part 132	Product I	3,022	45,325	32.8%	3.0%
10	Part 175	Product J	2,864	48,189	34.9%	3.3%
11	Part 255	Product K	2,844	51,033	36.9%	3.7%
12	Part 101	Product L	2,670	53,703	38.9%	4.0%
13	Part 265	Product M	2,665	56,368	40.8%	4.3%
14	Part 48	Product N	2,453	58,821	42.6%	4.7%
15	Part 2	Product O	2,222	61,043	44.2%	5.0%
16	Part 14	Product P	1,976	63,019	45.6%	5.3%
17	Part 70	Product Q	1,896	64,915	47.0%	5.7%
18	Part 117	Product R	1,888	66,803	48.4%	6.0%
19	Part 134	Product S	1,872	68,675	49.7%	6.3%
20	Part 170	Product T	1,687	70,362	50.9%	6.7%
21	Part 182	Product U	1,666	72,028	52.1%	7.0%
22	Part 28	Product V	1,646	73,674	53.3%	7.3%
23	Part 138	Product W	1,566	75,240	54.5%	7.7%
24	Part 23	Product X	1,530	76,770	55.6%	8.0%
25	Part 300	Product Y	1,057	77,827	56.3%	8.3%
26	Part 9	Product Z	1,050	78,877	57.1%	8.7%
27	Part 241	Product AA	1,022	79,899	57.8%	9.0%

FUNDAMENTALS OF INVENTORY MANAGEMENT AND CONTROL

A	B	C	D	E	F	G
Line No.	Part No.	Description	Annual Usage	Cumulative Usage	% Total Usage	% Total Items
28	Part 219	Product AB	1,022	80,921	58.6%	9.3%
29	Part 51	Product AC	1,001	81,922	59.3%	9.7%
30	Part 278	Product AD	997	82,919	60.0%	10.0%
31	Part 222	Product AE	991	83,910	60.7%	10.3%
32	Part 154	Product AF	986	84,896	61.5%	10.7%
33	Part 184	Product AG	972	85,868	62.2%	11.0%
34	Part 190	Product AH	968	86,836	62.9%	11.3%
35	Part 87	Product AI	964	87,800	63.6%	11.7%
36	Part 95	Product AJ	943	88,743	64.2%	12.0%
37	Part 6	Product AK	894	89,637	64.9%	12.3%
38	Part 142	Product AL	889	90,526	65.5%	12.7%
39	Part 210	Product AM	889	91,415	66.2%	13.0%
40	Part 13	Product AN	888	92,303	66.8%	13.3%
41	Part 121	Product AO	888	93,191	67.5%	13.7%
42	Part 3	Product AP	875	94,066	68.1%	14.0%
43	Part 235	Product AQ	867	94,933	68.7%	14.3%
44	Part 297	Product AR	861	95,794	69.3%	14.7%
45	Part 266	Product AS	856	96,650	70.0%	15.0%
46	Part 239	Product AT	846	97,496	70.6%	15.3%
47	Part 233	Product AU	843	98,339	71.2%	15.7%
48	Part 77	Product AV	800	99,139	71.8%	16.0%
49	Part 188	Product AW	795	99,934	72.3%	16.3%
50	Part 240	Product AX	788	100,722	72.9%	16.7%
51	Part 103	Product AY	779	101,501	73.5%	17.0%
52	Part 160	Product AZ	766	102,267	74.0%	17.3%
53	Part 211	Product BA	764	103,031	74.6%	17.7%
54	Part 243	Product BB	761	103,792	75.1%	18.0%
55	Part 201	Product BC	754	104,546	75.7%	18.3%
56	Part 202	Product BD	712	105,258	76.2%	18.7%
57	Part 75	Product BE	698	105,956	76.7%	19.0%
58	Part 206	Product BF	697	106,653	77.2%	19.3%
59	Part 200	Product BG	697	107,350	77.7%	19.7%
60	Part 124	Product BH	689	108,039	78.2%	20.0%
61	Part 208	Product BI	662	108,701	78.7%	20.3%
62	Part 253	Product BJ	644	109,345	79.2%	20.7%
63	Part 264	Product BK	640	109,985	79.6%	21.0%
64	Part 230	Product BL	614	110,599	80.1%	21.3%
65	Part 53	Product BM	590	111,189	80.5%	21.7%
66	Part 33	Product BN	587	111,776	80.9%	22.0%
67	Part 104	Product BO	566	112,342	81.3%	22.3%
68	Part 207	Product BP	564	112,906	81.7%	22.7%
69	Part 63	Product BQ	544	113,450	82.1%	23.0%
70	Part 275	Product BR	533	113,983	82.5%	23.3%

© American Management Association. All rights reserved.

APPENDIX A—INVENTORY   **169**

A	B	C	D	E	F	G
Line No.	Part No.	Description	Annual Usage	Cumulative Usage	% Total Usage	% Total Items
71	Part 155	Product BS	530	114,513	82.9%	23.7%
72	Part 7	Product BT	512	115,025	83.3%	24.0%
73	Part 90	Product BU	499	115,524	83.6%	24.3%
74	Part 59	Product BV	468	115,992	84.0%	24.7%
75	Part 122	Product BW	467	116,459	84.3%	25.0%
76	Part 35	Product BX	456	116,915	84.6%	25.3%
77	Part 67	Product BY	450	117,365	85.0%	25.7%
78	Part 92	Product BZ	444	117,809	85.3%	26.0%
79	Part 83	Product CA	443	118,252	85.6%	26.3%
80	Part 287	Product CB	433	118,685	85.9%	26.7%
81	Part 162	Product CC	420	119,105	86.2%	27.0%
82	Part 189	Product CD	420	119,525	86.5%	27.3%
83	Part 245	Product CE	398	119,923	86.8%	27.7%
84	Part 274	Product CF	382	120,305	87.1%	28.0%
85	Part 242	Product CG	355	120,660	87.3%	28.3%
86	Part 258	Product CH	354	121,014	87.6%	28.7%
87	Part 136	Product CI	353	121,367	87.9%	29.0%
88	Part 238	Product CJ	334	121,701	88.1%	29.3%
89	Part 115	Product CK	333	122,034	88.3%	29.7%
90	Part 94	Product CL	333	122,367	88.6%	30.0%
91	Part 64	Product CM	332	122,699	88.8%	30.3%
92	Part 298	Product CN	326	123,025	89.1%	30.7%
93	Part 295	Product CO	325	123,350	89.3%	31.0%
94	Part 30	Product CP	325	123,675	89.5%	31.3%
95	Part 11	Product CQ	323	123,998	89.8%	31.7%
96	Part 192	Product CR	321	124,319	90.0%	32.0%
97	Part 96	Product CS	321	124,640	90.2%	32.3%
98	Part 40	Product CT	298	124,938	90.4%	32.7%
99	Part 47	Product CU	285	125,223	90.7%	33.0%
100	Part 125	Product CV	269	125,492	90.8%	33.3%
101	Part 198	Product CW	260	125,752	91.0%	33.7%
102	Part 135	Product CX	258	126,010	91.2%	34.0%
103	Part 130	Product CY	256	126,266	91.4%	34.3%
104	Part 85	Product CZ	255	126,521	91.6%	34.7%
105	Part 216	Product DA	223	126,744	91.8%	35.0%
106	Part 193	Product DB	222	126,966	91.9%	35.3%
107	Part 285	Product DC	220	127,186	92.1%	35.7%
108	Part 288	Product DD	200	127,386	92.2%	36.0%
109	Part 26	Product DE	199	127,585	92.4%	36.3%
110	Part 176	Product DF	199	127,784	92.5%	36.7%
111	Part 186	Product DG	194	127,978	92.6%	37.0%
112	Part 173	Product DH	189	128,167	92.8%	37.3%
113	Part 81	Product DI	188	128,355	92.9%	37.7%

© American Management Association. All rights reserved.

170 FUNDAMENTALS OF INVENTORY MANAGEMENT AND CONTROL

A	B	C	D	E	F	G
Line No.	Part No.	Description	Annual Usage	Cumulative Usage	% Total Usage	% Total Items
114	Part 172	Product DJ	188	128,543	93.1%	38.0%
115	Part 144	Product DK	186	128,729	93.2%	38.3%
116	Part 12	Product DL	186	128,915	93.3%	38.7%
117	Part 141	Product DM	186	129,101	93.5%	39.0%
118	Part 15	Product DN	185	129,286	93.6%	39.3%
119	Part 227	Product DO	185	129,471	93.7%	39.7%
120	Part 191	Product DP	184	129,655	93.9%	40.0%
121	Part 272	Product DQ	178	129,833	94.0%	40.3%
122	Part 279	Product DR	156	129,989	94.1%	40.7%
123	Part 247	Product DS	150	130,139	94.2%	41.0%
124	Part 89	Product DT	144	130,283	94.3%	41.3%
125	Part 174	Product DU	143	130,426	94.4%	41.7%
126	Part 118	Product DV	133	130,559	94.5%	42.0%
127	Part 27	Product DW	116	130,675	94.6%	42.3%
128	Part 34	Product DX	116	130,791	94.7%	42.7%
129	Part 169	Product DY	116	130,907	94.8%	43.0%
130	Part 178	Product DZ	113	131,020	94.8%	43.3%
131	Part 84	Product EA	105	131,125	94.9%	43.7%
132	Part 204	Product EB	103	131,228	95.0%	44.0%
133	Part 273	Product EC	102	131,330	95.1%	44.3%
134	Part 24	Product ED	101	131,431	95.1%	44.7%
135	Part 114	Product EE	100	131,531	95.2%	45.0%
136	Part 57	Product EF	100	131,631	95.3%	45.3%
137	Part 168	Product EG	99	131,730	95.4%	45.7%
138	Part 187	Product EH	99	131,829	95.4%	46.0%
139	Part 214	Product EI	99	131,928	95.5%	46.3%
140	Part 220	Product EJ	98	132,026	95.6%	46.7%
141	Part 29	Product EK	98	132,124	95.6%	47.0%
142	Part 98	Product EL	98	132,222	95.7%	47.3%
143	Part 261	Product EM	97	132,319	95.8%	47.7%
144	Part 180	Product EN	97	132,416	95.9%	48.0%
145	Part 289	Product EO	96	132,512	95.9%	48.3%
146	Part 146	Product EP	96	132,608	96.0%	48.7%
147	Part 299	Product EQ	94	132,702	96.1%	49.0%
148	Part 68	Product ER	92	132,794	96.1%	49.3%
149	Part 41	Product ES	91	132,885	96.2%	49.7%
150	Part 38	Product ET	90	132,975	96.3%	50.0%
151	Part 140	Product EU	89	133,064	96.3%	50.3%
152	Part 16	Product EV	89	133,153	96.4%	50.7%
153	Part 128	Product EW	88	133,241	96.5%	51.0%
154	Part 25	Product EX	88	133,329	96.5%	51.3%
155	Part 45	Product EY	87	133,416	96.6%	51.7%
156	Part 1	Product EZ	86	133,502	96.6%	52.0%

© American Management Association. All rights reserved.

A	B	C	D	E	F	G
Line No.	Part No.	Description	Annual Usage	Cumulative Usage	% Total Usage	% Total Items
157	Part 246	Product FA	85	133,587	96.7%	52.3%
158	Part 108	Product FB	85	133,672	96.8%	52.7%
159	Part 231	Product FC	85	133,757	96.8%	53.0%
160	Part 21	Product FD	84	133,841	96.9%	53.3%
161	Part 183	Product FE	84	133,925	97.0%	53.7%
162	Part 248	Product FF	84	134,009	97.0%	54.0%
163	Part 199	Product FG	84	134,093	97.1%	54.3%
164	Part 120	Product FH	80	134,173	97.1%	54.7%
165	Part 224	Product FI	80	134,253	97.2%	55.0%
166	Part 256	Product FJ	76	134,329	97.2%	55.3%
167	Part 281	Product FK	76	134,405	97.3%	55.7%
168	Part 157	Product FL	76	134,481	97.4%	56.0%
169	Part 5	Product FM	75	134,556	97.4%	56.3%
170	Part 56	Product FN	75	134,631	97.5%	56.7%
171	Part 44	Product FO	74	134,705	97.5%	57.0%
172	Part 76	Product FP	74	134,779	97.6%	57.3%
173	Part 267	Product FQ	74	134,853	97.6%	57.7%
174	Part 262	Product FR	72	134,925	97.7%	58.0%
175	Part 225	Product FS	68	134,993	97.7%	58.3%
176	Part 276	Product FT	67	135,060	97.8%	58.7%
177	Part 43	Product FU	66	135,126	97.8%	59.0%
178	Part 10	Product FV	66	135,192	97.9%	59.3%
179	Part 126	Product FW	65	135,257	97.9%	59.7%
180	Part 296	Product FX	64	135,321	98.0%	60.0%
181	Part 277	Product FY	63	135,384	98.0%	60.3%
182	Part 42	Product FZ	63	135,447	98.1%	60.7%
183	Part 197	Product GA	62	135,509	98.1%	61.0%
184	Part 284	Product GB	61	135,570	98.1%	61.3%
185	Part 22	Product GC	61	135,631	98.2%	61.7%
186	Part 39	Product GD	61	135,692	98.2%	62.0%
187	Part 82	Product GE	58	135,750	98.3%	62.3%
188	Part 237	Product GF	56	135,806	98.3%	62.7%
189	Part 69	Product GG	56	135,862	98.4%	63.0%
190	Part 62	Product GH	56	135,918	98.4%	63.3%
191	Part 213	Product GI	56	135,974	98.4%	63.7%
192	Part 109	Product GJ	55	136,029	98.5%	64.0%
193	Part 149	Product GK	55	136,084	98.5%	64.3%
194	Part 159	Product GL	55	136,139	98.6%	64.7%
195	Part 113	Product GM	54	136,193	98.6%	65.0%
196	Part 110	Product GN	54	136,247	98.6%	65.3%
197	Part 218	Product GO	54	136,301	98.7%	65.7%
198	Part 46	Product GP	53	136,354	98.7%	66.0%
199	Part 112	Product GQ	52	136,406	98.7%	66.3%

© American Management Association. All rights reserved.

A	B	C	D	E	F	G
Line No.	Part No.	Description	Annual Usage	Cumulative Usage	% Total Usage	% Total Items
	Part 179	Product GR	52	136,458	98.8%	66.7%
201	Part 100	Product GS	52	136,510	98.8%	67.0%
202	Part 37	Product GT	52	136,562	98.9%	67.3%
203	Part 282	Product GU	50	136,612	98.9%	67.7%
204	Part 116	Product GV	48	136,660	98.9%	68.0%
205	Part 8	Product GW	46	136,706	99.0%	68.3%
206	Part 254	Product GX	45	136,751	99.0%	68.7%
207	Part 148	Product GY	45	136,796	99.0%	69.0%
208	Part 66	Product GZ	44	136,840	99.1%	69.3%
209	Part 18	Product HA	43	136,883	99.1%	69.7%
210	Part 119	Product HB	43	136,926	99.1%	70.0%
211	Part 52	Product HC	42	136,968	99.2%	70.3%
212	Part 123	Product HD	41	137,009	99.2%	70.7%
213	Part 55	Product HE	41	137,050	99.2%	71.0%
214	Part 147	Product HF	37	137,087	99.2%	71.3%
215	Part 161	Product HG	36	137,123	99.3%	71.7%
216	Part 127	Product HH	34	137,157	99.3%	72.0%
217	Part 74	Product HI	34	137,191	99.3%	72.3%
218	Part 250	Product HJ	33	137,224	99.3%	72.7%
219	Part 260	Product HK	32	137,256	99.4%	73.0%
220	Part 263	Product HL	32	137,288	99.4%	73.3%
221	Part 20	Product HM	28	137,316	99.4%	73.7%
222	Part 229	Product HN	26	137,342	99.4%	74.0%
223	Part 58	Product HO	25	137,367	99.4%	74.3%
224	Part 31	Product HP	25	137,392	99.5%	74.7%
225	Part 50	Product HQ	24	137,416	99.5%	75.0%
226	Part 217	Product HR	24	137,440	99.5%	75.3%
227	Part 232	Product HS	23	137,463	99.5%	75.7%
228	Part 234	Product HT	23	137,486	99.5%	76.0%
229	Part 257	Product HU	22	137,508	99.5%	76.3%
230	Part 280	Product HV	21	137,529	99.6%	76.7%
231	Part 80	Product HW	21	137,550	99.6%	77.0%
232	Part 88	Product HX	20	137,570	99.6%	77.3%
233	Part 49	Product HY	19	137,589	99.6%	77.7%
234	Part 212	Product HZ	18	137,607	99.6%	78.0%
235	Part 226	Product IA	18	137,625	99.6%	78.3%
236	Part 97	Product IB	18	137,643	99.6%	78.7%
237	Part 166	Product IC	18	137,661	99.7%	79.0%
238	Part 293	Product ID	18	137,679	99.7%	79.3%
239	Part 36	Product IE	18	137,697	99.7%	79.7%
240	Part 249	Product IF	17	137,714	99.7%	80.0%
241	Part 143	Product IG	16	137,730	99.7%	80.3%
242	Part 145	Product IH	16	137,746	99.7%	80.7%

© American Management Association. All rights reserved.

APPENDIX A—INVENTORY   **173**

A	B	C	D	E	F	G
Line No.	Part No.	Description	Annual Usage	Cumulative Usage	% Total Usage	% Total Items
243	Part 167	Product II	15	137,761	99.7%	81.0%
244	Part 268	Product IJ	15	137,776	99.7%	81.3%
245	Part 181	Product IK	14	137,790	99.8%	81.7%
246	Part 292	Product IL	14	137,804	99.8%	82.0%
247	Part 19	Product IM	14	137,818	99.8%	82.3%
248	Part 185	Product IN	14	137,832	99.8%	82.7%
249	Part 102	Product IO	13	137,845	99.8%	83.0%
250	Part 269	Product IP	12	137,857	99.8%	83.3%
251	Part 270	Product IQ	12	137,869	99.8%	83.7%
252	Part 158	Product IR	12	137,881	99.8%	84.0%
253	Part 228	Product IS	12	137,893	99.8%	84.3%
254	Part 205	Product IT	11	137,904	99.8%	84.7%
255	Part 223	Product IU	11	137,915	99.8%	85.0%
256	Part 17	Product IV	10	137,925	99.8%	85.3%
257	Part 156	Product IW	10	137,935	99.9%	85.7%
258	Part 171	Product IX	10	137,945	99.9%	86.0%
259	Part 137	Product IY	9	137,954	99.9%	86.3%
260	Part 203	Product IZ	9	137,963	99.9%	86.7%
261	Part 106	Product JA	9	137,972	99.9%	87.0%
262	Part 209	Product JB	8	137,980	99.9%	87.3%
263	Part 244	Product JC	8	137,988	99.9%	87.7%
264	Part 99	Product JD	8	137,996	99.9%	88.0%
265	Part 60	Product JE	8	138,004	99.9%	88.3%
266	Part 71	Product JF	8	138,012	99.9%	88.7%
267	Part 93	Product JG	8	138,020	99.9%	89.0%
268	Part 150	Product JH	7	138,027	99.9%	89.3%
269	Part 215	Product JI	7	138,034	99.9%	89.7%
270	Part 294	Product JJ	7	138,041	99.9%	90.0%
271	Part 236	Product JK	6	138,047	99.9%	90.3%
272	Part 86	Product JL	6	138,053	99.9%	90.7%
273	Part 32	Product JM	6	138,059	99.9%	91.0%
274	Part 129	Product JN	5	138,064	99.9%	91.3%
275	Part 164	Product JO	5	138,069	100.0%	91.7%
276	Part 283	Product JP	5	138,074	100.0%	92.0%
277	Part 252	Product JQ	5	138,079	100.0%	92.3%
278	Part 259	Product JR	5	138,084	100.0%	92.7%
279	Part 152	Product JS	5	138,089	100.0%	93.0%
280	Part 78	Product JT	4	138,093	100.0%	93.3%
281	Part 251	Product JU	4	138,097	100.0%	93.7%
282	Part 73	Product JV	4	138,101	100.0%	94.0%
283	Part 194	Product JW	4	138,105	100.0%	94.3%
284	Part 107	Product JX	3	138,108	100.0%	94.7%
285	Part 196	Product JY	3	138,111	100.0%	95.0%

© American Management Association. All rights reserved.

A	B	C	D	E	F	G
Line No.	Part No.	Description	Annual Usage	Cumulative Usage	% Total Usage	% Total Items
286	Part 177	Product JZ	3	138,114	100.0%	95.3%
287	Part 221	Product KA	3	138,117	100.0%	95.7%
288	Part 105	Product KB	3	138,120	100.0%	96.0%
289	Part 72	Product KC	2	138,122	100.0%	96.3%
290	Part 286	Product KD	2	138,124	100.0%	96.7%
291	Part 291	Product KE	2	138,126	100.0%	97.0%
292	Part 54	Product KF	2	138,128	100.0%	97.3%
293	Part 163	Product KG	2	138,130	100.0%	97.7%
294	Part 271	Product KH	1	138,131	100.0%	98.0%
295	Part 4	Product KI	1	138,132	100.0%	98.3%
296	Part 153	Product KJ	1	138,133	100.0%	98.7%
297	Part 91	Product KK	1	138,134	100.0%	99.0%
298	Part 151	Product KL	—	138,134	100.0%	99.3%
299	Part 61	Product KM	—	138,134	100.0%	99.7%
300	Part 165	Product KN	—	138,134	100.0%	100.0%

Appendix A—Formulas

A	B	C	D	E	F	G
Line No.	Part No.	Description	Annual Usage	Cumulative Usage	% Total Usage	% Total Items
1	79	Product A	8673	=0+D1	=E1/$E$300	=A1/$A$300
2	133	Product B	6970	=E1+D2	=E2/$E$300	=A2/$A$300
3	290	Product C	5788	=E2+D3	=E3/$E$300	=A3/$A$300
4	65	Product D	5690	=E3+D4	=E4/$E$300	=A4/$A$300
5	111	Product E	4899	=E4+D5	=E5/$E$300	=A5/$A$300
6	195	Product F	3669	=E5+D6	=E6/$E$300	=A6/$A$300
7	139	Product G	3364	=E6+D7	=E7/$E$300	=A7/$A$300
8	131	Product H	3250	=E7+D8	=E8/$E$300	=A8/$A$300
9	132	Product I	3022	=E8+D9	=E9/$E$300	=A9/$A$300
10	175	Product J	2864	=E9+D10	=E10/$E$300	=A10/$A$300
11	255	Product K	2844	=E10+D11	=E11/$E$300	=A11/$A$300
12	101	Product L	2670	=E11+D12	=E12/$E$300	=A12/$A$300
13	265	Product M	2665	=E12+D13	=E13/$E$300	=A13/$A$300
14	48	Product N	2453	=E13+D14	=E14/$E$300	=A14/$A$300
15	2	Product O	2222	=E14+D15	=E15/$E$300	=A15/$A$300
16	14	Product P	1976	=E15+D16	=E16/$E$300	=A16/$A$300
17	70	Product Q	1896	=E16+D17	=E17/$E$300	=A17/$A$300
18	117	Product R	1888	=E17+D18	=E18/$E$300	=A18/$A$300
19	134	Product S	1872	=E18+D19	=E19/$E$300	=A19/$A$300
20	170	Product T	1687	=E19+D20	=E20/$E$300	=A20/$A$300
21	182	Product U	1666	=E20+D21	=E21/$E$300	=A21/$A$300
22	28	Product V	1646	=E21+D22	=E22/$E$300	=A22/$A$300
23	138	Product W	1566	=E22+D23	=E23/$E$300	=A23/$A$300
24	23	Product X	1530	=E23+D24	=E24/$E$300	=A24/$A$300
25	300	Product Y	1057	=E24+D25	=E25/$E$300	=A25/$A$300
26	9	Product Z	1050	=E25+D26	=E26/$E$300	=A26/$A$300
27	241	Product AA	1022	=E26+D27	=E27/$E$300	=A27/$A$300

© American Management Association. All rights reserved.

176 FUNDAMENTALS OF INVENTORY MANAGEMENT AND CONTROL

A	B	C	D	E	F	G
Line No.	Part No.	Description	Annual Usage	Cumulative Usage	% Total Usage	% Total Items
28	219	Product AB	1022	=E27+D28	=E28/$E$300	=A28/$A$300
29	51	Product AC	1001	=E28+D29	=E29/$E$300	=A29/$A$300
30	278	Product AD	997	=E29+D30	=E30/$E$300	=A30/$A$300
31	222	Product AE	991	=E30+D31	=E31/$E$300	=A31/$A$300
32	154	Product AF	986	=E31+D32	=E32/$E$300	=A32/$A$300
33	184	Product AG	972	=E32+D33	=E33/$E$300	=A33/$A$300
34	190	Product AH	968	=E33+D34	=E34/$E$300	=A34/$A$300
35	87	Product AI	964	=E34+D35	=E35/$E$300	=A35/$A$300
36	95	Product AJ	943	=E35+D36	=E36/$E$300	=A36/$A$300
37	6	Product AK	894	=E36+D37	=E37/$E$300	=A37/$A$300
38	142	Product AL	889	=E37+D38	=E38/$E$300	=A38/$A$300
39	210	Product AM	889	=E38+D39	=E39/$E$300	=A39/$A$300
40	13	Product AN	888	=E39+D40	=E40/$E$300	=A40/$A$300
41	121	Product AO	888	=E40+D41	=E41/$E$300	=A41/$A$300
42	3	Product AP	875	=E41+D42	=E42/$E$300	=A42/$A$300
43	235	Product AQ	867	=E42+D43	=E43/$E$300	=A43/$A$300
44	297	Product AR	861	=E43+D44	=E44/$E$300	=A44/$A$300
45	266	Product AS	856	=E44+D45	=E45/$E$300	=A45/$A$300
46	239	Product AT	846	=E45+D46	=E46/$E$300	=A46/$A$300
47	233	Product AU	843	=E46+D47	=E47/$E$300	=A47/$A$300
48	77	Product AV	800	=E47+D48	=E48/$E$300	=A48/$A$300
49	188	Product AW	795	=E48+D49	=E49/$E$300	=A49/$A$300
50	240	Product AX	788	=E49+D50	=E50/$E$300	=A50/$A$300
51	103	Product AY	779	=E50+D51	=E51/$E$300	=A51/$A$300
52	160	Product AZ	766	=E51+D52	=E52/$E$300	=A52/$A$300
53	211	Product BA	764	=E52+D53	=E53/$E$300	=A53/$A$300
54	243	Product BB	761	=E53+D54	=E54/$E$300	=A54/$A$300
55	201	Product BC	754	=E54+D55	=E55/$E$300	=A55/$A$300
56	202	Product BD	712	=E55+D56	=E56/$E$300	=A56/$A$300
57	75	Product BE	698	=E56+D57	=E57/$E$300	=A57/$A$300
58	206	Product BF	697	=E57+D58	=E58/$E$300	=A58/$A$300
59	200	Product BG	697	=E58+D59	=E59/$E$300	=A59/$A$300
60	124	Product BH	689	=E59+D60	=E60/$E$300	=A60/$A$300
61	208	Product BI	662	=E60+D61	=E61/$E$300	=A61/$A$300
62	253	Product BJ	644	=E61+D62	=E62/$E$300	=A62/$A$300
63	264	Product BK	640	=E62+D63	=E63/$E$300	=A63/$A$300
64	230	Product BL	614	=E63+D64	=E64/$E$300	=A64/$A$300
65	53	Product BM	590	=E64+D65	=E65/$E$300	=A65/$A$300
66	33	Product BN	587	=E65+D66	=E66/$E$300	=A66/$A$300
67	104	Product BO	566	=E66+D67	=E67/$E$300	=A67/$A$300
68	207	Product BP	564	=E67+D68	=E68/$E$300	=A68/$A$300
69	63	Product BQ	544	=E68+D69	=E69/$E$300	=A69/$A$300
70	275	Product BR	533	=E69+D70	=E70/$E$300	=A70/$A$300

© American Management Association. All rights reserved.

A	B	C	D	E	F	G
Line No.	Part No.	Description	Annual Usage	Cumulative Usage	% Total Usage	% Total Items
71	155	Product BS	530	=E70+D71	=E71/$E$300	=A71/$A$300
72	7	Product BT	512	=E71+D72	=E72/$E$300	=A72/$A$300
73	90	Product BU	499	=E72+D73	=E73/$E$300	=A73/$A$300
74	59	Product BV	468	=E73+D74	=E74/$E$300	=A74/$A$300
75	122	Product BW	467	=E74+D75	=E75/$E$300	=A75/$A$300
76	35	Product BX	456	=E75+D76	=E76/$E$300	=A76/$A$300
77	67	Product BY	450	=E76+D77	=E77/$E$300	=A77/$A$300
78	92	Product BZ	444	=E77+D78	=E78/$E$300	=A78/$A$300
79	83	Product CA	443	=E78+D79	=E79/$E$300	=A79/$A$300
80	287	Product CB	433	=E79+D80	=E80/$E$300	=A80/$A$300
81	162	Product CC	420	=E80+D81	=E81/$E$300	=A81/$A$300
82	189	Product CD	420	=E81+D82	=E82/$E$300	=A82/$A$300
83	245	Product CE	398	=E82+D83	=E83/$E$300	=A83/$A$300
84	274	Product CF	382	=E83+D84	=E84/$E$300	=A84/$A$300
85	242	Product CG	355	=E84+D85	=E85/$E$300	=A85/$A$300
86	258	Product CH	354	=E85+D86	=E86/$E$300	=A86/$A$300
87	136	Product CI	353	=E86+D87	=E87/$E$300	=A87/$A$300
88	238	Product CJ	334	=E87+D88	=E88/$E$300	=A88/$A$300
89	115	Product CK	333	=E88+D89	=E89/$E$300	=A89/$A$300
90	94	Product CL	333	=E89+D90	=E90/$E$300	=A90/$A$300
91	64	Product CM	332	=E90+D91	=E91/$E$300	=A91/$A$300
92	298	Product CN	326	=E91+D92	=E92/$E$300	=A92/$A$300
93	295	Product CO	325	=E92+D93	=E93/$E$300	=A93/$A$300
94	30	Product CP	325	=E93+D94	=E94/$E$300	=A94/$A$300
95	11	Product CQ	323	=E94+D95	=E95/$E$300	=A95/$A$300
96	192	Product CR	321	=E95+D96	=E96/$E$300	=A96/$A$300
97	96	Product CS	321	=E96+D97	=E97/$E$300	=A97/$A$300
98	40	Product CT	298	=E97+D98	=E98/$E$300	=A98/$A$300
99	47	Product CU	285	=E98+D99	=E99/$E$300	=A99/$A$300
100	125	Product CV	269	=E99+D100	=E100/$E$300	=A100/$A$300
101	198	Product CW	260	=E100+D101	=E101/$E$300	=A101/$A$300
102	135	Product CX	258	=E101+D102	=E102/$E$300	=A102/$A$300
103	130	Product CY	256	=E102+D103	=E103/$E$300	=A103/$A$300
104	85	Product CZ	255	=E103+D104	=E104/$E$300	=A104/$A$300
105	216	Product DA	223	=E104+D105	=E105/$E$300	=A105/$A$300
106	193	Product DB	222	=E105+D106	=E106/$E$300	=A106/$A$300
107	285	Product DC	220	=E106+D107	=E107/$E$300	=A107/$A$300
108	288	Product DD	200	=E107+D108	=E108/$E$300	=A108/$A$300
109	26	Product DE	199	=E108+D109	=E109/$E$300	=A109/$A$300
110	176	Product DF	199	=E109+D110	=E110/$E$300	=A110/$A$300
111	186	Product DG	194	=E110+D111	=E111/$E$300	=A111/$A$300
112	173	Product DH	189	=E111+D112	=E112/$E$300	=A112/$A$300
113	81	Product DI	188	=E112+D113	=E113/$E$300	=A113/$A$300

178 FUNDAMENTALS OF INVENTORY MANAGEMENT AND CONTROL

A	B	C	D	E	F	G
Line No.	Part No.	Description	Annual Usage	Cumulative Usage	% Total Usage	% Total Items
114	172	Product DJ	188	=E113+D114	=E114/$E$300	=A114/$A$300
115	144	Product DK	186	=E114+D115	=E115/$E$300	=A115/$A$300
116	12	Product DL	186	=E115+D116	=E116/$E$300	=A116/$A$300
117	141	Product DM	186	=E116+D117	=E117/$E$300	=A117/$A$300
118	15	Product DN	185	=E117+D118	=E118/$E$300	=A118/$A$300
119	227	Product DO	185	=E118+D119	=E119/$E$300	=A119/$A$300
120	191	Product DP	184	=E119+D120	=E120/$E$300	=A120/$A$300
121	272	Product DQ	178	=E120+D121	=E121/$E$300	=A121/$A$300
122	279	Product DR	156	=E121+D122	=E122/$E$300	=A122/$A$300
123	247	Product DS	150	=E122+D123	=E123/$E$300	=A123/$A$300
124	89	Product DT	144	=E123+D124	=E124/$E$300	=A124/$A$300
125	174	Product DU	143	=E124+D125	=E125/$E$300	=A125/$A$300
126	118	Product DV	133	=E125+D126	=E126/$E$300	=A126/$A$300
127	27	Product DW	116	=E126+D127	=E127/$E$300	=A127/$A$300
128	34	Product DX	116	=E127+D128	=E128/$E$300	=A128/$A$300
129	169	Product DY	116	=E128+D129	=E129/$E$300	=A129/$A$300
130	178	Product DZ	113	=E129+D130	=E130/$E$300	=A130/$A$300
131	84	Product EA	105	=E130+D131	=E131/$E$300	=A131/$A$300
132	204	Product EB	103	=E131+D132	=E132/$E$300	=A132/$A$300
133	273	Product EC	102	=E132+D133	=E133/$E$300	=A133/$A$300
134	24	Product ED	101	=E133+D134	=E134/$E$300	=A134/$A$300
135	114	Product EE	100	=E134+D135	=E135/$E$300	=A135/$A$300
136	57	Product EF	100	=E135+D136	=E136/$E$300	=A136/$A$300
137	168	Product EG	99	=E136+D137	=E137/$E$300	=A137/$A$300
138	187	Product EH	99	=E137+D138	=E138/$E$300	=A138/$A$300
139	214	Product EI	99	=E138+D139	=E139/$E$300	=A139/$A$300
140	220	Product EJ	98	=E139+D140	=E140/$E$300	=A140/$A$300
141	29	Product EK	98	=E140+D141	=E141/$E$300	=A141/$A$300
142	98	Product EL	98	=E141+D142	=E142/$E$300	=A142/$A$300
143	261	Product EM	97	=E142+D143	=E143/$E$300	=A143/$A$300
144	180	Product EN	97	=E143+D144	=E144/$E$300	=A144/$A$300
145	289	Product EO	96	=E144+D145	=E145/$E$300	=A145/$A$300
146	146	Product EP	96	=E145+D146	=E146/$E$300	=A146/$A$300
147	299	Product EQ	94	=E146+D147	=E147/$E$300	=A147/$A$300
148	68	Product ER	92	=E147+D148	=E148/$E$300	=A148/$A$300
149	41	Product ES	91	=E148+D149	=E149/$E$300	=A149/$A$300
150	38	Product ET	90	=E149+D150	=E150/$E$300	=A150/$A$300
151	140	Product EU	89	=E150+D151	=E151/$E$300	=A151/$A$300
152	16	Product EV	89	=E151+D152	=E152/$E$300	=A152/$A$300
153	128	Product EW	88	=E152+D153	=E153/$E$300	=A153/$A$300
154	25	Product EX	88	=E153+D154	=E154/$E$300	=A154/$A$300
155	45	Product EY	87	=E154+D155	=E155/$E$300	=A155/$A$300
156	1	Product EZ	86	=E155+D156	=E156/$E$300	=A156/$A$300

© American Management Association. All rights reserved.

APPENDIX A—FORMULAS **179**

A	B	C	D	E	F	G
Line No.	Part No.	Description	Annual Usage	Cumulative Usage	% Total Usage	% Total Items
157	246	Product FA	85	=E156+D157	=E157/$E$300	=A157/$A$300
158	108	Product FB	85	=E157+D158	=E158/$E$300	=A158/$A$300
159	231	Product FC	85	=E158+D159	=E159/$E$300	=A159/$A$300
160	21	Product FD	84	=E159+D160	=E160/$E$300	=A160/$A$300
161	183	Product FE	84	=E160+D161	=E161/$E$300	=A161/$A$300
162	248	Product FF	84	=E161+D162	=E162/$E$300	=A162/$A$300
163	199	Product FG	84	=E162+D163	=E163/$E$300	=A163/$A$300
164	120	Product FH	80	=E163+D164	=E164/$E$300	=A164/$A$300
165	224	Product FI	80	=E164+D165	=E165/$E$300	=A165/$A$300
166	256	Product FJ	76	=E165+D166	=E166/$E$300	=A166/$A$300
167	281	Product FK	76	=E166+D167	=E167/$E$300	=A167/$A$300
168	157	Product FL	76	=E167+D168	=E168/$E$300	=A168/$A$300
169	5	Product FM	75	=E168+D169	=E169/$E$300	=A169/$A$300
170	56	Product FN	75	=E169+D170	=E170/$E$300	=A170/$A$300
171	44	Product FO	74	=E170+D171	=E171/$E$300	=A171/$A$300
172	76	Product FP	74	=E171+D172	=E172/$E$300	=A172/$A$300
173	267	Product FQ	74	=E172+D173	=E173/$E$300	=A173/$A$300
174	262	Product FR	72	=E173+D174	=E174/$E$300	=A174/$A$300
175	225	Product FS	68	=E174+D175	=E175/$E$300	=A175/$A$300
176	276	Product FT	67	=E175+D176	=E176/$E$300	=A176/$A$300
177	43	Product FU	66	=E176+D177	=E177/$E$300	=A177/$A$300
178	10	Product FV	66	=E177+D178	=E178/$E$300	=A178/$A$300
179	126	Product FW	65	=E178+D179	=E179/$E$300	=A179/$A$300
180	296	Product FX	64	=E179+D180	=E180/$E$300	=A180/$A$300
181	277	Product FY	63	=E180+D181	=E181/$E$300	=A181/$A$300
182	42	Product FZ	63	=E181+D182	=E182/$E$300	=A182/$A$300
183	197	Product GA	62	=E182+D183	=E183/$E$300	=A183/$A$300
184	284	Product GB	61	=E183+D184	=E184/$E$300	=A184/$A$300
185	22	Product GC	61	=E184+D185	=E185/$E$300	=A185/$A$300
186	39	Product GD	61	=E185+D186	=E186/$E$300	=A186/$A$300
187	82	Product GE	58	=E186+D187	=E187/$E$300	=A187/$A$300
188	237	Product GF	56	=E187+D188	=E188/$E$300	=A188/$A$300
189	69	Product GG	56	=E188+D189	=E189/$E$300	=A189/$A$300
190	62	Product GH	56	=E189+D190	=E190/$E$300	=A190/$A$300
191	213	Product GI	56	=E190+D191	=E191/$E$300	=A191/$A$300
192	109	Product GJ	55	=E191+D192	=E192/$E$300	=A192/$A$300
193	149	Product GK	55	=E192+D193	=E193/$E$300	=A193/$A$300
194	159	Product GL	55	=E193+D194	=E194/$E$300	=A194/$A$300
195	113	Product GM	54	=E194+D195	=E195/$E$300	=A195/$A$300
196	110	Product GN	54	=E195+D196	=E196/$E$300	=A196/$A$300
197	218	Product GO	54	=E196+D197	=E197/$E$300	=A197/$A$300
198	46	Product GP	53	=E197+D198	=E198/$E$300	=A198/$A$300
199	112	Product GQ	52	=E198+D199	=E199/$E$300	=A199/$A$300

© American Management Association. All rights reserved.

FUNDAMENTALS OF INVENTORY MANAGEMENT AND CONTROL

A	B	C	D	E	F	G
Line No.	Part No.	Description	Annual Usage	Cumulative Usage	% Total Usage	% Total Items
200	179	Product GR	52	=E199+D200	=E200/$E$300	=A200/$A$300
201	100	Product GS	52	=E200+D201	=E201/$E$300	=A201/$A$300
202	37	Product GT	52	=E201+D202	=E202/$E$300	=A202/$A$300
203	282	Product GU	50	=E202+D203	=E203/$E$300	=A203/$A$300
204	116	Product GV	48	=E203+D204	=E204/$E$300	=A204/$A$300
205	8	Product GW	46	=E204+D205	=E205/$E$300	=A205/$A$300
206	254	Product GX	45	=E205+D206	=E206/$E$300	=A206/$A$300
207	148	Product GY	45	=E206+D207	=E207/$E$300	=A207/$A$300
208	66	Product GZ	44	=E207+D208	=E208/$E$300	=A208/$A$300
209	18	Product HA	43	=E208+D209	=E209/$E$300	=A209/$A$300
210	119	Product HB	43	=E209+D210	=E210/$E$300	=A210/$A$300
211	52	Product HC	42	=E210+D211	=E211/$E$300	=A211/$A$300
212	123	Product HD	41	=E211+D212	=E212/$E$300	=A212/$A$300
213	55	Product HE	41	=E212+D213	=E213/$E$300	=A213/$A$300
214	147	Product HF	37	=E213+D214	=E214/$E$300	=A214/$A$300
215	161	Product HG	36	=E214+D215	=E215/$E$300	=A215/$A$300
216	127	Product HH	34	=E215+D216	=E216/$E$300	=A216/$A$300
217	74	Product HI	34	=E216+D217	=E217/$E$300	=A217/$A$300
218	250	Product HJ	33	=E217+D218	=E218/$E$300	=A218/$A$300
219	260	Product HK	32	=E218+D219	=E219/$E$300	=A219/$A$300
220	263	Product HL	32	=E219+D220	=E220/$E$300	=A220/$A$300
221	20	Product HM	28	=E220+D221	=E221/$E$300	=A221/$A$300
222	229	Product HN	26	=E221+D222	=E222/$E$300	=A222/$A$300
223	58	Product HO	25	=E222+D223	=E223/$E$300	=A223/$A$300
224	31	Product HP	25	=E223+D224	=E224/$E$300	=A224/$A$300
225	50	Product HQ	24	=E224+D225	=E225/$E$300	=A225/$A$300
226	217	Product HR	24	=E225+D226	=E226/$E$300	=A226/$A$300
227	232	Product HS	23	=E226+D227	=E227/$E$300	=A227/$A$300
228	234	Product HT	23	=E227+D228	=E228/$E$300	=A228/$A$300
229	257	Product HU	22	=E228+D229	=E229/$E$300	=A229/$A$300
230	280	Product HV	21	=E229+D230	=E230/$E$300	=A230/$A$300
231	80	Product HW	21	=E230+D231	=E231/$E$300	=A231/$A$300
232	88	Product HX	20	=E231+D232	=E232/$E$300	=A232/$A$300
233	49	Product HY	19	=E232+D233	=E233/$E$300	=A233/$A$300
234	212	Product HZ	18	=E233+D234	=E234/$E$300	=A234/$A$300
235	226	Product IA	18	=E234+D235	=E235/$E$300	=A235/$A$300
236	97	Product IB	18	=E235+D236	=E236/$E$300	=A236/$A$300
237	166	Product IC	18	=E236+D237	=E237/$E$300	=A237/$A$300
238	293	Product ID	18	=E237+D238	=E238/$E$300	=A238/$A$300
239	36	Product IE	18	=E238+D239	=E239/$E$300	=A239/$A$300
240	249	Product IF	17	=E239+D240	=E240/$E$300	=A240/$A$300
241	143	Product IG	16	=E240+D241	=E241/$E$300	=A241/$A$300
242	145	Product IH	16	=E241+D242	=E242/$E$300	=A242/$A$300

© American Management Association. All rights reserved.

APPENDIX A—FORMULAS   **181**

A	B	C	D	E	F	G
Line No.	Part No.	Description	Annual Usage	Cumulative Usage	% Total Usage	% Total Items
243	167	Product II	15	=E242+D243	=E243/$E$300	=A243/$A$300
244	268	Product IJ	15	=E243+D244	=E244/$E$300	=A244/$A$300
245	181	Product IK	14	=E244+D245	=E245/$E$300	=A245/$A$300
246	292	Product IL	14	=E245+D246	=E246/$E$300	=A246/$A$300
247	19	Product IM	14	=E246+D247	=E247/$E$300	=A247/$A$300
248	185	Product IN	14	=E247+D248	=E248/$E$300	=A248/$A$300
249	102	Product IO	13	=E248+D249	=E249/$E$300	=A249/$A$300
250	269	Product IP	12	=E249+D250	=E250/$E$300	=A250/$A$300
251	270	Product IQ	12	=E250+D251	=E251/$E$300	=A251/$A$300
252	158	Product IR	12	=E251+D252	=E252/$E$300	=A252/$A$300
253	228	Product IS	12	=E252+D253	=E253/$E$300	=A253/$A$300
254	205	Product IT	11	=E253+D254	=E254/$E$300	=A254/$A$300
255	223	Product IU	11	=E254+D255	=E255/$E$300	=A255/$A$300
256	17	Product IV	10	=E255+D256	=E256/$E$300	=A256/$A$300
257	156	Product IW	10	=E256+D257	=E257/$E$300	=A257/$A$300
258	171	Product IX	10	=E257+D258	=E258/$E$300	=A258/$A$300
259	137	Product IY	9	=E258+D259	=E259/$E$300	=A259/$A$300
260	203	Product IZ	9	=E259+D260	=E260/$E$300	=A260/$A$300
261	106	Product JA	9	=E260+D261	=E261/$E$300	=A261/$A$300
262	209	Product JB	8	=E261+D262	=E262/$E$300	=A262/$A$300
263	244	Product JC	8	=E262+D263	=E263/$E$300	=A263/$A$300
264	99	Product JD	8	=E263+D264	=E264/$E$300	=A264/$A$300
265	60	Product JE	8	=E264+D265	=E265/$E$300	=A265/$A$300
266	71	Product JF	8	=E265+D266	=E266/$E$300	=A266/$A$300
267	93	Product JG	8	=E266+D267	=E267/$E$300	=A267/$A$300
268	150	Product JH	7	=E267+D268	=E268/$E$300	=A268/$A$300
269	215	Product JI	7	=E268+D269	=E269/$E$300	=A269/$A$300
270	294	Product JJ	7	=E269+D270	=E270/$E$300	=A270/$A$300
271	236	Product JK	6	=E270+D271	=E271/$E$300	=A271/$A$300
272	86	Product JL	6	=E271+D272	=E272/$E$300	=A272/$A$300
273	32	Product JM	6	=E272+D273	=E273/$E$300	=A273/$A$300
274	129	Product JN	5	=E273+D274	=E274/$E$300	=A274/$A$300
275	164	Product JO	5	=E274+D275	=E275/$E$300	=A275/$A$300
276	283	Product JP	5	=E275+D276	=E276/$E$300	=A276/$A$300
277	252	Product JQ	5	=E276+D277	=E277/$E$300	=A277/$A$300
278	259	Product JR	5	=E277+D278	=E278/$E$300	=A278/$A$300
279	152	Product JS	5	=E278+D279	=E279/$E$300	=A279/$A$300
280	78	Product JT	4	=E279+D280	=E280/$E$300	=A280/$A$300
281	251	Product JU	4	=E280+D281	=E281/$E$300	=A281/$A$300
282	73	Product JV	4	=E281+D282	=E282/$E$300	=A282/$A$300
283	194	Product JW	4	=E282+D283	=E283/$E$300	=A283/$A$300
284	107	Product JX	3	=E283+D284	=E284/$E$300	=A284/$A$300
285	196	Product JY	3	=E284+D285	=E285/$E$300	=A285/$A$300

© American Management Association. All rights reserved.

182 FUNDAMENTALS OF INVENTORY MANAGEMENT AND CONTROL

A	B	C	D	E	F	G
Line No.	Part No.	Description	Annual Usage	Cumulative Usage	% Total Usage	% Total Items
286	177	Product JZ	3	=E285+D286	=E286/$E$300	=A286/$A$300
287	221	Product KA	3	=E286+D287	=E287/$E$300	=A287/$A$300
288	105	Product KB	3	=E287+D288	=E288/$E$300	=A288/$A$300
289	72	Product KC	2	=E288+D289	=E289/$E$300	=A289/$A$300
290	286	Product KD	2	=E289+D290	=E290/$E$300	=A290/$A$300
291	291	Product KE	2	=E290+D291	=E291/$E$300	=A291/$A$300
292	54	Product KF	2	=E291+D292	=E292/$E$300	=A292/$A$300
293	163	Product KG	2	=E292+D293	=E293/$E$300	=A293/$A$300
294	271	Product KH	1	=E293+D294	=E294/$E$300	=A294/$A$300
295	4	Product KI	1	=E294+D295	=E295/$E$300	=A295/$A$300
296	153	Product KJ	1	=E295+D296	=E296/$E$300	=A296/$A$300
297	91	Product KK	1	=E296+D297	=E297/$E$300	=A297/$A$300
298	151	Product KL	0	=E297+D298	=E298/$E$300	=A298/$A$300
299	61	Product KM	0	=E298+D299	=E299/$E$300	=A299/$A$300
300	165	Product KN	0	=E299+D300	=E300/$E$300	=A300/$A$300

© American Management Association. All rights reserved.

Appendix B

CONTINUATION SHEET FOR ACTIVITY 6–1 AND SELF-ASSESSMENT 6–2

Paragraph	Problems Identified	Problems Identified at Your Facility

Paragraph	Problems Identified	Problems Identified at Your Facility

Bibliography

Anderson, Barbara V. *The Art and Science of Computer Assisted Ordering: Methods for Management.* Westport, Conn.: Quorum Books, 1996.

Arnold, J. R. Tony, and Chapman, Stephen N. *Introduction to Materials Management, 4th ed.* Upper Saddle River, N.J.: Prentice Hall, 2001.

Bernard, Paul. *Integrated Inventory Management.* New York: John Wiley & Sons, Inc., 1999.

Brooks, Roger B., and Larry W. Wilson. *Inventory Record Accuracy: Unleashing the Power of Cycle Counting.* New York: John Wiley & Sons, 1995.

Collins, David Jarrett, and Nancy Nasuti Whipple. *Using Bar Coding: Why It's Taking Over, 2d ed.* Duxbury, Mass.: Data Capture Institute, 1994.

Cullinane, Thomas P., James A. Tompkins, and Jerry D. Smith. *How to Plan and Manage Warehouse Operations, 2d ed.* Watertown, Mass.: American Management Association, 1994.

Delaney, Patrick R., James R. Adler, Barry J. Epstein, and Michael F. Foran. *GAAP 98: Interpretation and Application of Generally Accepted Accounting Principles 1998.* New York: John Wiley & Sons, 1998.

Eisen, Peter J. *Accounting the Easy Way, 3rd ed.* New York: Barron's Educational Series, 1995.

Feld, William M. *Lean Manufacturing: Tools, Techniques, and How to Use Them.* Boca Raton: The St. Lucie Press/APICS Series on Resource Management, 2001.

Grieco, Peter L., Jr., Michael W. Gozzo, and C. J. (Chip) Long. *Behind Bars: Bar Coding Principles and Applications.* Palm Beach Gardens, Fla.: PT Publications, 1989.

Harmon, Craig K., and Russ Adams. *Reading Between the Lines: An Introduction to Bar Code Technology.* Peterborough, N.H.: Helmers Publishing, 1989.

Harris, George. *Fundamentals of Purchasing.* New York: AMACOM, 1999.

————. *Strategic Supply Management.* New York: AMACOM, 2001.

Henderson, Bruce, and Jorge Larco. *Lean Transformation.* Richmond: Oakley Press, 1999.

Langenwalter, Gary A. *Enterprise Resources Planning and Beyond: Integrating Your Entire Organization.* Boca Raton: St. Lucie Press, 2000.

Langenwalter, Gary A. *White Paper on Lean Manufacturing Methodologies.* Stow, Mass.: Manufacturing Consulting Partners. (complimentary copy available upon request by calling (978) 562-4632, or e-mailing Gary.Langenwalter@ mfgcons.com)

Landvater, Darryl. *World Class Production & Inventory Management.* New York: John Wiley & Sons, 1993.

Martinich, Joseph S. *Production and Operations Management: An Applied Modern Approach.* New York: John Wiley & Sons, 1997.

Melnyk, Steven, and R. T. "Chris" Christensen. "Understanding the Nature of Setups, Part Two: Setups and Lot Sizing." *APICS Online Edition. www.apics.org/magazine/apr97/basics.htm.* (September 9, 2000)

Meredith, Jack R., and Scott M. Shafer. *Operations Management for MBAs.* New York: John Wiley & Sons, 1999.

Oden, Howard, Gary Langenwalter, and Raymond Lucier, *Handbook of Material and Capacity Requirements Planning,* New York: McGraw-Hill, 1993.

Palmer, Roger C. *The Bar Code Book, 3rd ed: Reading, Printing, Specification, and Application of Bar Code and Other Machine Readable Symbols.* Peterborough, N.H.: Helmers Publishing, 1995.

Robeson, James F., and William C. Copacino. *The Logistics Handbook.* New York: The Free Press: A Division of Macmillan, Inc., 1994.

Rother, Mike, and John Shook, *Learning to See.* Brookline, Mass.: Lean Enterprise Institute, 1998. *www.lean.org*

Thomsett, Michael C. *The Little Black Book of Business Math.* New York: AMACOM, 1988.

————. *Winning Numbers: How to Use Business Facts and Figures to Make Your Point and Get Ahead.* New York: AMACOM, 1990.

Tompkins, James A., and Dale Harmelink. *The Distribution Management Handbook.* New York: McGraw-Hill, 1994.

Tompkins, James A., and Jerry D. Smith. *The Warehouse Management Book.* New York: McGraw Hill Book Company, 1988.

Waters, C. D. J. *Inventory Management and Control.* Chichester, West Sussex, England: John Wiley & Sons Ltd., 1992.

Womack, James P., and Daniel T. Jones. *Lean Thinking.* New York: Simon & Schuster, 1996.

Glossary

A-B-C categorization for warehouse layout The location of SKUs based on the speed with which they move through a facility, with A representing the most popular, fastest moving items, B representing the next most active, and C representing the slow movers

A-B-C analysis cycle counting A cycle counting method based on Pareto's law in which items are counted based on classification determined by value; value can be based on money, usage rate, or a combination of the two (usually usage times money)

accounts receivable Amounts due from customers resulting from sales activities

allocation The process of tying an item to a specific customer order, usually in a computer system

anticipation stock Inventory produced in anticipation of an upcoming season, such as fancy chocolates made up in advance of Mother's Day or Valentine's Day

average cost method A method of inventory valuation for accounting purposes that identifies the value of inventory and cost of goods sold by calculating an average unit cost for all goods available for sale during a given period of time

backflushing A software technique in which raw materials and other components going into a particular subassembly or final product are automatically relieved from stock by the computer system when that subassembly/product is completed

balance sheet Accounting document showing the financial position of a company on a specific date, listing assets and liabilities

bar coding An optical method using visible or invisible light reflecting off a printed pattern, or bar code, to achieve automatic identification

bill of materials (BOM) The recipe of raw materials, parts, subassemblies, etc., required to build or make something

book value The value of an item appearing as an asset on the balance sheet consisting of its original cost minus depreciation

buffer/safety inventory Inventory that serves to compensate for demand and supply uncertainties and enables firms to "decouple" and separate different parts of an operation so that they can function independently of one another

carrying costs (K factor) The cost represented by the number of pennies per inventory dollar per year a company is spending to house its inventory; generally expressed as a percentage (see **holding costs**)

charge coupled device scanner A type of scanner that has a depth of field of several inches, making contact with the label or other surface unnecessary, and can read very high bar code densities

Code 128 The preferred symbology for most new bar code applications

Code 39 The most widely used bar code in nonretail applications, in which three of the nine elements are wide and six are narrow

combination system A stock locator system in which items requiring special consideration are assigned specific locations while the bulk of the product mix is randomly located

consumables Category of inventory including items such as office supplies, cleaning materials, and packing materials

continuous symbology A bar code that starts with a bar, ends with a space, and has no gap between one character and another

cost of goods sold The item on an income statement that reflects the cost of inventory flowing out of a business

current ratio A ratio (current assets divided by current liabilities) that assesses the organization's overall liquidity and indicates its ability to meet its short-term obligations

cycle counting The frequent counting of a small cross-section of your inventory designed to eliminate the cause of errors by identifying items in error and triggering research to identify the cause of the errors

data characters The characters in a bar code symbol that contain the actual message within the code

dead stock Stock that cannot be sold

dependent demand The demand for raw materials, parts, and assemblies that depends on the demand for the final product (e.g., legs of a chair)

diminishing population cycle counting A cycle counting method in which each item in a defined population is counted before any item is counted over again; can be used as a stand-alone procedure or as part of the product category approach or the A-B-C approach, and ensures that all items in the population are counted at least once per cycle

direct thermal printing A bar-code print technology in which overlapping dots are formed on a heat-sensitive substrate (label or other foundation) by selectively heating elements in a printhead

discrete symbology A bar code with characters that start with a bar and end with a bar and have a space between each character

dot matrix impact printing A bar-code print technology in which a moving printhead, with rows of hammers, creates images through multiple passes over a ribbon

economic order quantity (EOQ) A type of fixed-order-quantity model that determines the amount of an item to be purchased or manufactured at one time; it is intended to minimize the combined costs of acquiring and carrying inventory. It should only be used for independent demand items

electronic data interchange (EDI) The paperless (electronic) exchange between companies of trading documents, such as purchase orders, shipment authorizations, advance shipment notices, and invoices, using standardized document formats

enterprise resources planning (ERP) A computer-based information system that integrates most of the critical functions of a manufacturing company, starting with MRP II functionality and adding human resources, manufacturing engineering, maintenance, quality, field service, full JIT support, manufacturing execution systems, logistics, distribution, full sales support, supply chain support, and executive decision support.

enterprise resources planning II (ERP II) Extends ERP to fully cover all areas of information required to operate a manufacturing company. Includes all ERP functions and adds: strategic planning, marketing, demand management, supply chain execution, customer relationship management, enterprise production systems, financial planning, product engineering, research and development, and sales and operations planning.

family grouping/like product approach An item placement theory that positions items with similar characteristics together, with the goal of achieving a natural grouping of items that will be received/stored/picked/shipped together

fill rate A measurement of the effectiveness of an organization's inventory efforts, usually expressed as a percentage

finished product Product ready for current customer sales

first-in, first-out (FIFO) A method of inventory valuation for accounting purposes that assumes that the first goods purchased are the first to be used or sold regardless of the actual movement of the physical units

fixed location system A stock locator system in which every item has a predetermined home and nothing else can live there

flow chart A chart that analyzes the sequence of events, showing the interdependence of events or which events are occurring simultaneously

free on board (F.O.B) Terms of sale that identify where the title passes from the seller to the buyer

holding, or carrying, costs The cost of capital tied up in inventory, storage costs, and costs of handling the product, including equipment, warehouse and stockkeeping staff, stock losses/wastage, and taxes

income statement An accounting report that identifies a company's revenues, expenses, and resulting profits for a given period of time

independent demand The demand for finished goods and spare parts for replacements influenced by market conditions outside the control of your organization's operations (e.g., by customers)

© American Management Association. All rights reserved.

ink jet printing A bar-code print technology in which a fixed printhead sprays tiny droplets of ink onto a substrate

in-transit inventory Inventory that is in transit from a supplier to your company, or from your company to a customer. See also **free on board; transit inventory.**

inventory A company's raw materials, work in process, supplies used in operations, and finished goods

inventory record accuracy (IRA) A means to track how well an organization's shelf count and record count match; designed to determine if stock records accurately reflect what is actually in the stockroom

inventory stratification An item placement theory based on the A-B-C categorization of SKUs and the utilization of the SKU's unloading/loading ratio

inventory turnover ratio A ratio that measures on average how many times inventory is replaced over a period of time, usually a year

item placement theories Theories addressing where a particular item or category of items should be placed within a facility

just-in-time (JIT) A philosophy of manufacturing based on planned elimination of all waste and continuous improvement of productivity

kanban A "visible record" that lets the supplier know it is time to process another unit of product.

laser (xerographic) printing A bar-code print technology in which a controlled laser beam creates an image on an electrostatically charged photoconductive drum; the charged areas attract toner particles that are transferred and fused onto the substrate

laser scanner A type of scanner that projects a beam of energy off a rotating prism or oscillating mirror; has a depth of field of several feet

last-in, first-out (LIFO) A method of inventory valuation for accounting purposes that assumes that the most recently purchased/acquired goods are the first to be used or sold regardless of the actual movement of the physical units

lean An approach to business that focuses on identifying what the customer values, then eliminating everything else; smoothing out the flow of materials and information; and pursuing perfection. Very similar to JIT.

light pen scanner A type of scanner that makes contact with the label or surface on which a pattern is printed and can be tied into various decoder types of equipment

location audit cycle counting A cycle counting method in which the stockroom(s) is (are) divided up in some logical method—by rooms, racks, bins, etc.—and a count is performed in the designated area on a regularly scheduled day

machine vision An automated method of identifying inventory in which cameras take pictures of objects, encode them, and send them to a computer for interpretation

magnetic stripes An automated method of identifying inventory in which a magnetic stripe, like those on credit cards, is encoded with information

manufacturing resources planning (MRP II) A computer-based information system that encompasses the basic manufacturing, materials, and accounting functions in a company, including: forecasting, order entry, customer service, master production scheduling, capacity requirement planning, inventory management, materials requirements planning, production activity control (shop floor control), purchasing, standard costing, and general accounting

master production schedule (MPS) The schedule that sets out what will be built, when, and in what quantities; it can cover either short or long time horizons

material requirements planning (MRP) A set of techniques that uses computerized bill of material data, inventory data, and the master production schedule to plan time-phased replenishment for each item to have just enough on hand when it is needed

memory system A stock locator solely system dependent on human recall; features include simplicity, relative freedom from paperwork or data entry, and maximum utilization of available space

min-max inventory control system A type of order point replenishment system where the "min" (minimum) is the order point, and the "max" (maximum) is the "order up to" inventory level; the order quantity is variable and is the result of the max minus available and on-order inventory

obsolete stock Inventory that cannot be sold as "current" product

optical character recognition (OCR) An automated method of identifying inventory in which numbers, letters, and characters are printed in a predetermined, standard character style or font

ordering, or acquisition, costs Costs incurred regardless of the actual value of the goods, including salaries of those purchasing the product, and costs of handling the inventory

order-point formulas Formulas used to determine how much of a given item needs to be ordered where there is independent demand

product categories cycle counting A cycle counting method in which the organization decides on how it wishes to categorize SKUs based on some characteristic(s), such as manufacturer or type of use; items matching these criteria are then counted either on the basis of a single event or by using the diminishing population technique for each separate category; cycle can be a single day or a defined number of times per year

quick, or acid-test, ratio A ratio that compares the organization's most liquid current assets to its current liabilities

quiet zone The space on each side of a bar code symbol that gives the scanner a starting point from which to start its measurement

radio frequency tags An automated method of identifying inventory in which data is encoded on a chip encased in a tag; in response to a radar pulse from a reader, a transponder in the tag sends a signal to the reader

random selection cycle counting A cycle counting method that counts randomly selected items each time

random system A stock locator system in which no item has a fixed home and may be placed wherever there is space

ratio An accounting tool used to compare key financial relationships within and among organizations; computed by dividing one number by another

raw materials Stock purchased from a supplier that will be used to produce partial subassemblies or completed goods

record count The amount reflected in the main database records

relieving The process of actually removing an item from stock in terms of both its paper life and its real life

reorder point (ROP) A set inventory level where, if the total stock on hand falls to or below that point, action is taken to replenish the stock; the order point is normally calculated as forecasted usage during the replenishment lead time plus safety stock

replenishment approach A type of inventory management associated with independent demand that assumes that market forces will exhibit a somewhat fixed pattern and calls for stock to be replenished as it is used in order to have items on hand for customers

replenishment cost (R factor) The cost of replenishing an item into inventory, including notifying the supplier, receiving the item, putting the item away, and paying the supplier. It does not include purchasing

requirements approach A type of inventory management associated with dependent demand that assumes no fixed pattern of market forces and calls for ordering materials needed to create an assembly or finished item on an as-needed basis

run chart A chart that measures a variable that changes over time; an x/y axis chart with the unit of measure appearing on the vertical y-axis, and the timeframe running along the horizontal x-axis

scanner An electro-optical device that reads a bar code by illuminating the symbol and measuring reflected light

service, repair, replacement, and spare items (S&R items) Items used to support products in the market

shelf count The actual balance on hand stock level for an SKU

specific cost method A method of inventory valuation for accounting purposes that assumes that the organization can track the actual cost of an item into, through, and out of the facility

standard cost method A method of inventory valuation for accounting purposes often used by manufacturing companies that gives a uniform value for an item throughout a given year; a best-guess approach based on known costs and expenses and anticipated changes

start and stop characters The characters in a bar code symbol that tell the scanner where the message is commencing

stock-keeping unit (SKU) An item at a particular geographic location; for example, one product stocked at the plant and at six different distribution centers would represent seven SKUs

stock-locator systems Systems that relate to the overall organization of SKUs within a facility and their impact on space planning; item placement theories dealing with the specific arrangement of product within an area of the warehouse; and practical methods of attaching addresses to stock items and tying items to their location addresses

surface acoustic wave An automated method of identifying inventory in which data is encoded on a chip encased in a tag, which, in response to a radar pulse from a reader, converts the pulse to an ultrasonic acoustic wave; this wave is converted back to an electromagnetic signal and sent back to the reader

symbologies The rules that control how information will be encoded in a bar code symbol

thermal transfer printing A bar-code print technology in which an image is transferred to a substrate (label or other foundation) from a ribbon that is heated by elements in the printhead

tolerances The acceptable plus-minus percentage of accuracy in calculating inventory record accuracy (IRA)

transit inventory Inventory en route from one place to another, moving from within the distribution channel toward a facility or en route from a facility to a customer

Uniform Commercial Code (UCC) An act that seeks to simplify and clarify the law governing commercial transactions; to permit the continued expansion of commercial practices through custom, usage, and *agreement* of the parties; and to make uniform the law among the various jurisdictions

universal product code (UPC) A highly structured and controlled symbology that is used only in general merchandise retailing

unloading/loading ratio A ratio reflecting the number of trips necessary to bring an item from a receiving point to a storage location compared to the number of trips required to transport it from a storage point to a point of use

variance report A report that compares an expectation with what actually occurred

work-in-process (WIP) A product or products in various stages of completion throughout the plant, including all material from raw materials that has been released for initial processing up to completely processed material awaiting final inspection and acceptance as finished product

"X" dimension The narrowest bar or space in a bar code, which determines how wide each narrow and wide bar or space will be

© American Management Association. All rights reserved.

zoning system A stock locator system based on an item's characteristics, such that only items with certain characteristics can live in a particular area and items with different attributes can't live there

Post-Test

Fundamentals of Inventory Management and Control
Third Edition

Course Code 95020

CREDIT: *On successful completion of this final exam, you will receive 1 CEU.*

INSTRUCTIONS: *Record your answers on one of the scannable forms enclosed. Please follow the directions on the form <u>carefully</u>. Be sure to keep a copy of the completed answer form for your records. <u>No photocopies will be graded.</u> When completed, mail your answer form to:*

American Management Association
Educational Services
P.O. Box 133
Florida, NY 10921

1. Counting a small cross-section of your inventory frequently is called:
   (a) annual physical inventory.
   (b) fair valuation determinism.
   (c) cycle counting.
   (d) inventory stratification.

2. A chart that analyzes the sequence and relationships of product moving through an inventory system is a:
   (a) run chart.
   (b) pareto chart.
   (c) flow chart.
   (d) variance report.

3. In EOQ, the cost of carrying inventory and the cost of acquiring inventory:
   (a) should be within 10 percent of one another.
   (b) are unrelated for purposes of purchasing and stocking.
   (c) should be equal, whenever possible.
   (d) cannot be calculated with any degree of certainty.

4. Human-dependent inventory location systems are:
   (a) fixed.
   (b) random.
   (c) memory.
   (d) combination.

5. Locating items within a facility according to product characteristics is arrangement by:
   (a) Pareto analysis.
   (b) family grouping.
   (c) items affected by market conditions outside the control of your organization's operations.
   (d) demand for items outside of their normal review cycle.

6. Sending routine business transactions between computers over telephone lines is called:
   (a) EDI.
   (b) file sharing.
   (c) ordering.
   (d) ERP.

7. Bar coding is:
   (a) a digital method of achieving automatic identification.
   (b) an optical method of achieving automatic identification.
   (c) an analog system.
   (d) dependent on digital duplexors.

8. From an accounting viewpoint, inventory is a (an):
   (a) liability.
   (b) appurtenance.
   (c) necessity.
   (d) asset.

9. The number of pennies per inventory dollar per year a company is spending to house its inventory is its:
   (a) ordering cost.
   (b) carrying cost.
   (c) rentable space cost.
   (d) usable space cost.

10. A bill of materials is most like a:
    (a) bill of lading.
    (b) production schedule.
    (c) packing slip.
    (d) recipe.

11. In a real-time inventory software system, items are allocated to a specific order at:
    (a) the time of system update.
    (b) the time of data input.
    (c) the time of customer service telling the customer that the items will ship.
    (d) the time of order shipment.

12. The necessity of planning around the largest quantity of an item that will be in the facility at one time is a characteristic of which product locator system?
    (a) Fixed
    (b) Random
    (c) Memory
    (d) Combination

13. The ratio computed as (Current Assets – Inventories) / Current Liabilities is called the:
    (a) current ratio.
    (b) inventory turnover ratio.
    (c) assets/liabilities ratio.
    (d) quick ratio.

14. Which inventory management system views inventory as waste?
    (a) ERP
    (b) ABC
    (c) ROP
    (d) Lean

15. Honeycombing is:
    (a) the warehousing situation where storage space is available but is not being fully utilized.
    (b) an order selection technique.
    (c) a pick-pack technique for order assembly.
    (d) a stock storage technique where floor stacked items are placed next to flow-through racking.

16. In which stock locator system does nothing have a home, but you know where everything is?
    (a) Fixed
    (b) Random
    (c) Memory
    (d) Combination

17. Materials entered into the production process but not yet completed are:
    (a) inventory stratification.
    (b) work in stasis.
    (c) work in process.
    (d) flow through.

18. A key reason an annual physical inventory is not useful in resolving inventory system problems is:
    (a) the audit trail is too long.
    (b) counters are unfamiliar with the system.
    (c) inventory valuation is tied to a single event.
    (d) every stockkeeping unit is counted.

19. Lean concepts dictate that:
    (a) organizations should not carry inventory in excess of what is needed for immediate needs.
    (b) organizations should carry no less than one week's worth of product requirements at any time.
    (c) organizations should organize their purchasing strategies around one week's worth of product movement.
    (d) organizations should only purchase a six-month supply of raw materials at any one time.

20. "F.O.B. origin" indicates that title to product will pass at:
    (a) the time the items arrive at the customer's site.
    (b) the time an order is originated and accepted.
    (c) the time items leave the shipper's dock.
    (d) the time an order is filled at the supplier's stockroom.

21. Which of the following is not a bar-code symbology?
    (a) UPC
    (b) Code 39
    (c) Code 128
    (d) Code 2000

22. The method of inventory that is most closely tied to actual physical flow of inventory is:
    (a) LIFO.
    (b) FIFO.
    (c) average cost.
    (d) standard cost.

23. Your company manufactures wooden chairs and tables. Which of the following is an example of dependent demand?
    (e) A one-time customer order for six chairs and one table
    (f) A standing customer order for 20 tables and 120 chairs every month
    (g) An internal requirement for 60 feet of dowel to make the rungs for 12 chairs
    (h) A customer order for one finished rung to replace a broken rung in their chair

24. Which has the greatest scope?
    (a) MRP II
    (b) ERP
    (c) MRP
    (d) ERP II

25. In reporting *up* a chain-of-command the amount of detail supplied differs from level to level in what way?
    (a) The amount of detail increases.
    (b) The amount of detail decreases.
    (c) The amount of detail remains fairly constant.
    (d) The amount of detail is not related to the direction of the information flow.

Index

A-B-C analysis cycle counting, 160–162
accessibility, space vs., 41
accounting, 3, 19, *see also* financial aspects of inventory
accounts receivable, 30
accuracy, inventory, 132–133, 145–148
acid-test ratio, *see* quick ratio
acquisition costs, *see* ordering costs
actual cost method, 20
adjustments, impact of tolerances on, 148
allocation, 138
alphabetic marking systems, 65
alphanumeric marking systems, 65–66
American Management Association, *xii*
American Standard Code of Information Interchange (ASCII), 57, 81, 82
annual inventory, cycle counting vs., 152
anticipation stock, 7
APICS, 132
ASCII, *see* American Standard Code of Information Interchange
asset(s), 22
    inventory as, 3, 22
    lending against, 30
Association for Manufacturing Excellence, 100
average cost method, 19–21

Backflushing, 134, 138, 143, 144
balance sheet, inventory on, 22, 23
bar coding, 63, 73–92
    applications of, 86–87
    components in systems of, 76
    and cycle counting, 90
    definition of, 74
    elements of symbols in, 76–78
    in maintenance programs, 89
    and physical inventory, 90–91
    printing basics in, 85–86
    in receiving/shipping, 88
    RF-capable, 68, 69
    scanning basics in, 83–85
    symbologies in, 78–83
    for tracking multiple manufacturing activities, 89
batch software systems, 138, 140, 143
bill of materials (BOM), 58, 108, 109, 115
book value, 29, 30
buffer inventory, 3, 4, 7, 8
bulk storage, location addressing systems for, 67
buying, replenishment vs., 117, 118

Capital structure, 29–30
card file tracking system, 68
carrying costs (K factor), 8, 31–34, 119–120
Cartesian coordinates, 67
CCDs (charge coupled devices), 84

channels of distribution, buffer stock in, 8
charge coupled devices (CCDs), 84
charts, 149–150
    flow, 151
    run, 150
closed-loop MRP II, 113, 114
Code 39, 80, 81
Code 128, 82
combination location systems, 51–52
consultants, 137
consumables, 6–7
continuous symbologies, 78–80
control group cycle counting, 154–155
control of inventory, *see* physical location and control
cost of goods sold, 22, 24, 26–27
cost(s), 7–8
    carrying, 8, 31–34, 119–120
    of defective products/services, 101
    of errors, 73–74
    of goods sold, 22, 24, 26–27
    of labor, 63
    opportunity, 8
    ordering, 4, 7, 8
    replenishment, 35, 117–120
    in ROP/EOQ systems, 117
    of storage, 8
    of supplier unreliability, 4
criticality, 147
cubic footage method, 45
current assets, 22
current ratio, 25–27

204 FUNDAMENTALS OF INVENTORY MANAGEMENT AND CONTROL

cycle counting, 151–163
  A-B-C analysis, 160–162
  annual inventory vs., 152
  to avoid failure of systems, 151–163
  and bar coding, 90
  control group, 154–155
  diminishing population, 157–158
  location audit, 155–157
  methodologies for, 153–154
  personnel for, 163
  product categories, 158–160
  random selection, 157
  specific objectives of, 152
  time of day for, 162–163

Damage, protection from, 41
data characters (bar codes), 78
dead stock, 28–35
  arguments for disposing of, 30–35
  convincing decision-makers to dispose of, 29–30
  reasons for keeping, 29
  S&R items as, 7
decision making
  on dead stock, 29–30
  on inventory investments, 18
  providing actual numbers for, 30
defects (as waste), 101
demand
  dependent, see dependent demand
  fluctuations in, 3–4
  independent, see independent demand
  patterns of, 137
  total, 111
Deming, W. Edwards, 100
dependent demand, 97, 110–112
Descartes, René, 67
diminishing population cycle counting, 157–158
direct thermal printing (bar codes), 86
discounts
  on dead stock, 29
  quantity, 4
discrepancies, "adjusting away" of, 133
discrete symbologies, 78–79
disposal (of dead stock), 34–35

distribution businesses, type of inventory in, 19
distribution channels, buffer stock in, 8
documentation, timing of, 139
dollars, accuracy defined/measured in, 132
dollar value, 146
dot matrix impact printing (bar codes), 86
drawers, location addressing systems for, 66
drop-shipping, 3
Drucker, Peter
  on control, 145
  on problem analysis, 133

EAN (European article numbering system), 80
economic order quantity (EOQ), 97–99
  assumptions in, 125–126
  calculation of, 125, 126
  costs in, 117–120
  migration to ERP from, 114–116
  origin of, 125
  setting up worksheet for, 127–128
EDI (electronic data interchange), 12
Educational Services, xi, xii
80-20 rule, 55
Einstein, Albert, on problem statements, 133
electronic data interchange (EDI), 12
elements (bar codes), 77
enterprise resource planning (ERP), 97–99, 113–117
  advantage of lean over, 98
  complexity of, 113, 114
  drawbacks of, 116, 117
  flow chart for, 115
  objectives of, 114
  origin of, 113
  ROP/EOQ vs., 114–116
EOQ, see economic order quantity
equity, 22
ERP, see enterprise resource planning
ERP II, 107
errors, cost of, 73–74
European article numbering system (EAN), 80

Fact-finding, 149
failure of systems, 131–164
  case example of, 133–145
  cycle counting to avoid, 151–163
  and fill rates, 148, 149
  and inventory record accuracy, 145–148
  metrics for identifying, 145–149
  tools for uncovering, 149–151
family grouping/like product approach, 59, 61
FIFO, see first-in, first-out
fill rates, 148, 149
financial aspects of inventory, 17
  and accounting for inventories, 19
  and inventory on balance sheet, 22, 23
  and inventory on income statement, 22–24
  and obsolete stock, 28–35
  and ordering cost/purchasing, 35
  and ratio analyses, 24–28
  and valuation of inventory, 19–21
finished goods inventory, 19
finished product, 4
first-in, first-out (FIFO), 19–21, 23
5-S program, 107
fixed location systems, 43–48
flow charts/charting, 151
  for ERP, 115
  value stream mapping as, 4
fluctuations in demand, 3–4
F.O.B. (free on board), 6
Ford, Henry, 99, 100
free on board (F.O.B.), 6

Grading of tests
  address for, xi
  policy for, xii
grid addressing system, 67

Hall, Bob, 100
handling, see item placement theory(-ies)
handling costs, 8
holding costs, see carrying costs
honeycombing, 43–46

Identification markings, 62–66, 75–76, see also bar coding

© American Management Association. All rights reserved.

income statement, inventory on, 22–24
independent demand, 96–97, 111–112
independent demand inventory, 120–125
information
  access to, 138
  coordinating flow of, 137
  in paper life of product, 10–11
  physical inventory vs., 3
ink jet printing (bar codes), 86
intangible assets, 22
in-transit inventory, 19
inventory
  accounting for, 19
  on balance sheet, 22
  costs of, 7–8
  definition of, 2
  on income statement, 22–24
  information vs., 3
  paper life of, 8–11
  purpose of, 3
  reasons for carrying, 3–4
  tangible nature of, 2–3
  traditional management approaches to, 3
  types of, 4–7, 19
  valuation of, 19–21
  as waste, 101
  see also specific topics
inventory analysis report, 33
inventory record accuracy (IRA), 145–148, 153
inventory stratification, 55–61
inventory turnover ratio, 26–28
IRA, *see* inventory record accuracy
item placement theory(-ies), 54–61
  family grouping as, 59, 61
  inventory stratification as, 55–60

*J*ust-in-time (JIT), 3, 97–99
  lean as replacement term for, 100
  origin of, 99, 100
  philosophy of, 101
  see also lean

*K*anbans, 105–106
key supplier agreements, 4
K factor, *see* carrying costs

*L*abor
  costs of, 63
  efficient utilization of, 31
  protection from damage vs. use of, 41
language, bar coding, *see* symbology(-ies) (bar coding)
laser printing (bar codes), 86
laser scanners, 84
last-in, first-out (LIFO), 19–21, 27
lead time, 146
lean, 3, 97–107
  advantage over ERP of, 98
  kanbans in, 105–106
  key steps in, 105
  philosophy of, 101
  as pull system, 105–107
  "staple yourself to an order" in, 101–105
  as term replacing JIT, 100
liabilities, 22
LIFO, *see* last-in, first-out
light pens, 84
like product approach, 59, 61
linear bar codes, 76–77
location addresses, 62–69
  significance of, 62–63
  tying SKUs to, 63–69
location audit cycle counting, 155–157
locator systems, 40–54
  combination, 51–52
  fixed, 43–48
  memory, 42–43
  purpose of, 40
  random, 50–51
  selection of, 41, 42
  zoning, 48–50
longer-term assets, 22

*M*achine resources, efficient utilization of, 31
machine vision, 75
MAD, *see* Mean Absolute Deviation
magnetic strip identification, 75
maintenance programs, bar coding in, 89
manufacturing companies
  bar coding for tracking activities in, 89
  current ratios in, 25
manufacturing resources planning (MRP II), 97–99, 113, 114

marking systems, 63–66, *see also* location addresses
master production schedule, 58
material locator systems, *see* locator systems
materials requirements planning (MRP), 58, 107–113
  conception of, 107
  coordinating flow of, 137
  demand in, 110–112
  planning process for, 112–113
  rows in, 109, 110
  time phasing in, 107–110
matrix bar codes, 77
Mean Absolute Deviation (MAD), 121–124
memory systems, 42–43
menu cards, 87
metrics, 145–149
minimum-maximum (min-max) inventory control system, 124–125
money, inventory as, 18, *see also* Financial aspects of inventory
motion (as waste), 101
MPR, *see* materials requirements planning
MRP II, *see* manufacturing resources planning

*N*on-value-added, 101
numeric marking systems, 65

*O*bsolete stock, 28, *see also* dead stock
OCR (optical character recognition), 75
Ohno, Taiichi, 99
opportunity cost, 8
optical character recognition (OCR), 75
order-filling operations, item placement for control of, 47–48
ordering costs, 4, 7, 8, *see also* replenishment costs
order point formulas, 120–125
overproduction (as waste), 101

*P*aper life, 1, 8–11
  electronic data interchange vs., 12
  real life vs., 1, 8–10
Pareto, Vilfredo, 55

Pareto's law, 55, 57–59, 61
physical inventory, *see* physical taking of inventory; real life inventory
physical location and control, 39–70
  combination systems for, 51–52
  common locator systems for, 40–42
  by family grouping, 59, 61
  fixed location systems for, 43–48
  by inventory stratification, 55–60
  and item placement theories, 54–55
  with location addresses and SKU identifiers, 62–69
  memory systems for, 42–43
  minimum-maximum system for, 124–125
  random location systems for, 50–51
  special considerations in, 61–62
  success factors for systems of, 62–63
  zoning systems for, 48–50
physical taking of inventory
  and bar coding, 90–91
  cycle counting vs., 152
planning and replenishment, 95–128
  approaches to, 97–100
  ERP/MRP II approach to, 107–117
  functionality comparison of approaches to, 108
  and inventory types, 96–97
  lean/JIT approach to, 99–107
  ROP/EOQ approach to, 117–128
planning grid, MRP, 112–113
"plus/minus" notation system, 11
point of use, 55, 56
popularity, 55
portable bar code scanners, 69
post-test, *xi, xii,* 197–201
pre-test, *xi–xvii*
price protection, 4
pricing agreements, 4
printing basics (bar coding), 85–86

process buffer, inventory as, 3
processing (as waste), 101
product categories cycle counting, 158–160
pull systems, 105–107
purchasing, 141
  patterns of, 137–138
  R factor exclusion of, 118

*Q*uadrant addressing system, 67
quality initiatives, 4, 106
quantity, buying in, 4
quantity discounts, 4
quick (acid-test) ratio, 26, 27
quiet zone (bar codes), 77

*R*acks, location addressing systems for, 66
radio frequency (RF) scanners, 63, 68
radio frequency tags, 76
random location systems, 50–51
random selection cycle counting, 157
ratio analyses, 24–28
  current ratio in, 25–27
  of honeycombing, 45, 46
  inventory turnover ratio in, 26–28
  quick ratio in, 26, 27
  unloading/loading ratio in, 59, 60
raw materials inventory, 4, 19
real life inventory, 1–3
  information vs., 3
  and paper life vs. real life, 8–10
recapture of space, 30
receiving/shipping, bar coding in, 88
record count, 1, 5, 69, 131
reorder point (ROP), 97–99
  costs in, 117–120
  definition of, 120
  determining, 123–124
  improvements of MRP over, 107
  migration to ERP from, 114–116
  order point formulas in, 120–125
repair items, 7
replacement items, 7
replenishment, 97, 117, 118, *see also* planning and replenishment

replenishment costs (R factor), 35
  balancing carrying costs and, 119–120
  calculating, 118
  in ROP/EOQ systems, 117–120
report generators, 57
reports
  inventory analysis, 33
  of stock movement, 63, 69
  variance, 151, 152
requirements approach, 97
resupply time, 4
review cycle, 124
R factor, *see* replenishment costs
RF scanners, *see* radio frequency scanners
ROP, *see* reorder point
rule-of-thumb method (carrying costs), 31–32
run charts, 150

*S*afety inventory, 7, 121–124
SAW (surface acoustic wave), 76
scan boards, 87
scanners (bar coding), 83–85
self-assessments
  for cost of errors, 73–74
  for current item placement, 62
  for inventory record accuracy, 132
  for needs determination, 82–83
  for organization of stock, 39–40
  for planning and replenishment, 96
  for slow-moving/obsolete/dead stock, 29–31
  for system-related problems, 136, 145
  for understanding accounting, 18
  for understanding inventory, 2
  for understanding stock locator systems, 53–54
  for understanding transit stock, 5–6
service, repair, replacement, and spare (S&R) items, 7
service industries, current ratios in, 25
shelf count inventory, 1, 69, 131

shelving, location addressing
systems for, 66
shipping, bar coding in, 88
single criterion cycle counting,
159
SKUs, *see* stock-keeping units
slow-moving stock, 28, *see also*
dead stock
software systems
batch, 138, 140
integration of, 137
variances in, 142–143
see also specific software
space
ability to locate item and utilization of, 41
accessibility vs., 41
fixed location systems and utilization of, 43–46
memory systems and utilization of, 42
random systems and utilization of, 50
recapture of, 30
zoning systems and utilization
of, 48
spare items, 7
specific cost method, 20
S&R (service, repair, replacement, and spare) items, 7
stacked bar codes, 77
standard cost method, 20
"staple yourself to an order,"
101–105
start characters (bar codes),
77–78
stock, *see* dead stock; inventory
stock-keeping units (SKUs)
A-B-C categorization of,
55–59, 167–174
assigned location for, 42, 43,
46, 48–50
for control group cycle counting, 154
creating matrix for, 59,
175–182
defining accuracy in terms of,
132

identification markings on,
62
location addresses for, 62–69
unloading/loading ratio for,
59, 60
unobscured, 63
stock locator systems, *see* locator
systems
stock movement reporting, 63,
69
stop characters (bar codes),
77–78
storage
conflicting considerations in,
41
costs of, 8
planning areas for, 51
see also item placement the-
ory(-ies)
stratification, inventory, 55–61
subcontract inventory, 19
suppliers, key supplier agreements with, 4
supply, unreliability of, 4
supply chain concepts and practices, 3, 111–112
supply time, reduction of, 3–4
surface acoustic wave (SAW),
76
symbology(-ies) (bar coding),
76–83
choosing, 82–83
Code 39 as, 80, 81
Code 128 as, 82
discrete vs. continuous,
78–80
elements of, 76–78
European article numbering
system as, 80
and structure of symbols,
77–78
universal product code as, 80,
81

*T*angible inventory, *see* real life
inventory
test counts, 145
thermal transfer (bar codes), 86

time phasing, 107–110
title, transfer of, 6
tolerances, 145–148
Toyota Production System, 100
traditional inventory management, reasons for carrying
inventory in, 3–4
transit inventory, 5–6
transportation (as waste), 101
turnover, 26, *see also* inventory
turnover ratio
two-dimensional bar codes, 77

*U*niform Commercial Code
(UCC), 6
universal product code (UPC),
80, 81
unloading/loading ratio, 59, 60
unreliability of supply, 4
UPC, *see* universal product code
usage rate, 146

*V*aluation of inventory, 19–21,
29, 30
value
book, 29, 30
definitions of, 55
dollar, 146
value added, 101
value stream mapping, 4
variance reports, 151, 152

*W*aiting (as waste), 101
wand scanners, 84
waste(s)
inventory as, 3
in JIT, 101, 105
work in process (WIP) inventory,
5, 19
worksheet, EOQ, 127–128
write-off, 29

"*X*" dimension (bar codes), 78
xerographic printing (bar codes),
86

*Z*ero Inventories (Bob Hall), 100
zoning systems, 48